365 Quick & Easy Microwave

Thelma Pressman

A JOHN BOSWELL ASSOCIATES BOOK

1817

HARPER & ROW, PUBLISHERS, New York
Grand Rapids, Philadelphia, St. Louis, San Francisco
London, Singapore, Sydney, Tokyo, Toronto

Dear Reader:

We welcome your recommendations for future 365
Ways books. Send your suggestions and a recipe, if
you'd like, to Cookbook Editor, HarperCollins
Publishers, 10 East 53rd Street, New York, NY 10022.
If we choose your title suggestion or your recipe we
will acknowledge you in the book and send you a free
copy.

Thank you for your support.

Sincerely yours,
The Editor

365 QUICK AND EASY MICROWAVE RECIPES. Copyright © 1989 by John Boswell
Management, Inc. All rights reserved. Printed in the United States of America. No part of
this book may be used or reproduced in any manner whatsoever without written permis-
sion except in the case of brief quotations embodied in critical articles and reviews. For
information address HarperCollins Publishers, Inc., 10 East 53rd Street, New York, NY
10022.

HarperCollins books may be purchased for educational, business, or sales promotional use.
For information please write: Special Markets Department, HarperCollins Publishers, Inc.,
10 East 53rd Street, New York, NY 10022.

Reissued in 1996.

Design: Nigel Rollings
Index: Maro Riofrancos

Library of Congress Cataloging-in-Publication Data

Pressman, Thelma.
    365 quick and easy microwave recipes / Thelma Pressman. — 1st ed.
        p.   cm.
    Includes index.
    ISBN 0-06-018657-7
    1. Microwave cookery. 2. Quick and easy cookery. I. Title. II. Title: Three
hundred and sixty-five quick and easy microwave recipes.
    TX832.P68   1989
    641.5'882—dc20   89-45057

96 97 98 99 00 DT/HC 10 9 8 7 6 5 4 3 2 1

Acknowledgments

To Paul Pressman, my deepest respect and gratitude for his invaluable help in the recipe development and testing that brought this book together, and to Mo, for always being there when needed.

Contents

An exercise in instant gratification. A dozen flavors of popcorn, Quick and Easy Enchiladas, and Cajun Onion Rings are among the choice munchies-in-minutes offered here.

Suggestions for easy entertaining range from the traditional—Chopped Chicken Liver or Crab-Stuffed Mushrooms—to the international—Taco Pie or Swiss Fondue—to the simply finger-licking good—Honey-Mustard Chicken Wings with Sesame Seeds or Polynesian Ribs.

For lunches, snacks and late-night noshing, choose from classics, such as a Reuben or Tuna-Cheddar Melt, pita sandwiches and an assortment of instant pizzas.

Microwaves are made for soup, whether it's a rich and creamy chowder, a nutritious vegetable puree, a hearty bean soup, a seafood stew that's a meal in a bowl or a light broth touched with exotic flavor.

Sixteen great ways to prepare skinless boneless chicken breasts elegantly or for everyday.

Meatballs in savory sauces, ground beef stews, chili, and a variety of meat loaves—each ready in a half hour or less.

Expert advice and dependable recipes for cooking all kinds of poultry, veal, pork and beef, including pot roast, in a fraction of the usual time.

Great ideas for shellfish, fish fillets, fish steaks and even whole trout.

Introduction

If you feel you aren't using your microwave oven to its fullest advantage, this book is for you. It's true the microwave can't do everything, but its talent lies in its speed and its ability to make cooking easier and cleaner than it's ever been before. The recipes I've developed for this book were chosen for their ability to take advantage of the microwave's speed and convenience. I hope you'll look inside whenever dinner has to be on the table in half an hour; whenever you have a craving for a quick snack; whenever you desire a perfectly cooked piece of fish or plate of vegetables with no guesswork involved.

Besides saving time cooking, the microwave also saves time cleaning up. You frequently can cook and serve in the same dish. And because there is a minimum of sticking or scorching, most cookware rinses out as if it were nonstick. Usually the plate itself can go right in the microwave. A number of my recipes require no utensils at all! They cook in microwaveable paper towels, on paper plates or in parchment.

To use this cookbook successfully, all you need are a few basic facts about the microwave.

- These recipes were tested in a 600 to 700 watt oven.
- This book assumes that all equipment used is microwave-safe.
- Only metal dishes specifically designed to go into a microwave should be used.
- Use only plastic wrap specifically designed to be microwave-safe. Always vent plastic wrap used as a cover by turning back one corner of the wrap or by poking two or three holes in the wrap with the tip of a small knife to allow the steam to escape.
- Remember that bowls, jars and casseroles can get hot. When in doubt, always use a mitt or pot holders to remove dishes from the oven. When possible, place dishes on a larger saucer or plate to make lifting easier.
- Use only microwave-safe glass and ceramic dishes. If you plan to cook regularly in the microwave it pays to invest in some inexpensive but convenient equipment.

Microwave Equipment

Here is my wish list of the most useful tools for microwave cooking:

Heatproof glass measures. These come in 1-cup, 2-cup, 4-cup and 2-quart size. They are inexpensive and extremely handy.

Casseroles made of glass, ceramic or other microwave-safe material. One-quart, 2-quart and 4-quart sizes are extremely useful. Whenever possible, purchase casseroles with covers.

Microwave rack. Used for elevating food, so there is air circulation, and moisture is not trapped underneath.

Microwave probe for measuring internal temperature of roasts and syrups. These usually come with the oven. If yours doesn't have one, invest in an instant-reading microwave thermometer.

Browning dish. If you want to cook burgers and other meats in your microwave and obtain that attractive, tasty caramelized coating, this is a worthwhile piece of equipment.

Microwave popcorn maker. Popcorn is the number one use for microwave ovens throughout the country. If you are part of the tidal wave of enthusiasts, it's worth buying one of these. Ordinary paper bags are dangerous (they can ignite), and throwaway microwave popcorn bags can get expensive. Buy this utensil once and use it all the time.

Chapter 1

Microwave Snack Packs

      If there's one thing the microwave is great at, it's instant gratification. With no preheating, no hot fat, no mess, no fuss, you can have a tasty snack whenever you're in the mood. And the microwave is superfast and efficient with small quantities, so you needn't feel guilty about noshing alone. There's no pot to dirty, no clean-up needed. Whether it's just you or the whole family that suddenly gets the munchies, indulge yourself instantly.

      Have a yen for Nachos? They're ready in a flash. Having a little VCR party? Try Quick and Easy Enchiladas—enough for six prepared in seconds. Want a big bowl of popcorn with no calories added? All it takes is a station break. Prefer yours flavored? We've got Cajun Popcorn, Garlic-Cheese, Chicken-Flavored, Lemon-Herb, and more. Only a few minutes between halves? No problem. Zap a trayful of tasty nibbles during the commercials. Choose Chicken Nuggets, Onion Rings or one of the marvelous melts (see Sandwiches, Pizzas, Tacos and Melts). Notorious for your sweet tooth? How about a Peach Caramel or Nutty Nectarine Sundae?

1   QUICK AND EASY ENCHILADAS
Prep: 5 minutes   Cook: 7 to 10 minutes   Serves: 6

1 10¾-ounce can condensed cream of chicken soup

1 7-ounce can chopped green chiles, drained

1 pint (2 cups) sour cream

12 6- to 7-inch corn tortillas

¾ pound Monterey jack cheese, shredded

1. In a medium bowl, combine soup, chiles and sour cream. Whisk to blend well. Spoon 2 tablespoons of mixture at one end of each tortilla. Sprinkle each with about 1 tablespoon cheese. Roll up and arrange seam-side down in shallow baking dish just large enough to hold enchiladas in a single layer.

2. Pour remaining sour cream mixture over enchiladas. Sprinkle remaining cheese on top. Cover dish with waxed paper. Cook on MEDIUM 7 to 10 minutes, until heated through.

2   QUESADILLAS
Prep: 5 minutes   Cook: 2 to 3 minutes   Makes: 4

1 7-ounce can whole green
   chiles, drained
4 8-inch flour tortillas

1 cup shredded Monterey jack
   or Cheddar cheese

1. Split whole chiles along one side and open up; discard stems and seeds. Place 1 chile on each tortilla and top with ¼ of the cheese. Roll up and secure with wooden toothpick. Repeat with remaining ingredients to make 4 quesadillas.

2. Place on a plate and cover with paper towel. Cook on HIGH 2 to 3 minutes, until cheese melts and quesadillas are warm.

3   POPCORN
Prep: 0   Cook: 3½ to 4½ minutes   Makes: about 3 quarts

½ cup popping corn

Melted butter and salt (optional)

1. Follow directions for your microwave popper. Place corn in popper as directed and cook on HIGH 3½ to 4½ minutes, or just until you no longer hear the corn popping frequently. Even if all the kenrnels have not popped at this time, the popped corn will begin to burn.

2. Turn popcorn out into bowl. Drizzle melted butter over corn if desired and salt to taste. Or try one of the flavored butters and seasonings that follow.

4   OLD-FASHIONED CARAMEL CORN
Prep: 5 minutes   Cook: 8 minutes   Makes: 4 quarts

Although this recipe makes use of a paper bag, do not use one to pop the corn.

1 cup brown sugar
¼ cup light corn syrup
1 stick butter or margarine
½ teaspoon salt

1 teaspoon vanilla extract
½ teaspoon baking soda
4 quarts popped corn

1. In a 2-quart glass measure, combine brown sugar, corn syrup, butter and salt. Cook on HIGH 2 minutes. Stir well. Cook on HIGH 3 minutes longer, stirring once. Stir in vanilla and baking soda. Caramel will foam up.

2. Place popped corn in a large paper bag (not recycled paper). Pour hot caramel over popcorn and fold edges of bag together to seal. Shake well.

3. Place bag in microwave and cook on HIGH 1 minute; shake bag. Cook 1 minute longer; shake bag. Cook 30 seconds; shake. Cook a final 30 seconds, shake again.

4. Pour caramel corn onto a baking sheet or sheet of aluminum foil. Let cool, then break into pieces. Store in an airtight container.

5 GARLIC-CHEESE POPCORN
Prep: 2 minutes   Cook: 1 to 2 minutes   Makes: 2 quarts

5 tablespoons butter
1 tablespoon minced garlic or
   1 teaspoon garlic powder
2 quarts popped corn

⅓ cup grated Parmesan or
   Romano cheese
Salt

1. In a 1-cup glass measure, combine butter and garlic. Cook on MEDIUM 1 to 2 minutes, until butter is melted and garlic is softened.

2. Stir garlic butter and pour over popped corn. Immediately sprinkle with cheese and toss. Season with salt to taste.

6 SCARBOROUGH FAIR POPCORN
Prep: 2 minutes   Cook: 1 minute   Makes: 2 quarts

Parsley, sage, rosemary and thyme are enough to make anyone nostalgic. Here's a sophisticated popcorn—fine for a snack, fancy enough for a party.

3 tablespoons butter
1 teaspoon minced lemon zest
1 teaspoon lemon juice
½ teaspoon dried parsley
   flakes
¼ teaspoon crushed sage

⅛ teaspoon rosemary, crushed
⅛ teaspoon thyme leaves,
   crushed
2 quarts popped corn
   Salt

1. In a 1-cup glass measure, combine butter, lemon zest, lemon juice, parsley, sage, rosemary and thyme. Cook on HIGH 45 to 60 seconds, until butter melts.

2. Stir and pour over popped corn. Toss to coat evenly. Season with salt to taste.

7 QUICK CARAMEL NUT CORN
Prep: 2 minutes   Cook: 6 to 7 minutes   Makes: 2½ quarts

1 8-ounce package caramels
   (about 28)
¼ cup sugar

¼ cup water
2 cups dry-roasted peanuts
2 quarts popped corn

1. In a 2-cup glass measure, combine caramels, sugar and water. Cook on HIGH 6 to 7 minutes, stirring several times, until mixture is at a full boil for 2 to 3 minutes.

2. In a large metal bowl, toss together peanuts and popped corn. Pour hot caramel over mixture and immediately toss with 2 large forks to coat evenly.

3. Spread out caramel nut corn on buttered cookie sheet and let cool. Then break into pieces.

8   SESAME POPCORN
Prep: 2 minutes   Cook: 1 to 2 minutes   Makes: 2 quarts

6 tablespoons butter
3 tablespoons minced
   scallions

2 tablespoons sesame seeds
2 quarts popped corn
   Salt

1. In a 1-cup glass measure, combine butter, scallions and sesame seeds. Cook on HIGH 1 to 2 minutes, until butter melts.

2. Stir and pour butter over popped corn. Toss and mix evenly. Season with salt to taste.

9   PEANUT BUTTER POPCORN
Prep: 2 minutes   Cook: 1 minute   Makes: 2 quarts

3 tablespoons butter
1 tablespoon peanut butter

2 quarts popped corn
   Salt

1. In a 1-cup glass measure, combine butter and peanut butter. Cook on HIGH 1 minute, or until hot.

2. Stir and pour over popped corn. Toss to coat evenly. Season with salt to taste.

10   MELLOW YELLOW CORN
Prep: 2 minutes   Cook: 1½ minutes   Makes: 2 quarts

¼ teaspoon crushed saffron
   threads, or substitute
   turmeric

3 tablespoons butter
2 quarts popped corn
   Salt

1. In a 1-cup glass measure, combine saffron and butter. Cook on MEDIUM 1½ minutes, or until butter melts.

2. Stir butter and pour over popped corn. Toss to coat evenly. Season with salt to taste.

11   NACHOS
Prep: 5 minutes   Cook: 5 to 6 minutes   Serves: 8 to 10

1 12-ounce bag tortilla chips,
   preferably round
1 16-ounce can refried beans
¾ cup shredded Monterey jack
   cheese

¾ cup shredded sharp
   Cheddar cheese
¼ cup sliced pickled jalapeño
   peppers

1. Arrange half the tortilla chips in a single layer in a round shallow dish. Top each with 1 teaspoon refried beans. Sprinkle both cheeses over chips and scatter jalapeño slices on top.

2. Cook on HIGH 2 to 3 minutes, until cheese melts. Repeat with remaining ingredients.

12   CHICKEN-FLAVORED POPCORN
Prep: 2 minutes   Cook: 1 to 2 minutes   Makes: 2 quarts

Everyone loves chicken, so why not on popcorn?

4 **tablespoons butter**
½ **teaspoon chicken bouillon granules**
¼ **teaspoon celery salt**

1 **teaspoon dried parsley flakes, crushed**
2 **quarts popped corn**

1. In a 1-cup glass measure, combine butter, bouillon granules, celery salt and parsley flakes. Cook on HIGH 1 to 2 minutes, until melted.

2. Stir and pour over popped corn. Toss to coat.

13   CAJUN POPCORN
Prep: 2 minutes   Cook: 1½ to 2 minutes   Makes: 2 quarts

3 **tablespoons butter**
½ **teaspoon salt**
¼ **teaspoon garlic powder**
¼ **teaspoon chili powder**
¼ **teaspoon crushed thyme**

⅛ **teaspoon cayenne pepper**
2 **tablespons grated Cheddar cheese**
2 **quarts popped corn**

1. In a 1-cup glass measure, combine butter, salt, garlic powder, chili powder, thyme, cayenne and cheese. Cook on MEDIUM 1½ to 2 minutes, until melted.

2. Stir well and pour over popped corn. Toss to coat evenly.

14   LEMON-HERB POPCORN
Prep: 2 minutes   Cook: 1 minute   Makes: 2 quarts

3 **tablespoons butter**
1 **teaspoon dried herb: dill, tarragon, oregano or thyme**

½ **teaspoon lemon juice**
2 **quarts popped corn**
  Salt

1. In a 1-cup glass measure, combine butter, herb and lemon juice. Cook on HIGH 45 to 60 seconds, until butter melts.

2. Stir and pour over popped corn. Toss to coat evenly. Season with salt to taste.

15   CHICKEN NUGGETS
Prep: 10 minutes   Cook: 7 to 9 minutes   Serves: 4

4 skinless, boneless chicken
   breast halves
1 egg
1 tablespoon vegetable oil

1½ cups Italian-seasoned bread
   crumbs
Spaghetti, barbecue or taco
   sauce, for dipping

1. Cut chicken into 1½-inch cubes. In a shallow bowl, whisk together egg and oil. Set crumbs on plate or sheet of waxed paper.

2. Dip each chicken piece in egg, then dredge in seasoned crumbs to coat. Pat gently to help crumbs adhere.

3. Arrange chicken nuggets in a circle on a 10-inch round shallow baking dish. Cover with waxed paper. Cook on MEDIUM-HIGH 7 to 9 minutes, until chicken is white throughout but still juicy. Turn dish if chicken appears to be cooking unevenly. Dip in desired sauce and eat.

16   OAT PECAN CRACKERS
Prep: 10 minutes   Cook: 3 to 4 minutes per batch   Makes: about 100

You can make as many or as few of these crackers as you like and refrigerate the extra dough in an airtight container for up to 3 days, or freeze for longer storage. They make a nice after-school or in-front-of-the-VCR snack.

2½ cups rolled oats
1½ cups flour
 ½ cup shelled pecans
 ⅓ cup shredded coconut
 2 tablespoons brown sugar
 1 teaspoon salt

⅔ cup water
½ cup vegetable oil
6 tablespoons sesame, poppy
   or caraway seeds
Coarse (kosher) salt

1. Place oats in a food processor and grind 5 seconds. Add flour, pecans, coconut, brown sugar and salt. Process until well blended. With the machine on, add water and oil and process until blended.

2. Divide dough into thirds. Roll out each piece on a lightly floured surface to a very thin rectangle at least 10 × 14 inches. Sprinkle 2 tablespoons seeds evenly over dough. Sprinkle with coarse salt to taste. Press gently to help seeds and salt adhere. With a sharp knife, cut dough into 2-inch squares.

3. Bake in batches, arranging 12 to 15 squares of dough on a shallow baking dish or sheet of parchment. Cook on HIGH 3 to 4 minutes, turning if dough appears to be cooking unevenly, until crackers are dry and firm. Repeat twice with remaining dough and seeds, or refrigerate or freeze for another time.

17   ONION RINGS
Prep: 10 minutes   Cook: 2 to 3 minutes   Makes: about 12

1 large sweet yellow onion	½ teaspoon paprika
1 egg	¼ teaspoon garlic powder
2 teaspoons olive oil	Coarse (kosher) salt
½ cup dry seasoned bread crumbs	

1. Cut onion into ½-inch-thick slices. Separate slices into rings, leaving 2 layers of onion in each ring.

2. In a small bowl, beat egg and oil together. Place bread crumbs on a plate or sheet of waxed paper. Toss with paprika and garlic powder. Dip each onion ring in egg, then dredge in bread crumbs to coat.

3. Place rings in a circle on a plate (paper is fine). Cover with a paper towel. Cook on HIGH 2 to 2½ minutes, until onion is slightly cooked. Season with salt to taste.

18   CAJUN ONION RINGS
Prep: 10 minutes   Cook: 2 to 3 minutes   Makes: about 12

1 large sweet yellow onion	½ teaspoon salt
1 egg	¼ teaspoon thyme
2 teaspoons vegetable oil	¼ teaspoon black pepper
½ cup dry bread crumbs	⅛ to ¼ teaspoon cayenne pepper, to taste
½ teaspoon paprika	

1. Cut onion into ½-inch-thick slices. Separate slices into rings, leaving 2 layers of onion in each ring.

2. In a small bowl, beat egg and oil together. In a shallow bowl, combine bread crumbs, paprika, salt, thyme, black pepper and cayenne. Toss to mix well.

3. Dip onion rings in egg, then dredge in seasoned bread crumbs to coat. Arrange in a circle on a paper plate. Cover with paper towel. Cook on HIGH 2 to 2½ minutes, until onion is slightly cooked.

19   PEACH CARAMEL SUNDAE
Prep: 2 minutes   Cook: 3 to 4 minutes   Serves: 1

¼ cup caramel sauce	1 slice pound cake
1 large ripe peach, sliced	1 large scoop vanilla ice cream

1. In a 1-cup glass measure or small bowl, cook caramel sauce on HIGH 1 to 2 minutes, until hot.

2. Place peach slices in another bowl or measure. Cook on HIGH 2 minutes, or until juices come to a boil.

3. To serve, place cake on plate, and set ice cream on top. Cover with hot caramel sauce and poached peaches.

20 CHILE-CHEESE BEAN DIP

Prep: 10 minutes   Cook: 5 to 7 minutes   Makes: about 2½ cups

Here's a sure winner anytime you need a savory snack. Cook and serve in the same bowl, and be sure to pass a big basket of tortilla chips on the side.

1 16-ounce can refried beans
2 cups shredded sharp
    Cheddar cheese
½ cup mild chunky-style salsa

1 7-ounce can diced green
    chiles, drained
½ teaspoon garlic powder
¼ teaspoon hot pepper sauce,
    or more to taste

1. Combine all of the ingredients in a 1½- to 2-quart bowl. Stir to blend well. Cover with waxed paper.

2. Cook on HIGH 3 minutes. Stir well. Cover and continue to cook 2 to 4 minutes, until cheese melts and dip is heated through.

21 POPCORN SUPERSNACK

Prep: 20 minutes   Cook: 15 minutes   Serves: 6

1 cup whole natural almonds
2 tablespoons butter
3 quarts popped corn
1 cup raisins
1 cup finely diced dried
    apricots

1 cup (firmly packed) light
    brown sugar
1 cup light corn syrup
⅓ cup evaporated milk
⅛ teaspoon salt

1. In a 9-inch pie plate, combine almonds and 1 tablespoon butter. Cook on HIGH 3 to 4 minutes, stirring twice, until lightly toasted. Chop very coarsely. In a large bowl, combine toasted almonds, popped corn, raisins and apricots

2. In a 4-quart glass bowl, combine brown sugar, corn syrup, evaporated milk, 1 tablespoon butter and salt. Cook on HIGH 5 minutes. Stir until sugar dissolves. Continue to cook until syrup reaches 234° on a microwave candy thermometer, 7 to 10 minutes; a small amount dropped in cold water will form a soft ball.

3. Immediately pour syrup over popcorn mixture. Quickly toss with 2 forks to lightly coat with syrup. Spread out on lightly buttered baking sheet and let cool, then break into chunks for eating.

22   NUTTY NECTARINE SUNDAE
Prep: 2 minutes   Cook: 3 to 5 minutes   Serves: 1

2 **tablespoons sliced almonds**
1 **teaspoon butter**
1 **ripe nectarine, sliced**

1 **large scoop butter pecan ice cream**

1. Combine nuts and butter in a small bowl. Cover with paper towel. Cook on HIGH 1 to 2 minutes, stirring once or twice, until lightly toasted.

2. Put nectarine slices in a small bowl or 1-cup glass measure. Cook on HIGH 2 to 3 minutes, just until juices come to a boil.

3. Set ice cream in an ice cream coupe or dessert dish. Top with poached nectarine and toasted almonds.

23   MEXICAN STUFFED MUSHROOMS
Prep: 10 minutes   Cook: 6 to 7 minutes   Makes: 24

24 **medium-large fresh mushrooms**
2 **ounces chorizo sausage or pepperoni, halved lengthwise and thinly sliced into 24 pieces**

1 **to 2 fresh or pickled jalapeño peppers, seeded and minced**
1½ **cups shredded Monterey jack cheese**
¼ **cup minced scallions**

1. Remove stems from mushrooms; reserve for another use. Arrange 12 mushroom caps in a 9-inch shallow round baking dish or pie plate, placing smaller mushrooms in center.

2. Set 1 piece of sausage in each mushroom. Sprinkle with half the jalapeños and half the cheese. Cook on HIGH 2 to 3½ minutes, just until cheese melts, sausage is hot and mushrooms are slightly soft to touch. Do not overcook.

3. Sprinkle half the scallions on top and serve hot. Repeat with remaining ingredients.

Chapter 2

Appetizers and Party Pleasers

Some studies have shown that the average American spends 8½ hours getting ready for a party. Not me! And not you, either, if you're smart and take advantage of your microwave's speed. Remember, it saves time not only cooking, but cleaning up as well.

Here are some of my favorite hors d'oeuvres, spreads and dips for easy entertaining. If you want to offer an assortment for a party, it's a good idea to pick a couple of recipes that can be made ahead and refrigerated, such as Caponata, Steamed Shrimp with Cocktail Dipping Sauce or Eggplant Yogurt Dip. Choose one or two that are good at room temperature, like Tex-Mex Tuna Dip or Brandied Liver Pâté. To save last-minute fuss, make only a couple of dishes that are served hot, such as Scallops Rumaki, wrapped in crisp bacon, Honey-Mustard Chicken Wings with Sesame Seeds, Polynesian Ribs or Taco Pie. I like to offer one as soon as guests arrive. The tantalizing aroma always helps to get the party started. I have the other all prepared and ready to go. Sometime when there is a lull in the middle of the evening, I pop it in the microwave for a few minutes, and surprise everyone with yet another treat.

Keep in mind that with the proper dishes, you can cook and serve from the same plate. So don't let time deter you. And don't think of the microwave just for everyday. It's your at-hand caterer, cleaner-upper and time-saver all in one. Look at your microwave and think—let's have a party.

---

24   SCALLOPS RUMAKI
Prep: 15 minutes   Cook: 6 to 8 minutes   Makes: 24

¼ cup soy sauce
1 tablespoon minced fresh ginger or ¾ teaspoon ground ginger
1 tablespoon minced garlic

12 wafer-thin slices bacon, cut in half
24 1-inch slices of scallion green
24 sea scallops

1. In a shallow bowl, combine soy sauce, ginger and garlic.

2. Wrap bacon around piece of scallion and scallop. Secure with wooden toothpick. Dip in sauce. Repeat with remaining ingredients.

3. Place 12 rumaki on an 8-inch plate. Cover with paper towel. Cook on HIGH 3 to 4 minutes, or until bacon is crisp and scallops are opaque throughout. Serve hot while you cook the remaining pieces.

25   SUPER-QUICK NACHOS
Prep: 10 minutes   Cook: 10 to 12 minutes   Makes: about 50

Mexican flavors have become something of a national obsession. Since the microwave is the perfect place to warm tortillas and melt cheese, it produces super nachos super quick.

1   pound lean ground beef
1   tablespoon chili powder
1   teaspoon ground cumin
½   teaspoon salt
¼   teaspoon pepper
1   large onion, chopped
1   16-ounce can refried beans
1   12-ounce package tortilla
    chips

1   cup shredded Monterey jack
    cheese
1   cup shredded Cheddar
    cheese
    Chopped scallions, sliced
    black olives and sliced
    pickled jalapeño peppers

1. In a 4-cup glass measure, place ground meat, chili powder, cumin, salt, pepper and onion. Cook on HIGH 3 minutes. Stir with a fork to break up any lumps. Cook for 2 minutes longer. Pour off fat.

2. Put refried beans in a bowl, cover with waxed paper and cook on HIGH for 3 minutes, until hot. Place tortilla chips on a 13-inch platter. Spoon refried beans over chips.

3. Sprinkle ground beef over beans; top with Monterey jack and Cheddar cheeses. Cook on HIGH 2 to 3 minutes, until cheeses are melted and nachos are heated through. Sprinkle as desired with scallions, olives and/or peppers. Serve hot.

26   BRANDIED LIVER PATE
Prep: 10 minutes   Cook: 5 minutes   Serves: 4 to 6

To make entertaining easy, prepare this savory spread up to 3 days in advance. Serve with crackers, melba toasts or party rye bread rounds.

½   pound chicken livers,
    trimmed and rinsed
⅓   cup minced shallots or
    onion
4   tablespoons butter
1½ tablespoons brandy

½   teaspoon salt
¼   teaspoon pepper
¼   teaspoon thyme
⅛   teaspoon nutmeg
    Sprigs of parsley

1. Cut livers into 1-inch pieces. Put livers, shallots and butter in a 1-quart casserole with lid. Cover and cook on MEDIUM 3 minutes; stir. Cook 1 to 2 minutes longer, just until livers are slightly pink inside; overcooking makes them bitter. Set aside, covered, and let cool slightly.

2. Transfer livers, shallots and juices to food processor or blender. Add brandy, salt, pepper, thyme and nutmeg. Puree until smooth.

3. Pack liver puree into lightly oiled 1-cup mold or small bowl. Cover and refrigerate until chilled and set, about 3 hours. Shortly before serving, run blunt knife around edge of mold to loosen pâté. Invert to unmold onto a serving dish. Garnish with sprigs of parsley.

27 STEAMED SHRIMP WITH COCKTAIL DIPPING SAUCE

Prep: 10 minutes   Cook: 6 minutes   Serves: 4 to 6

Everyone loves shrimp! Because of their high water content, the microwave cooks shrimp perfectly, keeping them succulent and juicy.

1 **pound large shrimp, shelled and deveined**
½ **cup ketchup**
1 **to 2 tablespoons prepared white horseradish**

2 **tablespoons lemon juice**
1 **teaspoon Worcestershire sauce**
Hot pepper sauce

1. In a 9-inch round or oval baking dish or pie plate, arrange shrimp with thickest section facing outside (tails toward center). Cover with waxed paper. Cook on HIGH 4 to 6 minutes, just until shrimp turn opaque. Remove shrimp as they *begin* to curl and let remaining shrimp finish cooking; overcooking will make them tough. Set aside to cool, then cover and refrigerate until chilled. (The shrimp can be cooked the night before your party.)

2. In a small bowl, combine ketchup, horseradish, lemon juice, Worcestershire and hot sauce to taste (the amount will depend on how hot you like your dip). To serve, set out the shrimp, preferably on a bed of crushed ice, with a bowl of the dipping sauce in the center.

28 EGGPLANT YOGURT DIP

Prep: 10 minutes   Cook: 9 minutes   Makes: 2 cups

Eggplant takes up to an hour to bake in a conventional oven. In the microwave, it needs little more than five minutes. Serve with toasted triangles of pita bread.

1 **eggplant (about 1 pound)**
1 **small onion, minced**
½ **green bell pepper**
1 **garlic clove, minced**
1 **teaspoon lemon juice**

½ **teaspoon salt**
⅛ **teaspoon pepper**
1 **cup plain yogurt**
Chopped parsley or scallion, for garnish

1. Leave peel on eggplant. Pierce with fork several times. If you have a rack for your microwave, place eggplant on rack. If not, wrap eggplant in paper towel, with extra folds underneath and set on floor of microwave. Cook on HIGH 6 to 7 minutes, or just until soft to the touch. Set aside to cool slightly.

2. Combine onion, green pepper, garlic and lemon juice in a bowl. Cook on HIGH 1½ to 2 minutes, until vegetables are limp.

3. Cut eggplant in half; scoop out pulp. Add eggplant to vegetables and blend well. Add salt and pepper. Stir in yogurt until well blended. Cover and refrigerate until chilled. Sprinkle with parsley before serving.

29   SAVORY STUFFED MUSHROOMS
Prep: 10 minutes   Cook: 4 to 6 minutes   Makes: 24

24 large fresh mushrooms
¾ cup shredded Cheddar
    cheese
 2 scallions, finely chopped
½ cup bread crumbs
 4 tablespoons melted butter
¼ teaspoon salt

⅛ teaspoon pepper
½ teaspoon marjoram or
    thyme
½ teaspoon Worcestershire
    sauce
    Dash of hot pepper sauce

1. Remove stems from mushrooms and finely chop. (A food processor does this quickly.) In a medium bowl, combine chopped mushroom stems with all of the remaining ingredients. Mix well.

2. Fill mushroom caps with bread crumb mixture, mounding slightly in center of each cap. Arrange 12 stuffed mushrooms in an 8-inch round shallow dish. Cook on HIGH 2 to 3 minutes, just until hot. Repeat with second batch.

30   SWISS FONDUE
Prep: 5 minutes   Cook: 6 to 7 minutes   Serves: 6 to 8

Serve with chunks of French bread and long forks for dipping. Or offer an assortment of crisp vegetable sticks.

 1 garlic clove, halved
 1 cup plus 2 tablespoons
    white wine
 1 pound Gruyère or Swiss
    cheese, shredded

 2 teaspoons cornstarch
    Dash of nutmeg and
    cayenne pepper

1. Rub inside of a 2-quart casserole with garlic. Add 1 cup wine and cook on HIGH 2 minutes. Gradually add cheese, stirring until it begins to melt. Dissolve cornstarch in 2 tablespoons wine and stir into cheese mixture, along with nutmeg and cayenne.

2. Cook on MEDIUM 3 minutes, stirring every minute to prevent boiling over. Serve at once.

31   HONEY-MUSTARD CHICKEN WINGS WITH SESAME SEEDS
Prep: 10 minutes   Cook: 16 to 17 minutes   Makes: 14

Marinate the chicken pieces for at least 2 hours, or overnight. Then cook them when your guests arrive.

 7 chicken wings or 14 chicken
    drumettes
½ cup honey
 1 tablespoon soy sauce

 2 teaspoons Dijon mustard
½ cup unhulled sesame seeds
½ teaspoon paprika

1. If using chicken wings, separate them at the joints into 3 sections. Discard the tips or save for stock. Place chicken in shallow dish.

2. In a 1-cup glass measure, combine honey, soy sauce and mustard. Stir to blend well. Cook on HIGH 1 minute. Brush chicken wings with honey mixture. Roll wings in sesame seeds to coat lightly. Sprinkle with paprika.

3. Arrange on a shallow 9-inch plate, like spokes on a wheel, with thickest portion facing outside of dish. Cover with a paper towel. Cook on HIGH 15 to 16 minutes, just until chicken begins to crisp slightly. (Turn plate partway through if chicken appears to be cooking unevenly.) Serve hot.

---

32 CAPONATA
Prep: 10 minutes   Cook: 23 minutes   Makes: 4 to 5 cups

This sweet-sour Italian eggplant spread is a perennial favorite. Serve with toast triangles or crackers.

1 large eggplant	½ cup coarsely chopped black
½ cup extra-virgin olive oil	olives
1 cup coarsely chopped onion	⅓ cup red wine vinegar
1 cup coarsely chopped celery	2 tablespoons sugar
1 cup chopped green bell	1 tablespoon capers
pepper	1½ teaspoons salt
1 cup tomato sauce	½ teaspoon pepper

1. Cut unpeeled eggplant into ½-inch cubes. Pour oil into a 2-quart casserole with cover and heat on HIGH 1½ minutes. Stir in eggplant, cover with lid and cook on HIGH 10 minutes, stirring twice.

2. Stir in onion, celery and green pepper. Cover and cook on HIGH 2 minutes. Stir in tomato sauce, olives, vinegar, sugar, capers, salt and pepper. Cook, uncovered, 10 minutes, stirring twice. Serve at room temperature or cover and refrigerate until chilled. The flavor improves upon standing.

---

33 TEX-MEX TUNA DIP
Prep: 5 minutes   Cook: 7 to 9 minutes   Makes: 3 cups

Serve with crackers, corn chips or fried corn tortilla strips.

2 tablespoons butter or	¾ pound Cheddar cheese,
margarine	shredded
1 medium onion, chopped	1 4-ounce can diced green
2 garlic cloves, minced	chiles, drained
2 tablespoons flour	¼ teaspoon hot pepper sauce
¼ teaspoon ground cumin	1 6½-ounce can tuna, drained
1 cup milk	

1. In a 2-quart bowl, place butter and onion. Cook on HIGH 2 minutes; stir. Continue to cook 2 to 3 minutes, until onion is soft. Stir in garlic, flour and cumin until well blended. Gradually stir in milk.

2. Cook 3 to 4 minutes, stirring once or twice, until thick. Gradually stir in cheese, chiles, hot sauce and tuna. Serve warm or at room temperature.

NOTE: To reheat, use MEDIUM to avoid overcooking cheese.

34   HOT BRIE AND CHUTNEY

Prep: 5 minutes   Cook: 5 to 7 minutes   Serves: 8

A perfect microwave recipe. Heat just before serving for best results.
Serve with crackers or French bread.

1 9-ounce glass jar of chutney, preferably Major Grey's	½ cup coarsely chopped salted roasted almonds
1 8-ounce round Brie cheese	2 tablespoons sliced scallion

1. Remove metal lid from jar of chutney. Cover jar with a paper towel. Cook
on MEDIUM 1½ to 2 minutes, until hot. Use mitt or pot holder to remove
jar.

2. Place Brie in center of a 9-inch microwave-safe serving dish with rim.
Cook on LOW 4 to 4½ minutes, turning plate if it appears to be heating
unevenly, until cheese is very warm and just beginning to melt.

3. Stir chutney and pour over Brie. Sprinkle with almonds and scallion.
Serve warm.

35   POLYNESIAN RIBS

Prep: 5 minutes   Cook: 50 to 55 minutes   Makes: about 30

3 pounds pork spareribs, cut by butcher crosswise into 2-inch sections	1 lemon, thinly sliced
	1 cup bottled teriyaki sauce
1 large onion, sliced	2½ tablespoons honey

1. Arrange ribs in a 3-quart baking dish, layering if necessary. Add hot
water to cover. Scatter onion and lemon slices over ribs. Cover and cook on
HIGH 7 minutes.

2. Reduce power to MEDIUM and cook 20 minutes. Turn ribs over and
rotate their position; place bottom ribs on top. Continue cooking, covered,
until ribs are fork tender, about 20 minutes. Drain off fat. Cut between ribs
to separate them.

3. Combine teriyaki sauce with honey. Dip each rib in sauce to coat completely. Arrange ribs in spoke pattern in a shallow round or oval baking
dish. Pour remaining sauce over ribs. Cover dish and cook on HIGH 5 to 7
minutes, until hot. Serve hot or at room temperature.

36   CRISPY CHICKEN WINGS PARMESAN

Prep: 10 minutes   Cook: 12 to 14 minutes   Makes: 12

6 chicken wings	½ teaspoon garlic powder
10 Ritz crackers, finely crushed	½ teaspoon paprika
¼ cup grated Parmesan cheese	½ teaspoon salt
1 tablespoon minced parsley	1 egg white

1. Separate chicken wings at the joints into 3 sections. Discard tips or save
for stock.

2. In a shallow bowl, combine cracker crumbs, cheese, parsley, garlic powder, paprika and salt. In another bowl, lightly beat egg white. Dip chicken pieces into egg white, then roll in seasoned crumbs to coat completely. Pat lightly to help crumbs adhere.

3. Arrange coated chicken wings on a plate in spoke fashion with thickest part closer to the rim. Cover with a paper towel. Cook on HIGH about 12 minutes, until crisp.

---

37 TACO PIE
Prep: 10 minutes   Cook: 11 to 14 minutes   Serves: 10 to 12

½ **pound bulk sausage**
½ **pound lean ground beef**
1 **garlic clove, crushed**
1 **large white onion, chopped**
1 **cup mild or hot salsa**
1 **16-ounce can refried beans**

2 **cups shredded Cheddar**
  cheese
1 **cup sour cream**
1 **medium tomato, chopped**
1 **2-ounce can sliced pitted**
  black olives, drained
1 **avocado, diced**

1. Crumble sausage and beef into a 2-quart casserole. Add garlic and onion. Cover with paper towel. Cook on HIGH 5 to 6 minutes, stirring after 3 minutes to keep meat crumbly. Pour off fat.

2. Stir salsa and refried beans into cooked meat. Spread mixture over bottom of a 10-inch deep-dish pie plate or quiche dish with raised edge. Cover with paper towel. Cook on HIGH 4 to 5 minutes, until very hot. Sprinkle cheese over top. Cook, uncovered, 2 to 3 minutes, until cheese melts. Spread sour cream over cheese and sprinkle tomato, olives and avocado evenly over the top. Serve at once, with tortilla chips for dipping.

---

38 MUSHROOM CAVIAR
Prep: 5 minutes   Cook: 5 minutes   Makes: about 1½ cups

2 **tablespoons pine nuts**
3 **tablespoons plus 1 teaspoon**
  butter
½ **pound fresh mushrooms**

2 **garlic cloves, minced**
1 **tablespoon dry white wine**
2 **tablespoons sour cream**
  Salt and pepper

1. Place nuts and 1 teaspoon butter in a 1-cup glass measure. Cook on HIGH 2 minutes, stirring once, until lightly toasted. Remove and let cool.

2. Coarsely chop mushrooms in a food processor. In a 4-cup glass measure, combine chopped mushrooms, garlic and 3 tablespoons butter. Cook on HIGH 2 minutes, stirring once. Add wine and cook 1 minute. Set aside and let cool.

3. Stir sour cream into mushroom mixture and season with salt and pepper to taste. Transfer to a food processor and pulse several times until finely chopped. Add toasted pine nuts and blend in. Cover and refrigerate until needed. Serve with crackers or slices of French bread.

39   CHOPPED CHICKEN LIVER
Prep: 15 minutes   Cook: 10 to 15 minutes   Serves: 6

Here's an old-fashioned recipe prepared in minutes using a couple of newfangled machines: the microwave and a food processor. Serve with rye bread or crackers.

1 pound chicken livers, trimmed and cut into 1-inch chunks
¼ cup Rendered Chicken Fat (recipe follows) or vegetable oil

1 large onion, chopped
1 teaspoon salt
¼ teaspoon pepper
2 hard-cooked eggs
   Minced parsley, for garnish

1. In a 1-quart casserole with cover, place livers and 2 tablespoons chicken fat. Cover and cook on MEDIUM 3 minutes. Stir, cover and continue to cook 3 to 4 minutes, or just until livers are barely cooked and still slightly pink inside. Set aside, covered, to cool slightly.

2. In a 4-cup glass measure, place remaining chicken fat and onion. Cover with waxed paper. Cook on HIGH 5 to 7 minutes, stirring once or twice, until onion begins to brown slightly. With a slotted spoon, transfer livers to a food processor. Add cooked onion mixture and salt and pepper. Process, turning the machine quickly on and off, until very coarsely chopped. Quarter 1 egg and add to liver mixture. Process until finely chopped; do not blend to a paste.

3. Transfer chopped liver to a bowl, cover and refrigerate until ready to serve. Shortly before serving, grate remaining egg and sprinkle over liver. Garnish with minced parsley.

40   RENDERED CHICKEN FAT
Prep: 10 minutes   Cook: 13 to 15 minutes   Makes: about ¾ cup

Here's an easy way to render fat with no mess. This recipe also works beautifully with goose or duck fat.

1 cup ½-inch pieces chicken, goose or duck fat and fatty skin

1 large onion, coarsely chopped

1. In a 4-cup glass measure, place fat and pieces of fatty skin. Cover with paper towel. Cook on HIGH until fat is melted and skin becomes crisp, about 10 minutes.

2. With slotted spoon, remove crisp skin (see NOTE). Add onion to fat and cook on HIGH 3 to 5 minutes, or until onion is lightly browned. Strain fat into a clean, dry heatproof jar (a canning jar works well). Let cool, then cover and store in refrigerator for up to 3 months.

NOTE: These crisp skins, or cracklings, are delicious sprinkled with coarse salt and folded into an omelet or sprinkled on top of a salad.

41   TURKEY AND SAUSAGE-STUFFED MUSHROOMS

Prep: 10 minutes   Cook: 12 to 15 minutes   Makes: 24

24 medium mushrooms
 1 medium onion, chopped
 1 teaspoon vegetable oil
 ¼ pound bulk sausage
 ¼ pound ground turkey

 3 ounces cream cheese
 ½ teaspoon thyme leaves
 1 teaspoon lemon juice
 2 tablespoons chopped
    parsley

1. Remove mushroom stems from caps. Chop stems fine in food processor.

2. In a 4-cup glass measure, combine onion and oil. Cook on HIGH 3 minutes. Add crumbled sausage and turkey. Cook 5 to 6 minutes, stirring twice to break up any lumps. Pour off fat. Stir in cream cheese, thyme, lemon juice, parsley and chopped mushroom stems.

3. Fill mushroom caps with about 1 teaspoon filling. Place 12 stuffed mushrooms in an 8-inch round shallow dish. Cook on HIGH 2 to 3 minutes, just until mushrooms are hot; do not overcook. Serve while you repeat with second batch.

42   MUSHROOMS STUFFED WITH SPINACH AND THREE CHEESES

Prep: 15 minutes   Cook: 9 minutes   Makes: 24

For easy entertaining, stuff these ahead of time and refrigerate until just before your party begins. If you have any filling left over, roll it into miniature balls and freeze until needed for next time.

 1 10-ounce package frozen
    chopped spinach
 ½ cup shredded Monterey jack
    cheese
 ¼ cup crumbled feta cheese

 ¼ cup grated Parmesan cheese
 ⅓ cup finely chopped scallions
24 large fresh mushrooms,
    stemmed

1. Place unopened box of frozen spinach on a plate. Cook on HIGH 3 minutes. Leave in box 5 minutes to complete thawing. Drain spinach; squeeze out as much moisture as possible.

2. In a medium bowl, combine spinach, jack cheese, feta cheese, Parmesan cheese and scallions; blend well. Stuff each mushroom cap with filling, piling high in center.

3. Place 12 mushrooms on an 8-inch plate, arranging smaller mushrooms in center. Cook on HIGH 2 to 3 minutes, just until mushrooms are slightly soft to the touch. Serve hot. Repeat with remaining batch.

43   CRAB-STUFFED MUSHROOMS
Prep: 15 minutes   Cook: 4 to 5 minutes   Makes: 24

These mushrooms can be stuffed early in the day and refrigerated. Remove them an hour or two before company arrives, so they can return to room temperature, and pop them in the microwave just before serving.

3   shallots or 1 small onion, minced
2   tablespoons butter or margarine
1   garlic clove, minced
¼   cup chopped parsley
1   tablespoon prepared white horseradish
6   ounces crabmeat, drained and flaked
24   medium mushrooms, stemmed

1. Place shallots and butter in a 1-quart bowl. Cook on HIGH 2 minutes. Stir in garlic, parsley, horseradish and crabmeat.

2. Stuff mushroom caps with crab filling. Arrange half the mushrooms on an 8-inch plate. Cook on HIGH 2 to 3 minutes, just until mushrooms are soft to the touch; do not overcook. Serve while you cook second batch.

---

44   MUSHROOMS STUFFED WITH SPINACH PESTO
Prep: 5 minutes   Cook: 10 to 12 minutes   Makes: 48

1   10-ounce package frozen chopped spinach
3   garlic cloves
2   medium shallots
3   tablespoons pine nuts
1   cup (lightly packed) fresh basil leaves
½   teaspoon salt
¼   teaspoon pepper
¼   cup grated Parmesan cheese
¼   cup extra-virgin olive oil
48   fresh medium mushrooms, stemmed

1. Place unopened box of spinach on a plate. Defrost on HIGH 3 minutes. Set aside in box for 5 minutes. Drain spinach well. Squeeze with hands to remove all excess moisture.

2. In a food processor, combine garlic, shallots and pine nuts; pulse to mince. Add basil, spinach, salt and pepper. Pulse until coarsely pureed. With machine on, add oil until blended. Refrigerate spinach pesto, covered, for up to 6 hours before using.

3. Fill each mushroom cap with spinach pesto. Place 16 mushrooms on an 8-inch serving plate. Cook on HIGH 2 to 3 minutes, just until mushrooms are warm and slightly soft to the touch. Do not overcook. Serve while you cook the other two batches.

45 PISTACHIO-STUFFED MUSHROOMS
Prep: 15 minutes   Cook: 5 to 7 minutes   Makes: 20

20 fresh medium mushrooms
¼ cup minced onion
3 tablespoons butter or margarine
⅓ cup dry bread crumbs
¼ cup chopped pistachios

2 tablespoons chopped parsley
¼ teaspoon marjoram
¼ teaspoon salt
⅛ teaspoon pepper

1. Trim stem ends of mushrooms. Remove stems and finely chop in a food processor or by hand. Reserve whole caps.

2. In a 4-cup glass measure, combine chopped mushrooms, onion and butter. Cook on HIGH 2 to 3 minutes, just until mushrooms are soft. Stir in bread crumbs, chopped nuts, parsley, marjoram, salt and pepper.

3. Stuff each mushroom cap with filling. Arrange in a 9-inch quiche dish or on a plate, with largest mushrooms around outside of dish. Cook on HIGH 3 to 4 minutes, just until mushrooms are slightly soft to the touch; do not overcook. Serve hot.

46 MUSHROOMS WITH GARLIC BUTTER AND PARMESAN CHEESE
Prep: 10 minutes   Cook: 5 minutes   Serves: 4 to 6

Have a plentiful supply of French bread on hand to sop up all the irresistible juices.

1 stick butter
5 garlic cloves, minced
1 pound fresh medium mushrooms

1 cup chopped fresh parsley
½ cup grated Parmesan cheese

1. In an 8-inch quiche dish or pie plate, cook butter and garlic on HIGH 2 minutes, stirring once. Stir in mushrooms. Cook 2 minutes longer, stirring once.

2. Stir in parsley and cheese and cook on HIGH 1 minute, or just until mixture is hot and mushrooms are tender. Serve at once, with toothpicks and slices of crusty bread.

Chapter 3

Sandwiches, Pizzas, Tacos and Melts

America is the land of the sandwich, and the nacho, and the pizza, and the taco and the melt. And nothing makes them faster than a microwave oven. Cheese melts beautifully to a soft, creamy consistency. Bacon cooks to a perfect crispy golden brown, and the grease disappears. For many of these recipes, all you need are microwave paper towels, and paper plates. There's nothing to dirty, nothing to clean up.

While ordinary bread must be toasted conventionally, the microwave is great for heating buns, muffins and tortillas. That's how I got the idea for using a flour tortilla as a base for pizza. Crisp it first in the microwave for 1 to 2 minutes, then pile on your choice of toppings—hot or cold. Try a Tortilla Pizza with spaghetti sauce, salami and mozzarella, or go designer with Tortilla Pizza with Peppers, Leeks and Goat Cheese. There's a Club Pizza layered with white-meat chicken, bacon, lettuce, tomato and cheese and a Vegetable Tortilla Pizza with broccoli, zucchini, red pepper and mushrooms.

Whether you're grabbing a quick lunch with a Tuna-Cheddar Melt, a Reuben Sandwich or a Sausage and Pepper Hero or looking for a late-night snack with Welsh Rabbit on Toast or a Ham and Cheese Melt, you'll find easy-to-follow recipes here for all your favorites.

---

47 TUNA-CHEDDAR MELTS

Prep: 10 minutes   Cook: 2 to 3 minutes   Serves: 4

1 6½- to 7-ounce can tuna
1 cup chopped celery
¼ cup chopped scallions
1 hard-cooked egg, chopped
¼ cup mayonnaise
1 tablespoon sweet pickle
    relish

1 teaspoon lemon juice
4 slices sharp Cheddar cheese
4 sesame hamburger buns or
    crusty sourdough rolls,
    split

1. Drain and flake tuna in a medium bowl. Add celery, scallions, egg, mayonnaise, relish and lemon juice. Mix well.

2. Spread tuna salad over bottom halves of buns. Cover each with a slice of cheese. Place on a paper towel-lined plate. Cook on HIGH 1 to 2 minutes, just until tuna is warm and cheese melts. Add bun tops. Cook on HIGH 45 to 60 seconds, to heat.

48 BARBECUED BEEF SANDWICHES
Prep: 5 minutes   Cook: 7 to 9 minutes   Serves: 4

This is a great way to use leftover roast beef.

1 pound thickly sliced
   leftover or deli roast beef
1 green bell pepper, coarsely
   chopped

1½ cups barbecue sauce
4 sesame seed hamburger
   buns or long crusty rolls

1. Cut beef slices into strips. Mix bell pepper and barbecue sauce in a 1-quart casserole. Cover and cook on HIGH 3 to 4 minutes, until hot.

2. Stir in beef strips. Cover and cook on MEDIUM 4 to 5 minutes, just until beef is hot. With slotted spoon, divide barbecued beef among buns. Spoon some sauce over each. Serve hot.

49 GRILLED HAMBURGER WITH ONION
Prep: 5 minutes   Cook: 5 minutes   Serves: 1

¼ pound lean ground beef
1 tablespoon ice water
1 teaspoon Worcestershire
   sauce
   Pinch of pepper

1 sweet onion slice, cut ½ inch
   thick
1 English muffin, split
   Ketchup and/or mustard

1. Preheat browning dish to its highest setting. Meanwhile, with a light hand, mix beef with ice water, Worcestershire and pepper. Shape into a patty about ¾ inch thick.

2. Place burger and onion slice next to each other on preheated browning dish. Cook on HIGH 3 minutes, or until browned on bottom. Turn both over and cook 1½ to 2 minutes, depending on whether you like your burgers rare, medium or well done. Meanwhile, toast muffin in toaster. Serve grilled hamburger and onion on toasted English muffin, with ketchup or mustard on the side.

50 BOARDWALK HOT DOG
Prep: 5 minutes   Cook: 1 to 1½ minutes   Serves: 1

1 knockwurst hot dog
1 hot dog bun
2 tablespoons drained
   sauerkraut (optional)

Garnishes: prepared
mustard, pickle relish,
chili, chopped onion,
shredded cheese

1. With small sharp knife, score hot dog in several places on opposite sides. Roll up hot dog in paper towel; place on paper plate. Cook on HIGH 1 to 1½ minutes (the longer time if you just removed the hot dog from the refrigerator).

2. Remove paper towel. Place hot dog in bun. If using sauerkraut, spoon over hot dog now. Cook on HIGH 15 seconds, just until bun is warm. Serve with choice of garnishes.

51 SAUSAGE AND PEPPER HEROES

Prep: 5 minutes   Cook: 6 minutes   Serves: 4

4 Italian sausages, sweet or
  hot to your taste
½ cup spaghetti or barbecue
  sauce, homemade or
  store-bought

2 medium bell peppers, cut
  into strips
4 hero rolls

1. Score sausages on opposite sides in several places. Roll each sausage in a paper towel. Place on plate. Cook on HIGH 3 minutes.

2. Combine sauce and peppers in small casserole. Cover and cook on HIGH 2 minutes.

3. Split rolls in half without cutting all the way through. Split each sausage in half lengthwise without cutting all the way through. Set 1 sausage on each roll. Top with sauce and peppers. Place each sandwich between paper towels. Cook on MEDIUM 1 minute, just to warm rolls. Serve at once.

52 REUBEN SANDWICH

Prep: 5 minutes   Cook: 5 minutes   Serves: 2

4 slices rye or pumpernickel
  bread
6 ounces thinly sliced corned
  beef

½ cup drained sauerkraut
3 tablespoons Thousand
  Island dressing
2 thick slices Swiss cheese

1. Toast bread in toaster. Place 2 slices on double layer of paper towels on a large plate. Layer corned beef, sauerkraut, dressing and cheese over bread, dividing evenly. Cook on HIGH 1 minute, or until corned beef and sauerkraut are hot.

2. Set remaining 2 toast slices on sandwiches. Cook on HIGH 45 seconds, just until tops are warmed. Serve hot.

53 VEGETABLE-FILLED PITA POCKETS WITH YOGURT-CUCUMBER DRESSING

Prep: 10 minutes   Cook: 7 to 9 minutes   Serves: 4

½ cup plain yogurt
1 teaspoon minced fresh dill
  or ½ teaspoon dried
1 teaspoon minced chives
¼ cup chopped cucumbers
  Salt and pepper
1 cup broccoli florets

1 cup thinly sliced carrots
1 cup thinly sliced
  mushrooms
3 scallions, thinly sliced
4 6-inch pita breads
1 cup alfalfa or radish sprouts

1. In a small bowl, combine yogurt, dill, chives and cucumbers. Season with salt and pepper to taste. Cover and refrigerate dressing until serving time.

2. Lay 4 sets of connected paper towels (2 to each) on counter. In a large mixing bowl, toss together broccoli, carrots, mushrooms and scallions.

Divide mixed vegetables among each set of paper towels, placing them in the center, directly over perforations. Fold long sides of towel toward center, enclosing food. Fold ends toward center, overlapping on top.

3. Briefly pass each bundle under running water until soaked but not dripping wet. Place bundles in a circle on a 9-inch plate, perforated side up. Cook on HIGH 6 to 8 minutes, or until vegetables are just tender.

4. Place pita breads between 2 paper towels. Cook on HIGH 1 minute, or until just heated through. Cut ½-inch slice from top of each pita. Fill with vegetables. Top with sprouts and yogurt-cucumber dressing.

54 CHEESE MUFFIN MELTS WITH TOMATO AND BACON
Prep: 5 minutes   Cook: 6 to 7 minutes   Serves: 2

6 slices bacon	8 slices (3 × 1-inch) Swiss,
2 English muffins, split	Cheddar or Monterey
4 teaspoons butter, softened	jack cheese
4 thick slices tomato	

1. Place bacon between paper towels on a paper plate. Cook on HIGH 4 to 5 minutes, or until crisp. Break each slice in half.

2. Arrange muffin halves on a plate. Spread each with 1 teaspoon butter. Top each with 1 tomato slice and 3 pieces of bacon. Overlap 2 slices of cheese on top. Cook on MEDIUM 1 to 2 minutes, until cheese melts. Serve hot.

55 SALAD TACO WITH CHEESE AND BEANS
Prep: 5 minutes   Cook: 1 minute   Serves: 1

Microwaving saves calories as well as time, since no oil is needed for the tortilla.

1 6- to 7-inch corn tortilla	½ cup chopped salad
¼ cup refried beans	vegetables: lettuce,
¼ cup shredded Cheddar	cucumber, tomato,
cheese	radishes, scallion
¼ cup diced avocado	Taco sauce

1. To make taco shell, place tortilla in center of paper towel. Fold 1 corner of towel toward center of tortilla and roll up tortilla with towel. Place loose corner down on plate. Cook on HIGH 1 minute. Remove towel.

2. Spread refried beans in taco shell. Top with cheese. Place taco on fresh paper towel. Cook on HIGH 30 to 45 seconds, just until cheese melts. Top with avocado and salad vegetables of choice. Serve with taco sauce on the side.

NOTE: To prepare 2 tacos, increase time 30 seconds. Add 15 seconds for each additional taco after that.

56   VEGETARIAN BURRITOS
Prep: 10 minutes   Cook: 5 to 7 minutes   Serves: 4 to 6

Serve with hot sauce and/or salsa and a big salad.

2 cups cooked pinto or black
   beans or 1 16-ounce can
   refried beans
4 scallions, chopped
1 7-ounce can chopped green
   chiles, drained

2 cups shredded Cheddar
   cheese
½ cup sour cream
1 tablespoon chili powder
½ teaspoon salt
6 10-inch flour tortillas

1. In a medium bowl, combine all ingredients except tortillas. Mix lightly to blend.

2. Place tortillas between 2 paper towels. Heat on HIGH 15 seconds to soften. Spoon ½ cup filling across center of each tortilla. Fold sides in and roll up tortilla.

3. Arrange burritos in a single layer in an 8-inch square baking dish. Cover with paper towel. Cook on HIGH 5 to 7 minutes, until hot throughout.

57   HOLIDAY TURKEY PITA SANDWICHES
Prep: 5 minutes   Cook: 5 to 6 minutes   Serves: 4

This is a sandwich for the day after Thanksgiving or Christmas or Easter or anytime you have leftover turkey. You may like it so much you'll buy deli turkey and packaged stuffing mix and enjoy it whenever you wish. For a real holiday touch, serve cranberry sauce (recipe follows) on the side.

2 cups diced cooked turkey
¾ cup poultry stuffing
1 cup chopped tomato
½ cup thinly sliced onion

1 cup cooked vegetables:
   carrots, peas, broccoli,
   zucchini or green beans
4 6-inch pita breads

1. Put the turkey in a medium bowl. Crumble in the stuffing. Add all the remaining ingredients except the pita breads and toss to mix.

2. Open one end of each pita bread with a knife or cut ½ inch off one side. Divide filling among breads. Wrap each in a paper towel. Cook on HIGH 5 to 6 minutes, until heated through.

58   FRESH CRANBERRY SAUCE
Prep: 5 minutes   Cook: 6 to 7 minutes   Makes: 2 cups

3 cups fresh cranberries
⅓ cup fresh orange juice

1 cup sugar
1 tablespoon minced orange
   zest

1. Combine all ingredients in a 2-quart glass measure or bowl. Cover with plastic wrap. Poke 2 or 3 holes in wrap with tip of small knife. Cook on HIGH 6 to 7 minutes until berries pop open.

2. Stir sauce and cool. Cover and refrigerate for up to 5 days before serving.

59 BURRITOS WITH CHORIZO AND POTATOES

Prep: 15 minutes   Cook: 9 to 12 minutes   Serves: 4 to 6

Serve with chopped salad and a dollop of sour cream.

¾ **pound chorizo sausage**
2 **large Idaho baking potatoes,**
   baked (p. 131), peeled
   and cut into ½-inch dice
2 **cups shredded sharp**
   Cheddar cheese

3 **medium tomatoes, chopped**
½ **teaspoon garlic powder**
½ **teaspoon ground cumin**
½ **teaspoon salt**
6 **10-inch flour tortillas**

1. Slice or break up sausage. Place in a 2-quart casserole or bowl. Cover with paper towel. Cook on HIGH 3 to 4 minutes, stirring once or twice to keep meat crumbly. Add all remaining ingredients except tortillas. Mix well.

2. Place tortillas between 2 paper towels. Heat on HIGH 15 seconds to soften. Spoon ½ cup sausage-potato filling across center of each tortilla. Fold sides in and roll up.

3. Arrange burritos in a 9-inch square baking dish. Cover with paper towel. Cook on HIGH 5 to 7 minutes, until heated through.

60 HAMBURGER HAMLET'S AVOCADO MELT WITH CHILI

Prep: 5 minutes   Cook: 1 to 2 minutes   Serves: 1

1 **cup corn chips**
½ **avocado**
¾ **cup chili, canned or**
   homemade

½ **cup shredded mozzarella**
   cheese

1. Sprinkle corn chips over bottom of a small, shallow oval or round dish. Cut avocado in two and place on chips. Cover with chili and sprinkle cheese on top.

2. Cook uncovered on HIGH 1 to 2 minutes, until chili is heated through and cheese melts. Serve with a fork.

61 HAM AND CHEESE MELT

Prep: 5 minutes   Cook: 1 minute   Serves: 1

2 **slices whole wheat bread,**
   toasted

2 **slices Swiss cheese**
1 **slice boiled ham**

1. Place a paper towel on counter. Place 1 slice of toast diagonally in center. Top with a slice of cheese, a slice of ham and another slice of cheese. Cover with remaining toast.

2. Fold 3 corners of paper towel toward center, covering sandwich like an envelope. Place folded-side down on plate. Cook on HIGH 30 to 45 seconds, until cheese melts.

TORTILLA PIZZAS

A flour tortilla makes an unconventional, but excellent low-cal base for a pizza that's perfect in the microwave, crisped in just about a minute. Here's an international collection of recipes to start you off. Soon you'll be inventing your own.

---

62   TORTILLA PIZZA
Prep: 5 minutes   Cook: 1½ to 2½ minutes   Serves: 1

1 **8-inch flour tortilla**
3 **tablespoons thick spaghetti
    sauce**
½ **cup shredded mozzarella
    cheese**

6 **thin slices salami, 3 inches
    in diameter**
1 **tablespoon grated Parmesan
    cheese**

1. Pierce tortilla several times with a fork. Place between 2 sheets of paper towel. Cook on HIGH 1½ minutes, just until tortilla is barely crisp. Transfer to a serving plate.

2. Spread spaghetti sauce over tortilla to within 1 inch of edge. Sprinkle with mozzarella cheese and top with salami. Sprinkle Parmesan cheese over all. Cook on HIGH 45 seconds, or just until cheese melts.

---

63   TORTILLA PIZZA WITH PEPPERS, LEEKS AND GOAT CHEESE
Prep: 10 minutes   Cook: 9 to 12 minutes   Serves: 1

1 **8-inch flour tortilla**
1 **medium leek (white and
    tender green), well rinsed
    and thinly sliced**
2 **tablespoons extra-virgin
    olive oil**

½ **cup sliced bell pepper**
¼ **cup crumbled mild goat
    cheese, such as
    Montrachet**

1. Pierce tortilla several times with a fork. Place between 2 sheets of paper towel. Cook on HIGH 1 to 1½ minutes, until tortilla is just barely crisp.

2. In a 4-cup glass measure, place leek and oil. Cover with waxed paper. Cook on HIGH 5 to 7 minutes, stirring once, until softened but still slightly crisp. Add pepper and cook 2 minutes.

3. Place crisped tortilla on a plate. Arrange leeks and peppers on top. Sprinkle goat cheese over vegetables. Cook on HIGH 30 to 45 seconds, just until cheese is hot. Serve immediately.

64   VEGETABLE TORTILLA PIZZA
Prep: 10 minutes   Cook: 3 to 5 minutes   Serves: 1

1 8-inch flour tortilla
¼ cup broccoli florets
¼ cup thinly sliced zucchini
2 tablespoons red bell pepper
   strips

3 medium mushrooms, sliced
¼ cup shredded Monterey jack
   cheese

1. Pierce tortilla several times with a fork. Place between 2 paper towels and cook on HIGH 1 to 1½ minutes, until barely crisp. Transfer to a serving plate.

2. Place 2 connected paper towels on counter. Toss together broccoli, zucchini, red pepper and mushrooms. Set vegetables on paper towel, directly over perforation in center. Fold over both sides and then the ends to enclose. Moisten packet under running water. Place, perforated side up, on plate. Microwave on HIGH 1½ to 2 minutes, until vegetables are crisp-tender.

3. Arrange vegetables on tortilla. Sprinkle cheese on top and cook on HIGH 45 to 60 seconds, just until cheese melts. Serve immediately.

65   HEARTLAND PIZZA
Prep: 10 minutes   Cook: 6 to 8 minutes   Serves: 1

1 8-inch flour tortilla
1 link sweet Italian sausage,
   casing removed
1 tablespoon Dijon mustard
¼ cup corn kernels

½ cup shredded Cheddar
   cheese
¼ cup chopped tomato
1 tablespoon chopped parsley

1. Pierce tortilla several times with a fork. Place between 2 paper towels. Cook on HIGH 1 to 1½ minutes, until tortilla is barely crisp. Remove from towels and set on a plate.

2. Crumble sausage into center of a paper towel. Fold to enclose sausage, with extra folds on bottom to absorb fat. Place on paper plate. Cook on MEDIUM 3 to 3½ minutes, until sausage is no longer pink. Crumble sausage with fork.

3. Spread mustard over tortilla to within ½ inch of edge. Sprinkle on crumbled sausage, corn, cheese, tomato and parsley. Cook on MEDIUM 2 to 3 minutes, until cheese melts. Serve immediately.

66 CLUB PIZZA
Prep: 10 minutes   Cook: 6 to 8 minutes   Serves: 1

The classic BLT in a new package.

6 wafer-thin slices of bacon
1 8-inch flour tortilla
1 tablespoon mayonnaise
2 ounces cooked roast turkey
   or chicken, shredded
   (about ⅓ cup)

½ cup chopped tomato
½ cup shredded Monterey jack
   cheese
½ cup shredded lettuce

1. Put bacon between 2 paper towels on a paper plate. Cook on HIGH 4 to 5 minutes until crisp; crumble.

2. Pierce tortilla several times with a fork. Place between 2 sheets of paper towel. Cook on HIGH 1 to 1½ minutes, just until tortilla is barely crisp. Transfer to serving plate.

3. Spread mayonnaise over tortilla to within ½ inch from edge. Sprinkle on bacon, shredded turkey, tomato and cheese. Cook on MEDIUM-HIGH 1 to 1½ minutes, just until cheese melts. Top with lettuce and serve.

67 GREEK TORTILLA PIZZA WITH SPINACH AND FETA
Prep: 10 minutes   Cook: 2 to 3 minutes   Serves: 1

1 8-inch flour tortilla
1 cup fresh spinach
⅓ cup crumbled feta cheese
2 tablespoons sliced scallion

⅓ cup diced tomato
1 tablespoon sliced black
   olives

1. Pierce tortilla several times with a fork. Place between 2 sheets of paper towel. Cook on HIGH 1 to 1½ minutes, until tortilla is barely crisp. Remove from towel and set on a plate.

2. Layer spinach leaves over tortilla. Sprinkle feta cheese over spinach. Top with scallion and tomato. Cook on HIGH 1 to 1½ minutes, until hot. Sprinkle with olives on top and serve.

68 WELSH RABBIT ON TOAST
Prep: 5 minutes   Cook: 12 minutes   Serves: 4 to 6

1 pound sharp Cheddar
   cheese, shredded
2 tablespoons butter
1 teaspoon Worcestershire
   sauce
½ teaspoon salt
½ teaspoon paprika

¼ teaspoon dry mustard
¼ teaspoon cayenne pepper
2 large eggs
1 cup beer or ale, at room
   temperature
6 thick slices French bread,
   toasted

1. In a 2-quart casserole, combine cheese, butter, Worcestershire, salt, paprika, mustard and cayenne. Cover with lid or waxed paper. Cook on

MEDIUM 3 minutes. Stir and continue cooking 3 minutes longer. Remove from microwave.

2. In a small bowl, beat eggs lightly. Gradually whisk ½ cup hot cheese into eggs. Slowly whisk eggs into remaining cheese mixture to blend well. Stir in beer. Cover and cook on MEDIUM 6 minutes, stirring once. To serve, set a piece of toast in each serving bowl and ladle hot cheese mixture over bread.

---

69 WARM SALMON SALAD IN A PITA POCKET
Prep: 10 minutes   Cook: 2 to 3 minutes   Serves: 4

1 7½-ounce can Sockeye red
    salmon
2 tablespoons mayonnaise
1 teaspoon lemon juice
2 scallions, chopped
1 celery rib, chopped

1 medium zucchini, chopped
4 pita breads
1 medium tomato, seeded and
    chopped
½ cup alfalfa sprouts
½ cup shredded lettuce

1. In a medium bowl, flake salmon. Add mayonnaise, lemon juice, scallions, celery and zucchini. Mix well. Slit each pita bread and fill the pockets with salmon salad. Place on a paper towel-lined plate; cover with a paper towel. Cook on HIGH 2 to 3 minutes, until heated through.

2. Place each sandwich on a plate and sprinkle tomato, sprouts and lettuce over salmon salad. Serve warm.

Chapter 4

Speedy Soups and Chowders

The trick to producing sensational soups and chowders in the microwave is in cooking the solids until they are tender before combining them with the liquid. Vegetable soups and seafood chowders are naturals for the microwave. When making a recipe with a large bone, such as a ham hock, it is important to give the ingredients a little longer to simmer on medium power to allow all the flavors to be drawn into the broth.

Many recipes here call for either homemade stock or canned broth. I feel that in most instances—while homemade is, of course, unbeatable for flavor—canned broth provides a more-than-acceptable base. When speed is of the essence, the savings it affords in time more than makes up for differences in taste. The only pitfall of canned broth is in its saltiness. Whenever possible, purchase reduced-sodium brands and always check the level of seasoning in a soup before adding any additional salt.

Choose here from hearty classics, such as Black Bean Soup with Sherry and Sour Cream, Easy New England Clam Chowder and Pea Soup with Sausages. Preface a dinner party with Speedy Crab Bisque, Rich Mushroom Soup or chilled Vichyssoise. Beat the clock with Instant Curried Tomato Soup, Tortilla Soup with Avocado and Lime or Cream of Broccoli Soup.

Since tasty soups are often made from tasty leftovers, I hope you will be encouraged to devise your own combinations. This collection just taps the surface of what you can do, but I hope that from it you will learn the techniques, tricks and types of equipment and ingredients appropriate for making great soups and chowders in the microwave.

70 ACORN SQUASH SOUP WITH MAPLE SYRUP

Prep: 10 minutes   Cook: 33 to 38 minutes   Serves: 6 to 8

Like the potato, squash is a vegetable made for the microwave, which cuts its cooking time from over an hour to just minutes.

2 acorn squash (1¼ pounds
 each)
1 large onion, chopped
3 tablespoons butter
2 10½-ounce cans chicken
 broth

½ cup heavy cream
2 tablespoons maple syrup
Dash of cayenne pepper
Salt

1. Pierce each squash several times with a long-pronged fork. Cook on HIGH 10 minutes. Turn over and cook 7 to 10 minutes longer, until squash are soft to the touch. Set aside and let cool slightly, then cut in half.

2. In a 3-quart casserole, place onion and butter. Cook on HIGH 5 minutes. Add chicken broth, cover and cook 6 minutes.

3. Seed squash and scoop out flesh. Working in batches in food processor or blender, puree squash with broth and onion until smooth. Return soup to casserole. Whisk in cream, maple syrup and cayenne. Cover with waxed paper and cook on HIGH 5 to 7 minutes, until simmering. Season with salt to taste.

---

71 BLACK BEAN SOUP WITH SHERRY AND SOUR CREAM

Prep: 15 minutes   Cook: 40 minutes   Serves: 6 to 8

1 large onion, chopped
1 small green bell pepper,
 chopped
3 large garlic cloves, chopped
1 large ham hock
1 bay leaf
2 10½-ounce cans beef broth
3 cups water

1 tablespoon red wine vinegar
2 15-ounce cans black beans,
 with liquid
½ cup dry sherry
Salt and pepper
1 cup sour cream
Sprigs of parsley

1. In a 5-quart casserole, combine onion, green pepper, garlic, ham hock, bay leaf, broth, water and vinegar. Cover with lid and cook on HIGH 10 minutes, or until boiling. Reduce power to MEDIUM-HIGH and cook, covered, 20 minutes.

2. Add beans with their liquid and sherry. Cover and cook on HIGH 10 minutes, or until hot. Season with salt and pepper to taste. Serve with a dollop of sour cream and garnish with a sprig of parsley.

72   EASY NEW ENGLAND CLAM CHOWDER
Prep: 10 minutes   Cook: 16 to 21 minutes   Serves: 4 to 6

4 slices bacon, diced
2 medium potatoes, peeled
     and cut into ½-inch cubes
1 medium onion, chopped
4 tablespoons butter
6 tablespoons flour
3 cups milk

1 10-ounce can whole baby
     clams, with liquid
1 6½-ounce can minced clams,
     with liquid
⅛ teaspoon thyme
     Dash of cayenne pepper
     Salt

1. Place bacon in a 3-quart casserole. Cook on HIGH 2 to 4 minutes, until crisp. Stir in potatoes and onion. Cover and cook on HIGH 8 to 10 minutes, stirring once, until potatoes are tender.

2. Put butter in a small bowl. Cook on HIGH 1 minute, or until melted. Stir in flour to make a paste. Stir into potato-onion mixture.

3. Add milk, whole and minced clams with liquid, thyme and cayenne. Mix well. Cover and cook on HIGH 1 minute. Stir vigorously. Continue to cook, covered, 4 to 5 minutes, until hot and slightly thickened. Season with salt to taste.

73   MANHATTAN CLAM CHOWDER
Prep: 10 minutes   Cook: 20 to 25 minutes   Serves: 4

2 large baking potatoes (about
     ½ pound each)
½ cup thinly sliced celery
1 carrot, finely diced
1 small onion, chopped
1 8-ounce bottle clam juice

1 14-ounce can peeled plum
     tomatoes, coarsely cut up,
     liquid reserved
½ teaspoon thyme leaves
2 6½-ounce cans minced
     clams, with liquid

1. Peel potatoes and cut into ½-inch dice. In a 3-quart casserole with lid, combine potatoes, celery, carrot, onion and clam juice. Cover and cook on HIGH, 15 to 20 minutes, stirring once or twice, until potatoes are fork tender.

2. Stir in tomatoes and liquid, thyme and clams with liquid. Cover and cook on HIGH 4 to 5 minutes, just until heated through.

74   INSTANT CURRIED TOMATO SOUP
Prep: 5 minutes   Cook: 12 minutes   Serves: 6

3 cups tomato juice
3 cups chicken broth
2 teaspoons lemon juice
1 teaspoon sugar
4 whole cloves

¼ teaspoon curry powder
     Salt and pepper
½ cup diced Monterey jack
     cheese

1. In a 3-quart casserole, combine tomato juice, broth and lemon juice. Cover with waxed paper. Cook on HIGH 7 minutes, or until simmering.

2. Stir in sugar, cloves and curry powder. Continue to cook on HIGH 5 minutes. Remove cloves. Season with salt and pepper to taste. Serve in mugs, with a sprinkling of diced cheese on top.

75   VICHYSSOISE
Prep: 20 minutes   Cook: 25 minutes   Serves: 4

Chilled, this soup is called Vichyssoise. It's also delicious hot, in which case it is plain old Potato and Leek Soup.

2 large baking potatoes, peeled and sliced	3½ cups chicken stock or canned broth
2 medium leeks (white and tender green), well washed and sliced	¾ cup heavy cream
	Salt and white pepper
	3 tablespoons minced chives

1. In a 3-quart casserole, place potatoes, leeks and 2 cups of stock. Cover and cook on HIGH 15 minutes, or until potatoes are fork tender.

2. Puree in a blender or food processor just until smooth. Do not overprocess, or potatoes will turn gummy. Return to casserole and stir in remaining 1½ cups stock. Cover and cook on HIGH 5 minutes.

3. Stir in cream and cook on HIGH 5 minutes. Season liberally with salt and white pepper. (The seasonings will fade as the soup chills.) Transfer to a covered container and refrigerate until chilled. Serve cold, garnished with minced chives.

76   RICH MUSHROOM SOUP
Prep: 5 minutes   Cook: 9 to 10 minutes   Serves: 4

This soup has an even more interesting taste if made with fresh oyster mushrooms, which are now available in many supermarkets.

1 pound fresh oyster mushrooms or white button mushrooms	½ teaspoon Worcestershire sauce
2 shallots, minced	¼ teaspoon thyme
2 tablespoons unsalted butter	½ teaspoon salt
3 cups milk	⅛ teaspoon white pepper
1 egg yolk	Hot pepper sauce
	Chopped parsley, for garnish

1. Trim stem ends of mushrooms. Cut mushrooms into ½-inch pieces. In a 2-quart bowl, combine mushrooms, shallots and butter. Cook on HIGH 3 minutes, stirring once.

2. Blend together milk, egg yolk, Worcestershire, thyme, salt and white pepper. Whisk in several drops of hot sauce. Add to mushrooms and stir to mix. Cook on HIGH 5 to 6 minutes, until heated through. Season with additional salt, white pepper and hot sauce to taste. Ladle into soup bowls and garnish with chopped parsley.

77   CREAMY CAULIFLOWER SOUP
Prep: 15 minutes   Cook: 11½ to 18 minutes   Serves: 3 to 4

3 **tablespoons butter or margarine**	1 **large cauliflower, broken into 1½-inch florets**
¼ **cup flour**	¼ **cup cream**
⅛ **teaspoon nutmeg**	**Salt and pepper**
4 **cups hot chicken stock or canned broth**	**Minced chives, for garnish**

1. In a 2-quart casserole, cook butter on HIGH 30 to 60 seconds, until bubbling. Stir in flour and nutmeg. Stir until smooth. Blend in chicken stock and cauliflower. Cover and cook on HIGH 10 to 15 minutes, until cauliflower is fork tender. Set aside, covered, for 10 minutes.

2. In a blender or food processor, puree soup in batches until smooth. Return to casserole and whisk in cream. Season with salt and pepper to taste. Cook on HIGH 1 to 2 minutes, until hot. Garnish with minced chives.

78   TEX-MEX TOMATO-CHEESE SOUP
Prep: 10 minutes   Cook: 13 to 15 minutes   Serves: 4

1 **large onion, finely chopped**	1 **7-ounce can diced green chiles, drained**
2 **tablespoons butter or margarine**	2 **cups shredded Cheddar cheese**
2 **garlic cloves, minced**	**Salt and pepper**
1 **28-ounce can peeled plum tomatoes, coarsely chopped, liquid reserved**	

1. In a 2-quart casserole, combine onion and butter. Cook on HIGH 5 minutes, stirring once. Add garlic, tomatoes with their liquid and chiles. Stir to blend. Cover and cook 7 to 9 minutes, until soup comes to full boil.

2. Stir in cheese. Cook, uncovered, until cheese melts, about 1 minute. Season with salt and pepper to taste. Serve immediately.

NOTE: To reheat, use MEDIUM power to avoid overcooking cheese.

79   SPEEDY CRAB BISQUE
Prep: 5 minutes   Cook: 7 to 9 minutes   Serves: 4 to 6

6 **ounces crabmeat**	1 **cup half-and-half or light cream**
1 **10¾-ounce can condensed cream of celery soup**	¼ **cup dry sherry or white wine**
1 **10¾-ounce can condensed cream of asparagus soup**	**Dash of cayenne pepper**
	Sour cream and parsley sprigs

1. If crab is frozen, thaw and drain, reserving liquid. If canned, drain, reserving liquid.

2. In a blender or food processor, combine celery and asparagus soups, half-and-half, sherry and reserved crab liquid. Puree until smooth.

3. Pour puree into a 2-quart casserole. Cover with waxed paper. Cook on HIGH 6 to 7 minutes, stirring twice, until simmering. Stir in crab and cayenne; cook 1 to 2 minutes longer. Serve hot, with a dollop of sour cream and a parsley sprig in each bowl.

80   CIOPPINO
Prep: 15 minutes   Cook: 31 to 35 minutes   Serves: 6 to 8

2 large leeks (white and tender green), well washed and thinly sliced	½ teaspoon oregano
	½ teaspoon salt
	½ teaspoon pepper
1 large onion, chopped	1 cup dry white wine
2 garlic cloves, crushed	2 pounds assorted fish, such as rockfish, cod, sea bass, cut into 2-inch chunks
¼ cup olive oil	
1 28-ounce can peeled plum tomatoes, coarsely chopped, liquid reserved	½ pound scallops or shrimp
	½ pound precooked crab legs, broken into pieces
1 6-ounce can tomato paste	

1. In a 4-quart casserole, combine leeks, onion, garlic and oil. Cover and cook on HIGH 8 to 9 minutes, until leeks and onion are soft.

2. Add tomatoes with liquid, tomato paste, oregano, salt and pepper. Cover and cook on HIGH 10 to 12 minutes, until boiling. Stir in wine and cook 3 minutes.

3. Add fish, scallops and crab. Cover and cook on HIGH until fish is opaque in center, about 10 minutes. Let stand, covered, 10 minutes before serving.

81   PEA SOUP WITH SAUSAGES
Prep: 5 minutes   Cook: 14 minutes   Serves: 4 to 6

½ cup chopped carrots	2 soup cans of water
½ cup chopped celery, with leaves	1 12-ounce kielbasa sausage, sliced
1 small onion, minced	1 bay leaf
2 tablespoons butter	Salt and pepper
2 11½-ounce cans condensed green pea soup	

1. In a 2-quart casserole, combine carrots, celery, onion and butter. Cover and cook on HIGH 4 minutes.

2. Add condensed soup, water, sausage slices and bay leaf. Cover and cook, stirring twice, on MEDIUM-HIGH 10 minutes, or until carrots are tender. Remove bay leaf. Season with salt and pepper to taste. Serve hot.

82   ITALIAN CLAM SOUP
Prep: 20 minutes   Cook: 20 to 25 minutes   Serves: 4

Serve in wide-brimmed soup plates with plenty of freshly made garlic bread. Be sure to have an extra empty bowl on the table for shells.

¼ **cup extra-virgin olive oil**
3 **large garlic cloves, minced**
1 **28-ounce can peeled plum tomatoes, coarsely chopped, liquid reserved**
½ **cup dry red wine**
3 **dozen hard-shelled clams, such as cherrystone or littleneck, well scrubbed**

1 **cup boiling water**
1 **tablespoon chopped fresh oregano or ½ teaspoon dried**
Garlic Toast (recipe follows)
2 **tablespoons chopped parsley**

1. In a 2-quart casserole with cover, place oil and garlic. Cook on HIGH 45 seconds. Stir in tomatoes with liquid and wine. Cover and cook on HIGH 10 minutes. Set aside.

2. Place clams and boiling water in a shallow baking dish. Cover and cook on HIGH 8 to 10 minutes, removing clams as they open. (Do not overcook, or clams will toughen.) Discard any clams that do not open.

3. Strain clam juices through double thickness of cheesecloth. Add to casserole. Cook on HIGH 2 to 3 minutes, until boiling. Stir in oregano and add clams in shells. To serve, place 1 slice of Garlic Toast in each of 4 soup plates. Ladle clams and soup over bread. Garnish with chopped parsley. Pass remaining toasts on the side.

83   GARLIC TOAST
Prep: 5 minutes   Cook: 2 to 3 minutes   Makes: 1 loaf

1 **long loaf French or sourdough bread**

⅓ **cup olive oil**
2 **garlic cloves, halved**

1. Cut bread into ½-inch-thick slices. Brush one side of each slice with oil and rub with cut side of garlic.

2. Place bread oiled-sides up on a microwave rack or on 3 folded sheets of paper towels. Cook on HIGH 2 to 3 minutes, or until dried.

84   CREAM OF SPINACH SOUP
Prep: 10 minutes   Cook: 13 to 15 minutes   Serves: 4 to 6

2 **10-ounce packages frozen chopped spinach**
2 **cups milk**
1½ **cups chicken stock or canned broth**

2 **thin slices onion**
3 **tablespoons flour**
¼ **teaspoon nutmeg**
Salt and pepper

1. Place unopened boxes of spinach on a plate and cook on HIGH 5 minutes. Set aside in closed box for 5 minutes longer to complete thawing.

Squeeze spinach dry.

2. In a food processor or blender, combine half the spinach, milk and chicken stock with the onion, flour and nutmeg. Puree until smooth. Pour into a 2-quart casserole. Repeat with remaining spinach, milk and stock. Whisk to blend the two batches. Cover and cook on MEDIUM 8 to 10 minutes, stirring twice, until thickened. Season with salt and pepper to taste.

---

85   CHILE-CHEESE SOUP
Prep: 5 minutes   Cook: 16 to 17 minutes   Serves: 4

Instead of bread, serve this tasty soup with soft, warm corn tortillas.

1 large onion, finely chopped	1 4-ounce can diced green
1 large red bell pepper, finely	chiles, with liquid
chopped	1 4-ounce jar pimientos,
2 tablespoons vegetable oil	coarsely chopped
1 28-ounce can peeled plum	½ teaspoon salt
tomatoes, coarsely	¼ teaspoon pepper
chopped, liquid reserved	½ pound Monterey jack
	cheese, shredded

1. In a 3-quart casserole, combine onion, red pepper and oil. Cook on HIGH 7 minutes, stirring once. Stir in tomatoes with liquid, chiles with liquid, pimientos, salt and pepper.

2. Cover and cook on HIGH 8 to 9 minutes, until soup comes to a full boil. Stir in cheese and cook 1 minute, or until just melted. Season with additional salt and pepper to taste.

---

86   FRESH VEGETABLE SOUP
Prep: 15 minutes   Cook: 27 to 37 minutes   Serves: 6 to 8

½ pound green beans	1 garlic clove, minced
2 zucchini	4 cups water
2 yellow summer squash	1 teaspoon basil
2 celery ribs	1 teaspoon salt
2 yams or sweet potatoes,	½ teaspoon pepper
peeled	½ cup chopped parsley
1 small onion	

1. Cut green beans, zucchini, summer squash, celery, yams and onion into small dice (¼- to ⅜-inch). Place diced vegetables in a 4-quart bowl. Add garlic, water, basil, salt, pepper and ⅓ cup parsley. Cover and cook on HIGH 25 to 35 minutes, stirring once, until all vegetables are tender. Set aside, covered, for 15 minutes.

2. Puree half the vegetables in a food processor or blender. Return soup to bowl and season with additional salt and pepper to taste. Cover and cook on HIGH 1 to 2 minutes to reheat. Serve, garnished with remaining chopped parsley.

87   CREAM OF BROCCOLI SOUP
Prep: 20 minutes   Cook: 21 to 22 minutes   Serves: 4 to 6

1 **medium onion, chopped**	1½ **pounds broccoli, stems**
3 **tablespoons butter or**	**peeled**
margarine	½ **cup heavy cream**
4 **cups hot chicken stock or**	**Salt and pepper**
canned broth	1 **cup grated Cheddar cheese**

1. In a 3-quart casserole with lid, combine onion and butter. Cook on HIGH 5 minutes, stirring once. Stir in 2 cups heated stock.

2. Slice broccoli stems into ½-inch rounds. Cut florets into 1- to 1½-inch pieces. Add broccoli stems and florets to stock. Cover and cook on HIGH 12 minutes, or until broccoli is tender. Let stand, covered, 5 minutes.

3. Puree soup in batches in blender or food processor. Return to casserole, add remaining stock and cream and cook on HIGH 4 to 5 minutes until hot. Season with salt and pepper to taste. Stir in cheese and serve.

88   TORTILLA SOUP WITH AVOCADO AND LIME
Prep: 20 minutes   Cook: 12 minutes   Serves: 4

½ **cup finely chopped onion**	2 **tablespoons minced cilantro**
1 **tablespoon corn oil**	¾ **cup finely diced tomato**
2 **10¾-ounce cans chicken**	¾ **cup finely diced avocado**
broth	1 **tablespoon fresh lime juice**
½ **cup water**	1 **corn tortilla, cut into ¼-inch**
½ **to 1 minced seeded jalapeño**	**strips**
pepper, or cayenne	**Lime wedges**
pepper to taste	

1. In a 2-quart glass measure, cook onion and oil on HIGH 2 minutes. Add chicken broth, water, jalapeño and 1 tablespoon cilantro. Cook 7 minutes, or until boiling.

2. Stir in tomato, avocado and lime juice. Cook on HIGH 3 minutes. Stir in tortilla strips and remaining cilantro. Serve at once, with lime wedges on the side to squeeze into the soup.

89   CREAMY POTATO SOUP
Prep: 10 minutes   Cook: 20 minutes   Serves: 2

Thick and creamy, this soup tastes sinfully rich, but it's not. The velvety texture comes from pureed vegetables, not from cream.

2 **large baking potatoes (about**	2½ **cups chicken stock or**
½ pound each), peeled	**canned broth**
1 **medium onion**	1½ **cups milk**
1 **small carrot, peeled**	**Salt and pepper**
1 **small celery stalk**	

1. Cut potato, onion, carrot and celery into 1-inch pieces. In a 2-quart casserole, place vegetables and chicken stock. Cover and cook on HIGH 15 minutes, or just until vegetables are tender. Set aside, covered, and let cool slightly

2. Puree soup in batches in a blender or food processor. Return to casserole and stir in milk. Cook, uncovered, on HIGH 4 to 5 minutes, until hot. Season with salt and pepper to taste.

90 POTATO, LEEK AND FENNEL SOUP
Prep: 25 minutes   Cook: 32 to 33 minutes   Serves: 6

½ **pound fennel**
2 **cups coarsely chopped**
   onions
3 **cups diced leeks (white and**
   tender green)
2 **medium potatoes, peeled**
   and diced

3 **tablespoons butter or**
   margarine
4 **cups hot chicken stock or**
   canned broth
1 **cup half-and-half or milk**
   Salt and pepper

1. Trim root and stalks off fennel. Chop 2 tablespoons of green fronds and reserve for garnish. Thinly slice fennel bulb and place in a 4-quart casserole. Add onions, leeks, potatoes and butter. Cover and cook on HIGH 10 minutes, stirring after 5 minutes.

2. Add 2 cups hot stock, cover and cook on MEDIUM-HIGH 20 minutes. Puree in batches in blender or food processor. Return soup to casserole. Add remaining 2 cups stock and half-and-half. Season with salt and pepper to taste. Cook on HIGH 2 to 3 minutes, or until heated through. Garnish with chopped fennel greens.

91 CORN CHOWDER
Prep: 10 minutes   Cook: 22 to 25 minutes   Serves: 4 to 6

½ **pound bacon, diced**
3 **medium baking potatoes,**
   peeled and cut into 1-inch
   chunks
1 **medium onion, chopped**
1½ **cups milk**

1 **17-ounce can cream-style**
   corn
1 **7-ounce can corn kernels,**
   drained
½ **teaspoon pepper**
   Hot pepper sauce
   Salt

1. Place bacon in a 4-cup glass measure. Cover with paper towel. Cook on HIGH 5 to 6 minutes, until bacon is crisp. Remove bacon with slotted spoon and set aside. Discard all but 1 tablespoon bacon drippings.

2. Place potatoes, onion and 1 tablespoon bacon drippings in a 2-quart casserole. Cover and cook on HIGH 7 minutes, stirring once.

3. Stir in milk, cream-style corn and corn kernels. Cover and cook on HIGH 10 to 12 minutes, until potatoes are tender. Add pepper and season with hot sauce and salt to taste.

92   MUSSEL SOUP PROVENCALE

Prep: 15 minutes   Cook: 20 to 25 minutes   Serves: 6

I like to use cultivated mussels when I can find them. They are farmed in the ocean and tend to be uniformly cleaner and sweeter. This is a very rich, very special soup for a very special occasion.

2 pounds mussels, scrubbed and debearded	½ teaspoon fennel seeds
	¼ teaspoon thyme
2 large carrots, coarsely chopped	2 cups fish stock or 1 cup bottled clam juice diluted with 1 cup water
2 celery ribs, coarsely chopped	
	1½ cups dry white wine
2 medium leeks (white and tender green), well rinsed and coarsely chopped	2 egg yolks
	2 cups heavy cream
	¼ teaspoon saffron threads
2 garlic cloves, chopped	Salt and white pepper

1. In a 4-quart casserole, place mussels, carrots, celery, leeks, garlic, fennel seeds, thyme, fish stock and wine. Cook on HIGH 12 to 15 minutes, or until mussels open. Discard any mussels that do not open. Strain liquid through a sieve lined with a double thickness of cheesecloth. Rinse out casserole and return liquid to it. Pick out and reserve 6 mussels in their shells. Remove remaining mussels from shells and coarsely chop. Add chopped mussels to liquid in casserole. Discard vegetables.

2. In medium bowl, whisk egg yolks lightly. Whisk cream into egg yolks. Gradually whisk in 2 cups hot mussel soup to warm mixture. Whisk egg yolk mixture into remaining soup in casserole. Crumble in saffron and season with salt and pepper to taste. Cover and cook on HIGH 7 to 10 minutes, until hot. Do not boil, or soup will curdle. To serve, place 1 mussel in shell in each of 6 soup bowls and ladle on hot soup.

Chapter 5

Chicken in a Hurry

The microwave was made for juicy, tender skinless, boneless chicken breasts. With no interference from skin or bone, cooking is rapid and complete. The beauty of this delicate meat is its lightness—both in terms of calories and cholesterol—and its versatility.

Chicken breasts can be used as a base for exciting dishes like Chicken Breasts with Artichokes and Garlic, Chicken with Fresh Plum Sauce and Chicken Breasts with Tomatoes, Basil and Goat Cheese. They make easy ethnic dishes like Chicken Parmesan and Peking Chicken. You can create a meal in a dish—or in a packet—with Dilled Chicken Breasts with Carrots, Zucchini and Potatoes or Chicken and Vegetables en Papillote.

En papillote means in paper, and cooking chicken breasts in parchment is a favorite technique of mine. It seals in all the flavor and juices, and I use it in a number of these recipes. Rolls of parchment are available in cookware shops. Tear off lengths as you need them. To form the packet, fold a sheet in half and trim the edges to form a half-moon shape. Open up and place the food in the center, just to one side of the crease. Fold the parchment back over and fold and pleat the edges to seal. There's not even a plate to clean up. The chicken steams inside the paper until it's perfectly cooked. To serve, place the parchment packets on dinner plates and snip open the tops.

---

93 CHICKEN BREASTS WITH LEMON, SOY AND GINGER

Prep: 5 minutes   Cook: 5 to 7 minutes   Serves: 2

2 skinless, boneless chicken
   breast halves
¼ cup sliced onion
2 tablespoons soy sauce
2 teaspoons lemon juice

2 teaspoons minced fresh
   ginger
1 garlic clove, minced
¼ teaspoon pepper

1. Put chicken in a small shallow baking dish. Scatter onion over chicken. Combine all remaining ingredients and pour over chicken.

2. Cover with waxed paper. Cook on HIGH 5 to 7 minutes.

94 CHICKEN BREASTS WITH ARTICHOKES AND GARLIC

Prep: 5 minutes   Cook: 5 to 6 minutes   Serves: 2

Garlic cloves cooked in their skins become very soft and mild. Squeeze the garlic onto slices of French bread for a tasty spread, or mash into a baked potato.

2 skinless, boneless chicken breast halves	½ teaspoon herbes de Provence or rosemary
1 6-ounce jar marinated artichoke hearts	Salt, pepper and paprika to taste
12 garlic cloves, in their skins	

1. Tear off two 10 × 14-inch pieces of parchment. Fold in half and trim edges to form a half-moon shape. Place a chicken breast half to one side of crease on each piece of parchment. Arrange half the artichokes and garlic around each piece of chicken. Season with herbes, salt, pepper and paprika.

2. Fold over the parchment edges to close and crimp to seal. Place on a plate. Cook on HIGH 5 to 6 minutes, just until the chicken is white throughout but still juicy. Let stand 2 to 3 minutes. Serve in the parchment on a dinner plate.

95 TARRAGON CHICKEN SALAD VINAIGRETTE

Prep: 10 to 15 minutes   Cook: 6 to 7 minutes   Serves: 2

2 skinless, boneless chicken breast halves	1½ tablespoons white wine vinegar
½ teaspoon tarragon	½ teaspoon Dijon mustard
1 small lemon, thinly sliced	⅓ cup extra-virgin olive oil
½ cup broccoli florets	Salt and pepper
⅓ cup julienned carrots	2 tablespoons sliced scallions
½ red bell pepper, cut into thin strips	Lettuce leaves

1. Place chicken breast halves side by side in center of a double layer of microwave paper towels. Sprinkle tarragon over chicken and arrange lemon slices on top. Fold towels around chicken to enclose completely. Hold under running water to wet towels; let excess water drain off. Place wrapped chicken in a shallow baking dish. Cook on HIGH 3 to 4 minutes, until chicken is just white throughout but still juicy. Set aside still wrapped in towels.

2. Divide broccoli, carrots and bell pepper between 2 double layers of paper towels. Wrap each bundle separately. Wet under faucet and set on plate. Microwave on HIGH 3 minutes, until vegetables are crisp-tender and still brightly colored. Rinse under cold running water to stop cooking; drain well. Transfer to a medium bowl.

3. In a small bowl, whisk together vinegar and mustard. Slowly blend in olive oil. Season vinaigrette with salt and pepper to taste. Pour about half

the vinaigrette over vegetables, add scallions and toss to coat.

4. Slice chicken breasts crosswise into 4 large pieces. Line 2 plates with lettuce leaves. Reassemble each breast in center of each plate. Surround with vegetables and drizzle remaining vinaigrette over chicken.

---

96 CHICKEN PARMESAN
Prep: 10 minutes   Cook: 9 to 12 minutes   Serves: 4

4 skinless, boneless chicken breast halves	½ teaspoon garlic powder
1 egg	¼ cup plus 2 tablespoons grated Parmesan cheese
1 tablespoon olive oil	4 large slices mozzarella cheese
½ cup Italian-flavored bread crumbs	1 cup marinara sauce, homemade or prepared
½ teaspoon basil, crushed	

1. Rinse chicken and wipe dry. In a pie plate, beat egg and oil until well blended. On a plate or sheet of waxed paper, toss together bread crumbs, basil, garlic powder and ¼ cup Parmesan cheese.

2. Dip each chicken breast into egg to coat, then dredge in bread crumbs. Press lightly to help them adhere. Arrange chicken in a 12-inch round shallow baking dish in ring fashion, with ends touching. Cover with paper towel. Cook on HIGH 7 to 9 minutes, until chicken is just white throughout but still juicy; turn dish if chicken appears to be cooking unevenly.

3. Remove paper towel and place 1 slice mozzarella cheese on top of each piece of chicken. Spoon sauce over cheese. Cook, uncovered, 2 to 3 minutes, until sauce is hot and cheese melted. Sprinkle remaining Parmesan cheese on top and serve.

---

97 GINGERED CHICKEN BREASTS WITH SNOW PEAS, SWEET PEPPER AND MUSHROOMS
Prep: 10 minutes   Cook: 5 to 6 minutes   Serves: 2

2 bok choy stalks	2 skinless, boneless chicken breast halves
1 small red bell pepper	
4 large mushrooms	2 teaspoons minced fresh ginger
½ small onion	
16 snow peas	2 teaspoons soy sauce

1. Remove and reserve green leaves from bok choy. Cut 1 white stalk into thin strips. Reserve other stalk for another use. Cut pepper into thin strips. Thinly slice mushrooms and onion.

2. Cut out two 10 × 14-inch pieces of parchment. Fold in half. Trim edges to form a half-moon shape; unfold. Place 1 bok choy leaf on each. Arrange ¼ of vegetables on each. Place chicken on top of vegetables. Sprinkle 1 teaspoon ginger and soy over each. Top with remaining vegetables, dividing evenly.

3. Fold up edges of parchment; crimp and pleat to seal. Place on a plate. Cook on HIGH 5 to 6 minutes. Let stand 2 minutes before opening to serve.

98   CURRIED CHICKEN BREASTS WITH SWEET PEPPERS

Prep: 15 minutes   Cook: 11 to 12 minutes   Serves: 4

2 garlic cloves, minced
1 tablespoon minced fresh
  ginger
½ teaspoon whole cumin seeds
1 tablespoon vegetable oil
½ teaspoon ground coriander
¼ teaspoon ground cumin
¼ teaspoon curry powder
⅛ to ¼ teaspoon cayenne
  pepper
½ teaspoon salt

3 medium bell peppers, red
  and/or green, cut into 1-
  inch squares
1 medium onion, cut into 1-
  inch pieces
1½ tablespoons lemon juice
1 pound skinless, boneless
  chicken breasts, cut into
  1-inch cubes
1 large tomato, cut into 10
  wedges

1. In a 2-quart casserole, place garlic, ginger, cumin seeds and oil. Cook on HIGH 2 minutes. Stir in coriander, ground cumin, curry powder, cayenne, salt, bell peppers, onion and lemon juice. Cook on HIGH 3 minutes.

2. Stir in chicken; cover with waxed paper. Cook on HIGH 5 minutes, stirring once. Add tomato and toss gently to mix. Continue to cook 1 to 2 minutes, until chicken is just cooked through. Serve over rice.

99   CHICKEN BREASTS IN JALAPENO CREAM SAUCE

Prep: 5 minutes   Cook: 16 to 17 minutes   Serves: 4

¼ cup minced onion
¾ cup chicken broth
½ teaspoon marjoram or
  thyme leaves
1 bay leaf
4 skinless, boneless chicken
  breast halves
½ teaspoon salt

¼ teaspoon white pepper
2 large jalapeño peppers,
  stemmed and seeded
2 garlic cloves
½ cup crème fraîche or sour
  cream
1½ teaspoons cornstarch
  Minced parsley, for garnish

1. In a 12-inch round or oval baking dish, combine onion, chicken broth, marjoram and bay leaf. Arrange chicken breasts in a circle, with ends touching. Season with salt and white pepper. Cover with waxed paper or parchment and cook on HIGH 5 minutes. Turn chicken over, cover again and continue to cook 4 to 5 minutes, just until chicken is white throughout but still juicy. Remove chicken to a plate; cover with aluminum foil to keep warm. Strain broth from dish; reserve ½ cup.

2. In a food processor or blender, combine jalapeños, garlic and reserved ½ cup broth. Puree until smooth. Pour into a 4-cup glass measure. Cook on HIGH 5 minutes. Blend together crème fraîche and cornstarch. Gradually whisk into hot broth. Cook on MEDIUM 1½ to 2 minutes, or until slightly thickened. Season with additional salt and white pepper to taste. Pour over chicken breasts and garnish with minced parsley.

100 CHICKEN WITH FRESH PLUM SAUCE
Prep: 5 minutes   Cook: 10 to 12 minutes   Serves: 2

I like this sauce on the tart side. If you prefer yours sweeter, increase the sugar to 2 tablespoons. You can use this same recipe all summer long, substituting peaches or apricots as the fruit season changes.

- 4 large fresh plums, sliced
- 1 tablespoon sugar
- 1½ teaspoons minced fresh ginger
- 2 skinless, boneless chicken breast halves

- ¼ teaspoon salt
- ½ teaspoon pepper
- ½ teaspoon paprika
- 2 very thin lemon slices

1. Arrange plum slices in a small baking dish. Sprinkle sugar and ginger over plums. Place chicken on top and season with salt, pepper and paprika. Cut each lemon slice in half and place over chicken.

2. Cover with waxed paper. Cook on MEDIUM 10 to 12 minutes, basting with juices after 6 minutes, until chicken is just white throughout but still juicy. Transfer chicken to a plate and spoon plum sauce on top.

101 PEKING CHICKEN
Prep: 10 minutes   Cook: 9 to 10 minutes   Serves: 4 to 6

Flour tortillas take the place of Peking pancakes, and lean chicken replaces duck, but the savory flavors are the same as in the classic dish. Allow time for the chicken to marinate.

- 1 tablespoon brown sugar
- 1 tablespoon rice vinegar or apple cider vinegar
- 2 teaspoons soy sauce
- ½ teaspoon cinnamon
- ½ teaspoon ground ginger
- 4 skinless, boneless chicken breast halves

- 2 packages 6-inch flour tortillas
- 2 bunches of scallions, quartered lengthwise and cut into 2-inch slivers
- 1 cup hoisin sauce or Chinese plum sauce
    Sprigs of cilantro or parsley

1. In a small bowl, combine brown sugar, vinegar, soy sauce, cinnamon and ginger. Brush mixture all over chicken, cover and refrigerate for at least 3 hours, or overnight.

2. In a 12-inch round baking dish, arrange chicken in ring fashion, with ends touching. Cover with waxed paper. Cook on HIGH 7½ to 8 minutes, just until chicken loses its pinkness in the thickest part.

3. Remove tortillas from package and wrap each stack in a microwave paper towel. Cook one stack on HIGH 1 to 2 minutes, just until warm to the touch. Heat remaining stack as needed. To serve, slice chicken and place on a platter. Pass small dishes of sliced scallions, hoisin sauce, sprigs of cilantro and warm tortillas. To eat, spread sauce on tortilla, place chicken, scallions and cilantro inside, roll up and eat with your hands.

102   CHICKEN AND POTATOES

Prep: 10 minutes   Cook: 13 to 15 minutes   Serves: 4

⅓ cup extra-virgin olive oil
1 garlic clove, crushed
   through a press
½ teaspoon rosemary,
   crumbled
1 teaspoon salt
1 teaspoon pepper

2 medium baking potatoes,
   peeled and sliced
4 skinless, boneless chicken
   breast halves
1 cup dry bread crumbs
1 teaspoon paprika

1. In a shallow dish, combine olive oil, garlic, ¼ teaspoon rosemary and ½ teaspoon each salt and pepper. Roll potato slices in seasoned oil and place in shallow 10-inch round baking dish. Cover with a lid or microwave-safe plastic wrap. If using wrap, pierce in 2 or 3 places with the tip of a knife. Cook on HIGH 5 minutes.

2. Meanwhile, add chicken to remaining seasoned oil and turn to coat. Place bread crumbs on a plate and toss with remaining ¼ teaspoon rosemary and ½ teaspoon each salt and pepper. Dredge chicken breasts in crumbs to coat; press lightly to help them adhere.

3. Arrange chicken in a circle, with ends touching on top of potatoes. Sprinkle with paprika. Cover with waxed paper. Cook on HIGH 8 to 10 minutes, until chicken is white throughout and potatoes are tender. Let stand, covered, for 5 minutes before serving.

103   DILLED CHICKEN BREASTS WITH CARROTS, ZUCCHINI AND POTATOES

Prep: 15 minutes   Cook: 10 minutes   Serves: 4

2 medium carrots, peeled and
   thinly sliced diagonally
1 medium zucchini, sliced
1 medium onion, sliced
2 medium red potatoes, thinly
   sliced
   Salt and pepper

4 skinless, boneless chicken
   breast halves
2 tablespoons minced fresh
   dill or 2 teaspoons dried
2 tablespoons sliced scallions
12 thin lemon slices
1 cup chicken broth

1. Divide carrots, zucchini, onion and potatoes into 4 equal portions. For each serving, arrange one portion of vegetables in center of 2 connected microwave paper towels. Season with salt and pepper to taste. Place chicken on top of vegetables. Season lightly with salt and pepper and sprinkle ½ tablespoon fresh dill or ½ teaspoon dried and scallions over each serving. Cover each with 3 lemon slices. Wrap paper towel around chicken and vegetables, tucking ends under to enclose completely.

2. Arrange bundles in a circle in a 10-inch round baking dish and pour ¼ cup chicken broth over each bundle to moisten. Cook on HIGH 10 minutes, until chicken is white throughout and potato is tender. Let stand 2 minutes before opening to serve.

104   CHICKEN AND VEGETABLES EN PAPILLOTE

Prep: 15 minutes   Cook: 10 to 12 minutes   Serves: 4

2 small zucchini, cut into thin strips
2 celery ribs, cut into thin strips
1 medium potato, peeled and cut into thin strips

1 medium onion, thinly sliced
Salt and pepper
4 skinless, boneless chicken breast halves
1 teaspoon paprika
4 teaspoons chopped parsley

1. Tear off four 10 × 14-inch sheets of parchment; butter parchment. Fold over and trim edges to form half-moon shape; unfold. Arrange ¼ of the zucchini, celery, potato and onion on each piece of parchment to one side of crease. Season with salt and pepper to taste. Place a chicken breast half on top of vegetables. Season lightly with salt and pepper. Sprinkle ¼ teaspoon paprika and 1 teaspoon parsley over each piece of chicken.

2. Fold over edges of parchment; crimp and pleat to seal. Arrange the packets in a circle on a round or oval baking dish. Cook on HIGH 10 to 12 minutes, until chicken is cooked through. Place each packet on a plate, cut open the top and serve.

105   CHICKEN FAJITAS

Prep: 10 minutes   Cook: 10 to 12 minutes   Serves: 2 to 3

These tender strips of chicken wrapped in a tortilla are great for parties, suppers and snacking. Allow several hours for the chicken to marinate.

2 tablespoons soy sauce
2 tablespoons fresh lime juice
3 tablespoons vegetable oil
2 skinless, boneless chicken breast halves
1 medium onion, thinly sliced

6 8-inch flour tortillas
1 large tomato, chopped
1 cup shredded lettuce
Garnishes: salsa, guacamole and sour cream

1. In an 8-inch pie plate, combine soy sauce, lime juice and 2 tablespoons oil. Add chicken and turn to coat with marinade.

2. In a 2-cup glass measure, combine onion and 1 tablespoon oil. Cook on HIGH 5 minutes. Add onions to chicken. Turn chicken again, cover and marinate in refrigerator 2 to 3 hours, turning occasionally.

3. Cook chicken in marinade with onion, covered with paper towel on HIGH 4 to 6 minutes, stirring once. With 2 forks, tear chicken into strips.

4. Wrap tortillas in paper towel and cook on HIGH 45 seconds, or until warm. To serve, spoon equal amounts of chicken and onion into tortilla. Add tomato, lettuce and garnishes as desired. Roll up and eat.

106 CHICKEN BREASTS WITH FRESH FENNEL
Prep: 5 minutes   Cook: 13 minutes   Serves: 4

Fresh fennel is sometimes labeled anise. In Italian markets it is called "finocchio." It looks like an overgrown celery with feathery green fronds on the ends.

1 **fennel bulb (about 1 pound), cut into thin strips**
1 **medium onion, thinly sliced**
2 **garlic cloves, minced**
1 **tablespoon olive oil**

4 **skinless, boneless chicken breast halves**
½ **teaspoon salt**
¼ **teaspoon pepper**
  Chopped fennel green (optional)

1. In a 12-inch round shallow baking dish or quiche pan, place fennel strips, onion, garlic and oil. Toss to mix. Cover with waxed paper and cook on HIGH 5 minutes, stirring once.

2. Arrange chicken on top of fennel in a circle, with ends touching. Season with salt and pepper. Sprinkle fennel green on top. Cover with waxed paper and cook on HIGH 8 minutes, or until chicken is just white throughout. Serve fennel and juices on top of chicken.

107 CHICKEN BREASTS WITH TOMATOES, BASIL AND GOAT CHEESE
Prep: 10 minutes   Cook: 4 to 6 minutes   Serves: 2

4 **large tomato slices**
4 **teaspoons shredded fresh basil or ½ teaspoon dried**
3 **ounces mild goat cheese, such as Montrachet, cut into 8 thin rounds**

2 **skinless, boneless chicken breast halves**
1 **large garlic clove, minced**

1. Tear off two 10 × 14-inch sheets of parchment. Fold in half. Trim edges to form a half-moon shape. Open up and layer to one side of crease on each: 1 tomato slice, 1 teaspoon fresh basil or ⅛ teaspoon dried, 2 cheese rounds, 1 chicken breast half, half the garlic, 1 tomato slice, the remaining basil and 2 cheese rounds.

2. Fold up edges of parchment and crimp to seal. Place both on a plate. Cook on HIGH 4 to 6 minutes, until chicken is just white throughout. Let stand 2 minutes before opening to serve.

108   POACHED CHICKEN BREASTS WITH ORANGE SAUCE

Prep: 5 minutes   Cook: 7 to 10 minutes   Serves: 2

2 skinless, boneless chicken breast halves	1 cup orange juice, preferably fresh
½ teaspoon tarragon	1 teaspoon grated orange zest
Salt and pepper	1 tablespoon cornstarch

1. Place 2 connected paper towels on a plate. Place chicken in center, over perforations. Sprinkle with tarragon and season with salt and pepper to taste. Fold over the long and then the short sides to enclose the chicken. Turn over so folds are on bottom. Pour ¼ cup water evenly over packet. Cook on HIGH 4 to 6 minutes, until chicken is firm to the touch. Set aside, covered, while you make the sauce.

2. In a 2-cup glass measure, combine orange juice, grated zest and cornstarch. Stir to dissolve cornstarch. Cook on HIGH 2½ to 4 minutes, stirring several times, until sauce thickens and turns clear. Transfer chicken to serving plates. Pour sauce over chicken and serve.

Chapter 6

What to Do with a Pound of Ground Beef

There's nothing more versatile than ground beef. It's a family favorite that's tasty, nutritious and kind to your budget. The microwave is a whiz at burgers, especially if you have a browning dish. For time, it's unbeatable for chili and hamburger stews, such as Picadillo, loaded with almonds, raisins and olives, and Italian Meatballs in Sauce. But one of its most efficient contributions is in the art of the meat loaf.

No more waiting for over an hour. In the microwave, you can whip up a variety of savory loaves in 25 minutes or less. Here are a range of recipes from the familiar Old-Fashioned Meat Loaf, just like you'd find in your local diner, to a flavorful Country Terrine with Fresh Mushrooms, Basil and Tomatoes, to an elegant Lemon Meat Loaf and a company-quality Meat Loaf with Wild Rice, Sausage and Mushrooms.

What to do with that package of ground beef that's been sitting in the back of your freezer for months? Defrost it in the microwave and surprise your family with an easy Two-Alarm Chili or Swedish Meatballs in Lingonberry Sauce.

---

109 MEAT LOAF WITH SUN-DRIED TOMATOES
Prep: 10 minutes   Cook: 25 to 30 minutes   Serves: 8

1 large onion, chopped
1 celery stalk, chopped
4 garlic cloves, minced
2 tablespoons olive oil
1 teaspoon basil
1 teaspoon oregano
1 teaspoon thyme leaves
1½ pounds lean ground beef

¾ pound bulk pork sausage
2 eggs, lightly beaten
¼ cup dry bread crumbs
¼ cup chopped parsley
1½ teaspoons salt
1 teaspoon pepper
4 ounces sun-dried tomatoes
    packed in oil, diced

1. In a 4-cup glass measure, place onion, celery, garlic and oil. Cook on HIGH 4 minutes, stirring once. Blend in basil, oregano and thyme.

2. In a large bowl, combine beef, sausage, eggs, bread crumbs, parsley, salt and pepper, Mix with your hands to blend well. Blend in cooked vegetables and sun-dried tomatoes. Pack lightly into a 9 × 5 × 3-inch loaf pan.

3. Cover pan with waxed paper. Cook on HIGH 20 to 25 minutes, until meat loaf registers 160 degrees on instant-reading thermometer or on oven probe. Pour off any extra juices. Let stand for 10 minutes before slicing. Serve hot or cold.

110 COUNTRY TERRINE WITH FRESH MUSHROOMS, BASIL AND TOMATOES

Prep: 30 minutes   Cook: 19 to 24 minutes   Serves: 8

1 cup chopped onions
1 tablespoon minced garlic
2 teaspoons olive oil
1 pound lean ground beef
¾ pound ground pork
¼ pound chicken livers, trimmed and chopped
1 cup fresh bread crumbs
2 eggs, lightly beaten

1 tablespoon Worcestershire sauce
1½ teaspoons salt
½ teaspoon pepper
¼ pound fresh mushrooms, sliced (about 1 cup)
3 medium tomatoes, peeled, seeded and chopped
3 tablespoons minced fresh basil or 1 teaspoon dried

1. In a 4-cup glass measure, cook onions, garlic and oil on HIGH 4 minutes, stirring once. Transfer to a large bowl. Add beef, pork, chicken livers, bread crumbs, eggs, Worcestershire, salt and pepper. Blend well.

2. Place half the meat mixture into a 9 × 5 × 3-inch loaf pan. Pat lightly to flatten the top. Arrange half the mushroom slices on top in a single layer. Combine the tomatoes and basil and spoon ⅔ on top of the mushrooms. Arrange the remaining mushrooms over the tomatoes. Spoon remaining meat mixture on top and flatten gently.

3. Cover with waxed paper. Cook on HIGH 15 to 20 minutes, until meat loaf is cooked through. (It should register 160 degrees in the center on an instant-reading thermometer.) Turn pan if loaf appears to be cooking unevenly. Let stand at least 5 minutes. Pour off juices. Invert loaf onto serving platter. Spoon remaining tomato-basil mixture over top. Serve hot or cold.

111 LEMON MEAT LOAF

Prep: 10 minutes   Cook: 10 to 12 minutes   Serves: 4

1 egg, lightly beaten
¼ cup fresh lemon juice
2 teaspoons minced lemon zest
1 teaspoon salt
¼ teaspoon pepper
¾ cup stale bread cubes
1 pound lean ground beef

2 tablespoons chopped fresh basil or 1 teaspoon dried
2 tablespoons chopped scallion
3 garlic cloves, minced
2 tablespoons chopped parsley
¼ cup cold water
¼ cup ketchup

1. In a medium bowl, beat together egg, lemon juice, lemon zest, salt and pepper. Add bread cubes and toss to mix. Add beef, basil, scallion, garlic, parsley and water. Mix with your hands. Pack lightly into a 5 × 7½-inch loaf pan.

2. Cover with waxed paper. Cook on HIGH 8 to 10 minutes. Spread ketchup over top and cook 1 to 2 minutes longer.

112 OLD-FASHIONED MEAT LOAF
Prep: 10 minutes   Cook: 12 to 14 minutes   Serves: 6

1½ pounds ground chuck
 1 egg, lightly beaten
 1 cup tomato sauce
 1 medium onion, chopped
 1 small green bell pepper,
      chopped

 2 slices white bread,
      crumbled
 ¾ teaspoon salt
 ¼ teaspoon pepper

1. In a large bowl, combine beef, egg, ½ cup tomato sauce, onion, bell pepper, crumbled bread, salt and pepper. Pack lightly into a 6-cup ring mold or 9 × 5 × 3-inch loaf pan.

2. Cover with paper towel. Cook on HIGH 10 to 12 minutes, just until loaf begins to pull away from edges. Turn dish if loaf appears to be cooking unevenly.

3. Pour off any juices. Spoon remaining tomato sauce over meat loaf. Cook, uncovered, on HIGH 2 minutes.

113 SURPRISE MEAT LOAF

Prepare Old-Fashioned Meat Loaf as described above, but use loaf pan and tuck 2 hard-cooked eggs into the center of the meat. Cooking time will be the same.

114 MEAT LOAF PARISIENNE
Prep: 15 minutes   Cook: 30 to 35 minutes   Serves: 6 to 8

The combination of three meats makes this meat loaf reminiscent of a French-style pâté. For a party buffet, serve chilled, with grainy mustard, cornichons (tiny sour gherkin pickles) and crusty French bread.

 ¼ pound chicken livers,
      rinsed, dried and
      trimmed
 ½ cup milk
 1 egg
 1 tablespoon Worcestershire
      sauce
 1 cup fresh bread crumbs
 ½ teaspoon thyme
 ¼ teaspoon ground allspice
 1 teaspoon salt

 ¼ teaspoon pepper
 10 medium mushrooms
 1 large carrot
 1 small onion
 2 garlic cloves
 2 tablespoons butter
 1 pound ground beef
 ½ pound ground veal
 ¼ pound ground pork
 1 tablespoon Dijon mustard
 1 tablespoon dry white wine

1. In a food processor, puree livers with milk, egg and Worcestershire. Scrape into medium bowl. Add bread crumbs, thyme, allspice, salt and pepper. Blend well.

2. In a food processor (or by hand), finely chop mushrooms, carrot, onion and garlic. Place in a 4-cup glass measure with butter. Cook on HIGH 5 minutes, stirring once. Add to liver-bread crumb mixture.

3. Add beef, veal and pork. Mix with your hands to blend well. Pack lightly into a 9 × 5 × 3-inch loaf pan. Combine mustard and wine and brush over top of loaf.

4. Cover with waxed paper. Cook on HIGH 25 to 29 minutes, turning if loaf is cooking unevenly, until loaf begins to pull away from side of pan and registers 160 degrees on microwave probe or instant-reading thermometer. Let stand 10 minutes before slicing.

---

115 MEAT LOAF WITH WILD RICE, SAUSAGE AND MUSHROOMS

Prep: 20 minutes   Cook: 18 to 21 minutes   Serves: 8

For this larger recipe, a microwave bundt pan works best. It unmolds easily and makes an attractive presentation. The recipe can be made ahead and reheated.

2 **pounds lean ground beef, preferably chuck**	¼ **teaspoon pepper**
1 **cup corn bread stuffing mix**	1 **10½-ounce package frozen white and wild rice in cooking pouch**
1 **8-ounce can tomato sauce**	
½ **cup chopped onion**	½ **cup sliced fresh mushrooms**
¼ **cup chopped celery**	½ **cup diced Polish kielbasa sausage, casing removed**
2 **eggs**	
½ **teaspoon thyme**	½ **cup shredded Swiss cheese**
1 **teaspoon salt**	2 **tablespoons minced parsley**

1. In a large bowl, combine beef, stuffing mix, tomato sauce, onion, celery, eggs, thyme, salt and pepper. Mix well. Turn into a 10-cup bundt pan; press meat up against sides and center tube to make a well around the middle.

2. Pierce rice pouch. Cook on HIGH 3 to 4 minutes to defrost. Layer mushrooms, rice and sausage in well in center of meat loaf. Press edges of meat loaf over filling to cover completely.

3. Cover with waxed paper. Cook on HIGH 14 to 16 minutes, until probe or instant-reading thermometer registers 160 degrees. Pour off juices. Invert loaf onto serving platter. Sprinkle cheese and parsley over top. Return to microwave and cook on HIGH for about 10 seconds, until cheese just melts.

116   MEAT LOAF FLORENTINE
Prep: 10 minutes   Cook: 27 to 32 minutes   Serves: 6 to 8

2 10-ounce packages frozen
   chopped spinach
2 pounds lean ground beef
1 medium onion, chopped
4 garlic cloves, minced
1 tablespoon soy sauce
2 eggs, beaten

½ cup fresh bread crumbs
1½ teaspoons salt
¾ teaspoon pepper
½ cup sliced scallions
1 2-ounce jar pimientos,
   drained and diced

1. Place frozen spinach in package on plate. Cook on HIGH 7 minutes. Meanwhile, in a large bowl, combine beef, onion, half the garlic, the soy sauce, eggs, bread crumbs, 1 teaspoon salt and ½ teaspoon pepper. Mix well but with a light touch. Turn meat mixture out onto a sheet of waxed paper. Pat into an 8 × 12-inch rectangle.

2. Drain spinach and squeeze dry. Place in medium bowl. Add scallions, pimientos and remaining garlic, ½ teaspoon salt and ¼ teaspoon pepper. Blend well. Spread spinach mixture over meat, leaving a 1-inch border all around. Roll up meat from a short end, using paper to help lift. Place meat seam-side down in a 9 × 5 × 3-inch loaf pan.

3. Cover with waxed paper. Cook on HIGH 20 to 25 minutes, until center is no longer pink and edges pull away from sides of pan. Let stand 5 minutes. Pour off any excess liquid. Garnish with additional pimiento, if desired, for color.

117   REUBEN MEAT LOAF
Prep: 15 minutes   Cook: 21 to 27 minutes   Serves: 4 to 6

1½ pounds lean ground beef
   chuck
1½ cups rye bread crumbs
2 eggs, lightly beaten
½ cup chopped onion
¼ cup sweet pickle relish
¼ cup Russian dressing

1 tablespoon Worcestershire
   sauce
1 teaspoon salt
¼ teaspoon pepper
1 8-ounce can sauerkraut,
   drained
1½ cups shredded Swiss cheese

1. In a large mixing bowl, combine ground beef, bread crumbs, eggs, onion, pickle relish, Russian dressing, Worcestershire sauce, salt and pepper. Mix with hands or wooden spoon to blend well. On a sheet of plastic wrap, shape meat mixture into a 7 × 14-inch rectangle.

2. Evenly layer sauerkraut and then 1 cup cheese over meat, leaving a 1-inch border around edges. Starting at a shorter end, roll up meat jelly-roll fashion, using the plastic wrap to help lift. Place meat seam-side down in a 9 × 5 × 3-inch loaf pan. Cover with waxed paper. Cook on HIGH 5 minutes.

3. Reduce power to MEDIUM and cook 15 to 20 minutes, just until meat is cooked through. Turn dish if loaf appears to be cooking unevenly. Pour off drippings. Sprinkle ½ cup cheese over top of loaf. Cook on MEDIUM 1 to 2 minutes, until cheese melts.

118 PICADILLO
Prep: 10 minutes   Cook: 8 to 20 minutes   Serves: 4

This savory ground beef stew is traditionally served over rice with black beans.

1 medium onion, chopped	½ teaspoon oregano
1 green bell pepper, chopped	½ teaspoon salt
1 garlic clove, minced	½ teaspoon pepper
2 tablespoons olive oil	⅛ teaspoon cinnamon
1 pound ground beef	½ cup raisins
¼ cup tomato paste	⅓ cup slivered almonds
½ cup dry sherry	1 3½-ounce jar pimiento-
1 tablespoon red wine vinegar	stuffed olives, sliced
½ teaspoon ground cumin	

1. In a 2-quart casserole, combine onion, green pepper, garlic and oil. Cook on HIGH 4 minutes. Add ground beef. Cook 2 minutes. Stir to break up any lumps. Cook 3 minutes longer; drain off fat.

2. In a small bowl, blend tomato paste, sherry and vinegar. Stir into meat mixture. Add cumin, oregano, salt, pepper and cinnamon. Cover and cook on HIGH 6 minutes. Stir in raisins, almonds and olives. Continue to cook, uncovered, 3 to 5 minutes, until sauce thickens.

---

119 MEATBALLS MEXICANA
Prep: 15 minutes   Cook: 10 to 12 minutes   Makes: 36

Serve over rice as a main course, or in a chafing dish with toothpicks for a party.

1 pound lean ground beef	1 large garlic clove, minced
1 slice firm-textured white bread, dipped in water and squeezed dry	½ teaspoon salt
	¾ teaspoon chili powder
	½ teaspoon ground cumin
1 egg, lightly beaten	⅛ teaspoon pepper
¼ cup chopped cilantro or parsley	1 4-ounce can diced green chiles
½ cup minced onion	1 cup tomato puree

1. In a medium bowl, combine beef, bread, egg, cilantro, ¼ cup onion, garlic, salt, ¼ teaspoon chili powder, ¼ teaspoon cumin, pepper and half the chiles. Mix well. With a light touch, shape into about 3 dozen 1-inch meatballs.

3. Arrange meatballs in a circle on a round microwave rack set in a shallow baking dish. Cover with paper towel. Cook on HIGH 5 to 7 minutes, or just until meatballs are cooked through. Turn rack if they appear to be cooking unevenly. Transfer meatballs to chafing dish or shallow serving dish and cover to keep warm.

3. In a 2-cup glass measure, combine tomato puree and remaining chiles, ¼ cup onion, ½ teaspoon chili powder and ¼ teaspoon cumin. Cover with waxed paper. Cook on HIGH 5 minutes, stirring once. Pour over meatballs.

120 DELI MEATBALL HEROES
Prep: 20 minutes   Cook: 9 to 10 minutes   Serves: 4

To whip this up in an instant, make the meatballs ahead and freeze in plastic bags. Microwave on DEFROST, or 30 percent power, for 5 to 7 minutes and then let stand for 5 to 10 minutes to thaw completely.

1 pound lean ground beef	½ teaspoon pepper
1 cup cooked rice	2 cups thick spaghetti sauce,
1 small onion, minced	store-bought or
2 eggs, beaten	homemade
2 teaspoons Italian seasoning	1 large loaf Italian bread
1 teaspoon salt	

1. In a medium bowl, combine beef, rice, onion, eggs, Italian seasoning, salt and pepper; blend well. With a light touch, shape into 8 meatballs without packing the meat.

2. Arrange meatballs in a circle on a microwave cooking rack or platter. Cover with paper towel. Cook on HIGH 3 minutes. Turn meatballs over and cook 2 minutes longer.

3. Transfer meatballs to a 2-quart casserole. Add sauce. Cover and cook on HIGH 4 minutes, until heated through. Split loaf of bread in half. Spoon meatballs and sauce onto bottom of loaf. Cover with top and cut into 4 servings. Serve with plenty of napkins.

121 ITALIAN MEATBALLS IN SAUCE
Prep: 20 minutes   Cook: 27 minutes   Serves: 6 to 8

While the cooking time on this recipe is longer than usual for a microwave, it is hours shorter than the comparable dish on a conventional stove. Serve over spaghetti with a green salad or antipasto to start. This dish is even better reheated the next day.

2 pounds lean ground beef,	1 teaspoon Worcestershire
preferably chuck	sauce
1 medium onion, chopped	1 teaspoon salt
2 eggs, lightly beaten	¼ teaspoon pepper
1 cup fresh bread crumbs	Mama's Italian Tomato
2 teaspoons Italian seasoning	Sauce (recipe follows)
¼ cup ketchup	

1. In a large bowl, combine all ingredients except tomato sauce. Mix with your hands to blend well. Shape lightly into about 3 dozen 1½-inch meatballs.

2. Set half of the meatballs on a microwave rack with a dish underneath. Cover with paper towels and cook on HIGH 3 minutes. Turn and cook 3 minutes longer. Transfer to a 3-quart casserole. Repeat with remaining meatballs. Add sauce to casserole, cover with waxed paper and cook meatballs on MEDIUM 15 minutes.

122   MAMA'S ITALIAN TOMATO SAUCE
Prep: 5 minutes   Cook: 25 minutes   Makes: about 1 quart

This sauce keeps well in the refrigerator for up to 3 days, and it can be frozen for months.

2 medium onions, chopped	1 teaspoon basil
3 garlic cloves, minced	1 teaspoon oregano
2 tablespoons olive oil	½ teaspoon sugar
1 35-ounce can peeled plum	¼ teaspoon black pepper
tomatoes, with liquid	⅛ teaspoon cayenne pepper
1 6-ounce can tomato paste	

1. Place onions, garlic and oil in a 3-quart casserole. Cook on HIGH 5 minutes.

2. Add all remaining ingredients. Cover and cook on HIGH 10 minutes. Stir. Reduce power to MEDIUM and cook, covered, 10 minutes longer.

123   BURGERS AMERICAN-STYLE
Prep: 5 minutes   Cook: 5 to 8 minutes   Serves: 4

If you plan to cook beef regularly in the microwave, it's worth investing in a browning dish. Here's the all-American favorite with no splatter, no mess. Dress up with all the fixings—lettuce, tomato, onion, pickle chips, mustard, mayo and ketchup—and let everyone have it their way at your house.

4 slices bacon	½ teaspoon salt
1 pound lean ground beef	¼ teaspoon pepper
1 small onion, chopped	4 hamburger buns, split
3 tablespoons ketchup	

1. Place bacon between 2 layers of paper towels on a paper plate. Cook on HIGH 3 to 4 minutes, until crisp. Set aside.

2. Combine beef, onion, ketchup, salt and pepper in bowl. Mix with a light touch; do not pack meat. Shape into 4 patties.

3. Preheat browning dish according to manufacturer's instructions. Place burgers in dish and cook on HIGH 1½ to 2 minutes, or until browned on the bottom. Turn patties over and cook 1 to 2 minutes, depending on your preference for rare, medium or well done. Sandwich burgers between buns and top each with a slice of bacon.

124   CHEESEBURGERS AMERICAN-STYLE

Prepare burgers as described above, but as soon as burgers are cooked, top each with a slice of Colby, Cheddar or Swiss cheese and let stand until just melted.

125   GINGER MEATBALLS

Prep: 5 minutes   Cook: 5 to 7 minutes   Makes: 36

Great party pick-ups! To serve as a main course, spoon over Japanese soba noodles with a splash of extra teriyaki sauce or over linguine.

1 **pound lean ground beef**	¼ **cup bottled teriyaki sauce**
¼ **cup fresh bread crumbs**	1 **teaspoon ground ginger**

1. In a medium bowl, mix all ingredients. With a light touch, shape into about 3 dozen 1-inch balls.

2. Place meatballs on a round microwave rack. Cover with paper towels. Cook on HIGH 5 to 7 minutes, or until just cooked through. Turn rack if meatballs appear to be cooking unevenly.

126   SWEDISH MEATBALLS IN LINGONBERRY SAUCE

Prep: 20 minutes   Cook: 14 to 15 minutes   Makes: about 40

Serve on small plates with forks or toothpicks, or offer as a main course with boiled potatoes.

½ **cup finely chopped onion**	1 **teaspoon sugar**
2 **tablespoons vegetable oil**	¼ **teaspoon grated nutmeg**
1 **pound lean ground beef**	¼ **teaspoon ground allspice**
chuck	¼ **cup chopped green bell**
¼ **pound ground pork**	**pepper**
½ **cup bread crumbs**	3 **tablespoons chopped celery**
¾ **cup milk**	1 **teaspoon flour**
1½ **teaspoons salt**	1 **12-ounce jar lingonberries**
½ **teaspoon pepper**	2 **tablespoons dry white wine**

1. In a 1-cup glass measure, combine onion and 1 tablespoon oil. Cook on HIGH 2 minutes. In medium bowl, combine beef, pork, bread crumbs, milk, salt, pepper, sugar, nutmeg and allspice. Shape into 1½-inch balls.

2. Arrange meatballs in circle on a round microwave rack set in a shallow baking dish. Cover with paper towel and cook on HIGH 7 to 8 minutes, or just until meatballs are cooked through. Turn rack if meatballs appear to be cooking unevenly. Transfer to a chafing dish or shallow serving dish and cover to keep warm.

3. In a 1-quart glass measure, combine green pepper, celery and remaining 1 tablespoon oil. Cook on HIGH 3 minutes. Stir in flour, mixing to blend well. Add lingonberries and wine. Cook 2 minutes, or until sauce is heated through and slightly thickened. Pour over meatballs and serve hot.

127   JALAPEÑO BURGERS

Prep: 10 minutes   Cook: 3 to 4 minutes   Serves: 4

1 **pound lean ground beef**	½ **teaspoon salt**
1 **small onion, chopped**	4 **hamburger buns, split**
2 **tablespoons chopped jalapeño peppers, fresh or pickled**	¼ **cup guacamole, homemade or thawed frozen (optional)**

1. In a medium bowl, combine beef, onion, jalapeños and salt. Mix well with a light touch. Shape into 4 patties.

2. Preheat browning dish according to manufacturer's instructions. Place patties in dish. Cook on HIGH 1½ to 2 minutes, until bottoms are brown and slightly crisp. Turn burgers over and cook 1½ to 2 minutes, depending on your preference for rare, medium or well done. Place burgers in buns. Top with a dollop of guacamole, if desired.

128   JALAPEÑO CHEESEBURGERS

Prepare as above, but as soon as burgers are done, top each with a thin slice of Cheddar or Monterey jack cheese.

129   BEEF TACOS

Prep: 15 minutes   Cook: 9 to 10 minutes   Makes: 10 tacos

1 **pound lean ground beef**	2 **cups shredded Cheddar or Monterey jack cheese**
2 **teaspoons chili powder**	**Garnishes: shredded lettuce,**
½ **teaspoon garlic powder**	**radishes, sliced scallions,**
½ **teaspoon ground cumin**	**chopped avocado,**
½ **teaspoon salt**	**chopped cucumber,**
⅛ **teaspoon cayenne pepper**	**chopped tomatoes**
1 **16-ounce can refried beans**	**Taco sauce and/or salsa**
10 **taco shells**	

1. Place beef in a medium bowl. Add chili powder, garlic powder, cumin, salt and cayenne. Mix well. Cook on HIGH 2 minutes. Stir to break up any lumps. Continue to cook 3 minutes longer. Drain off any fat.

2. Place refried beans in a 2-cup glass measure or bowl. Cover with waxed paper and cook on HIGH 2 minutes, until heated through.

3. Arrange taco shells upright in microwave taco rack or shallow dish that will hold them upright. Spread about 2 tablespoons refried beans in the bottom of each taco shell. Divide meat evenly among shells. Sprinkle cheese over meat. Cook on HIGH about 2 minutes, until cheese melts and filling is hot. Serve at once, with remaining refried beans, assorted garnishes and taco sauce.

130   TWO-ALARM CHILI
Prep: 10 minutes   Cook: 30 to 35 minutes   Serves: 4 to 6

1 large onion, chopped
1 tablespoon vegetable oil
1 pound lean ground beef
2 garlic cloves, minced
1 14-ounce can peeled plum
    tomatoes, with liquid,
    coarsely chopped
1 6-ounce can tomato paste

1 16-ounce can pinto beans,
    with liquid
1 7-ounce can chopped green
    chiles, drained
2 tablespoons chili powder
1 teaspoon ground cumin
¼ teaspoon crushed hot red
    pepper

1. In a 2-quart casserole, place onion and oil. Cook on HIGH 4 minutes, stirring once. Add beef and cook 2 minutes. Stir to break up lumps. Cook 3 minutes longer.

2. Add all remaining ingredients. Cook, uncovered, stirring once or twice, 20 to 25 minutes, until slightly thickened.

Chapter 7

Other Meats You Really Can Cook in a Microwave

While chicken cutlets and ground meat work especially well in the microwave, you can cook a variety of cuts in the same clean, quick way with excellent results, if you know how. Remember, thicker, tender cuts will do best. Liquid can act as a buffer to help keep them soft and succulent. Stewing meats need longer cooking on medium power in a moist environment to tenderize them and allow the flavors to blend.

All kinds of poultry do well in the microwave. Chicken, turkey and Cornish game hens alike cook for roughly the same length of time—7 minutes per pound. I've developed a little trick of adding on an extra 5 to 10 minutes on low or defrost to ensure that the meat is cooked through to the bone.

So enlarge your microwave meat and poultry repertoire. Surprise your family with a whole Roast Chicken with Savory Mushroom Stuffing or a Glazed Boneless Pork Loin in half an hour. Try Beef Fajitas or Pork Ribs with Sweet-and-Sour Cabbage. Go for classics, like Chicken with 40 Cloves of Garlic or Savory Pot Roast with Vegetables. Or experiment with Chinese Sweet and Sour Pork with Peppers and Pineapple or Thai Chicken Salad. Whatever you choose to cook for dinner, you can cook it faster and easier in the microwave.

---

131 POT ROAST COOKED IN BEER
Prep: 10 minutes   Cook: 1 hour 22 minutes   Serves: 6 to 8

3 tablespoons flour	2 medium onions, sliced
1 3½-pound boneless beef chuck roast	1 green bell pepper, chopped
	½ teaspoon salt
2 12-ounce cans beer	½ teaspoon black pepper

1. Rub flour over roast. Place in a large oven cooking bag or 3-quart casserole with lid. Pour beer over meat. Add onions, bell pepper, salt and black pepper. If using bag, tie top loosely and place in deep bowl; if using casserole, cover with lid. Cook on HIGH 7 minutes. Reduce power to MEDIUM and cook 30 minutes.

2. Turn roast over. Cook on MEDIUM 30 minutes. Turn roast again and cook on MEDIUM 15 minutes longer. Let stand 15 minutes before serving. Carve roast against the grain. Spoon vegetables and a little sauce over meat.

132   SESAME CHICKEN AND CABBAGE SALAD
Prep: 20 minutes   Cook: 5 to 7 minutes   Serves: 4

2 ounces snow pea pods
2 tablespoons sesame seeds
½ cup rice wine vinegar
5 tablespoons peanut oil
1 tablespoon Asian sesame oil
2 teaspoons soy sauce
½ teaspoon sugar
½ teaspoon dry mustard
1 garlic clove, crushed

2 thin slices of fresh ginger,
   finely minced
¼ teaspoon pepper
2 cups shredded cabbage
2 cups shredded romaine
   lettuce
2 cups leftover cooked
   chicken, shredded

1. Wrap snow peas in paper towel, moisten under faucet and place on a plate. Cook on HIGH 2 minutes. Slice lengthwise into thin strips.

2. Put sesame seeds in a 1-cup glass measure and cook on HIGH 1 to 2 minutes, stirring once, until lightly toasted. Set aside. In a small bowl, combine vinegar, 3 tablespoons peanut oil, sesame oil, soy sauce, sugar, mustard, garlic, ginger and pepper. Whisk dressing to blend well.

3. Put cabbage in a 1-quart casserole. Add 2 tablespoons peanut oil. Toss to coat. Cover with lid. Cook on HIGH 2 to 3 minutes, until cabbage is slightly wilted but still crisp.

4. Pour dressing over hot cabbage and toss. Transfer to a large serving bowl. Add lettuce, pea pods, chicken and half of toasted sesame seeds. Toss to mix. Sprinkle remaining sesame seeds on top.

133   CHICKEN THIGHS STUFFED WITH WILD RICE AND CHESTNUTS
Prep: 15 minutes   Cook: 15 minutes   Serves: 6

6 large chicken thighs
1 recipe Wild Rice and
   Chestnuts (p. 103)
1 teaspoon flour
1 teaspoon salt
½ teaspoon pepper
½ teaspoon paprika

6 medium carrots, peeled and
   sliced crosswise on the
   diagonal
1 teaspoon minced fresh dill
   or ½ teaspoon dried
1 tablespoon melted butter

1. Gently pull skin away from meat on each thigh to loosen, but without separating or tearing it. Stuff Wild Rice and Chestnuts between skin and meat. Arrange thighs in a ring in a shallow round baking dish just large enough to hold thighs in a single layer.

2. Combine flour, salt, pepper and paprika. Sprinkle liberally over chicken thighs. Mound carrots in center of dish. Combine dill and butter. Drizzle over carrots. Cover dish with lid or vented microwave-safe plastic wrap. Cook on HIGH 15 minutes, or 7 minutes per pound of chicken thighs, until there is no trace of pink near bone. Turn dish if thighs appear to be cooking unevenly.

134 BEEF JERKY
Prep: 30 minutes   Cook: 70 to 80 minutes   Makes: about 1 pound

Because the microwave is good at removing moisture, it can add as a dehydrator. Beef jerky is great for nibbles or an outdoor snack. Partially freeze the steak before you begin this recipe so it will be easier to slice. You will need a rack to make this.

3 **tablespoons soy sauce**	2 **teaspoons minced fresh**
2 **tablespoons dry white wine**	**ginger**
2 **tablespoons honey**	½ **teaspoon cayenne pepper**
2 **teaspoons Asian sesame oil**	1½ **pounds flank steak, all fat**
3 **garlic cloves, crushed**	**removed**

1. In a large shallow glass dish, combine soy sauce, wine, honey, sesame oil, garlic, ginger and cayenne. Mix marinade well.

2. Cut steak crosswise in half. Then cut each half lengthwise into very thin strips, ⅛ inch thick or less. Add steak strips to marinade and toss to coat evenly. Marinate at room temperature, tossing occasionally, 2 hours.

3. Remove meat from marinade and arrange half the strips, flat and close together, on a microwave bacon rack. Cover with paper towels and cook on MEDIUM-LOW 20 minutes. Rotate strips so that drier strips are in center. Cover with fresh paper towel and cook on MEDIUM-LOW 15 to 20 minutes, until meat is dry but still slightly pliable. Remove to a large wire rack and let stand overnight. Repeat with remaining strips.

135 THAI CHICKEN SALAD
Prep: 10 minutes   Cook: 4 to 6 minutes   Serves: 4

1 **whole chicken breast,**	2 **tablespoons minced fresh**
boned and halved	**mint or 1 teaspoon dried**
6 **carrots, peeled and cut into**	¼ **cup red wine vinegar or rice**
thin strips	**vinegar**
2 **small zucchini, cut into thin**	1 **tablespoon water**
strips	½ **teaspoon salt**
⅓ **cup chopped dried apricots**	¼ **teaspoon sugar**
1 **8¾-ounce can apricot halves,**	⅛ **to ¼ teaspoon crushed hot**
drained and coarsely	**pepper**
chopped	3 **tablespoons vegetable oil**

1. Wrap each half of chicken breast in a paper towel. Hold under faucet until wet. Place on plate. Cook on HIGH 4 to 6 minutes, just until chicken is cooked through. Let cool in towel. Remove skin and tear chicken into shreds. In a large bowl, combine chicken, carrots, zucchini, apricots and mint. Toss to mix.

2. In a small bowl, combine vinegar, water, salt, sugar and hot pepper. Whisk in vegetable oil. Pour dressing over salad and toss until well blended. Cover and refrigerate until serving time. This salad is best served slightly chilled.

136 ROAST CHICKEN WITH SAVORY MUSHROOM STUFFING
Prep: 20 minutes   Cook: 42 minutes   Serves: 4

1 4-pound whole chicken, liver reserved	½ teaspoon tarragon
1 medium onion, chopped	1½ teaspoons salt
2 garlic cloves, minced	1 teaspoon pepper
2 tablespoons olive oil	3 cups stale bread cubes
½ pound mushrooms, chopped	¼ to ⅓ cup chicken broth
½ cup finely diced baked ham	2 tablespoons flour
⅓ cup chopped parsley	1 teaspoon paprika
	¾ teaspoon garlic powder

1. Rinse chicken inside and out. Pat dry with paper towels. Trim liver; finely dice. Place liver in a 1-cup glass measure. Cover and cook on MEDIUM 2 minutes. Stir; set aside, covered.

2. In a 2-quart bowl, combine onion, garlic and 1 tablespoon oil. Cook on HIGH 3 minutes. Stir in mushrooms. Cook 2 minutes. Add cooked liver, ham, parsley, tarragon, ¾ teaspoon salt and ½ teaspoon pepper. Mix well. Toss in bread cubes. Stir in just enough chicken broth to moisten without making stuffing wet.

3. Spoon stuffing into large cavity of chicken and into neck. Push some stuffing underneath loose breast skin near neck. Use wooden toothpicks to truss chicken closed. Place chicken breast-side up in shallow baking dish. Rub remaining oil over chicken. Combine flour, paprika and garlic powder; sprinkle over chicken. Cover with waxed paper and cook on HIGH 15 minutes. Brush chicken with drippings and carefully turn over. Cover again with waxed paper and cook 10 minutes longer.

4. Carefully turn chicken breast-side up; baste with drippings. Reduce power to MEDIUM, and cook 10 minutes, until skin is lightly colored and juices from thigh run clear when pierced to the bone. Let chicken stand, covered, 5 minutes before carving.

137 LIVER AND ONIONS
Prep: 10 minutes   Cook: 12 to 15 minutes   Serves: 3 to 4

1 large onion, thinly sliced	1 teaspoon salt
2 tablespoons vegetable oil	½ teaspoon pepper
1 pound chicken livers	¼ teaspoon garlic powder

1. In a 2-quart casserole, toss onion slices with oil. Cook on HIGH 4 minutes. Remove onions to a serving bowl and set aside.

2. Rinse livers and drain well. Trim off tough membranes. Cut livers into chunks. Place in same casserole onions cooked in (do not wash). Season with salt, pepper and garlic powder. Cover with lid and cook on MEDIUM 6 to 7 minutes, stirring once, until just cooked through.

3. Reheat onion in a bowl on HIGH 30 seconds. With slotted spoon, remove livers from casserole, add to onions and toss. Serve at once.

138 VEAL WITH LEMON AND GARLIC
Prep: 5 minutes   Cook: 2 minutes   Serves: 1

It's nice to dine well when you're eating alone. If you have company, add 1½ minutes of cooking time for each additional serving.

¼ **pound veal scallopine**	⅛ **teaspoon white pepper**
1 **teaspoon Worcestershire**	3 **thin lemon slices**
sauce	4 **garlic cloves, unpeeled**

1. Tear off a 10 × 14-inch sheet of parchment. Fold in half and trim edges to form an oval. Place veal to one side of crease. Sprinkle with Worcestershire and pepper. Arrange lemon slices on top. Place garlic cloves around meat. Fold to close paper, roll up edges and crimp to seal.

2. Place packet in microwave and cook on HIGH 2 minutes, until veal is just done. Do not overcook. Serve right from parchment.

139 SAVORY POT ROAST WITH VEGETABLES
Prep: 25 minutes   Cook: 1 hour 15 minutes   Serves: 4 to 6

"Quick" is a relative term. An hour and 15 minutes sounds like a long time when you're talking about microwave cooking. But to make pot roast, compare that to 2 to 3 hours, or longer, in a conventional oven.

2 **tablespoons Worcestershire**	4 **medium potatoes, peeled**
sauce	**and halved**
3 **tablespoons flour**	2 **large carrots, peeled and cut**
1 **8-ounce can tomato sauce**	**into 2-inch pieces**
1 **tablespoon brown sugar**	2 **parsnips, peeled and cut**
½ **teaspoon salt**	**into 2-inch pieces**
½ **teaspoon dry mustard**	1 **green bell pepper, cut into**
½ **teaspoon fennel seeds**	**1-inch squares**
¼ **teaspoon pepper**	1 **large onion, cut into 6**
3 **garlic cloves, crushed**	**wedges**
1 **4-pound boneless chuck**	
roast, fat trimmed	

1. In a bowl, mix Worcestershire and flour to a paste. Stir in tomato sauce, brown sugar, salt, mustard, fennel, pepper and garlic. Set sauce aside.

2. Place roast in 14 × 20-inch oven roasting bag with a 1-inch strip cut off open end or in a 4-quart casserole with lid. Spoon sauce over meat. Add potatoes, carrots, parsnips, green pepper and onion to bag. Shake bag to distribute liquid.

3. Tie end of bag closed loosely with reserved strip or cover casserole. Arrange bag with tied end facing up. Cook on MEDIUM 30 minutes. Carefully turn bag over and cook 30 minutes longer. Check pot roast. If it looks dry, add ¼ cup water. Continue to cook on MEDIUM 10 to 15 minutes, until meat is fork tender. Let stand in bag 25 minutes before slicing.

140 MARINATED FILLET OF BEEF
Prep: 10 minutes   Cook: 15 to 20 minutes   Serves: 6

The king of roasts, always served rare, is a perfect cut for the microwave. It comes out tender and succulent. An oven cooking bag holds in all the moisture and provides an even oven-like environment within the microwave.

1 2½- to 3-pound fillet of beef	1 cup canned beef broth
2 garlic cloves, minced	½ cup chili sauce
1 medium onion, sliced	½ cup dry red wine
½ pound mushrooms, sliced	¼ cup flour

1. Place roast in a shallow glass dish. Sprinkle garlic, onion and mushrooms on top. Combine beef broth, chili sauce and red wine. Spoon over roast. Cover and marinate in refrigerator for 2 to 4 hours, turning occasionally.

2. Cut 2-inch strip off open end of regular-size oven cooking bag; reserve strip. Place flour in bag. Remove meat from marinade and pour marinade and vegetables into bag. Turn to mix and absorb flour. Add fillet, distributing the liquid and vegetables evenly. Tie bag loosely at top with reserved strip to keep juices in. Place in shallow dish.

3. Cook fillet on HIGH 10 minutes. Carefully turn bag over to rotate meat, leaving open end pointed up. Cook on MEDIUM-HIGH 5 to 10 minutes, just until roast reaches 130 degrees on a microwave probe or instant-reading thermometer. Let stand 10 minutes, then carve into thick slices. Serve with mushrooms and onions.

141 BEEF FAJITAS
Prep: 10 minutes   Cook: 11 to 12 minutes   Serves: 2 to 3

½ pound flank steak, trimmed	1 medium onion, thinly sliced
2 tablespoons soy sauce	6 8-inch flour tortillas
3 tablespoons vegetable oil	1 large tomato, chopped
2 tablespoons fresh lime juice	1 cup shredded lettuce
¼ teaspoon ground cumin	Garnishes: salsa,
⅛ teaspoon black pepper	guacamole, sour cream
⅛ teaspoon cayenne pepper	

1. Slice steak thinly against the grain. In an 8-inch pie plate, combine soy sauce, 2 tablespoons oil, lime juice, cumin, black pepper and cayenne. Stir vigorously with a fork to blend well. Add steak slices and turn to coat.

2. In a 1-cup glass measure, combine onion and 1 tablespoon oil. Cook on HIGH 5 minutes. Add to meat and toss. Cover and refrigerate 4 to 6 hours.

3. To cook, cover pie plate with paper towel. Cook steak and onion with marinade on MEDIUM-HIGH 5 to 6 minutes, just until meat is slightly pink. Do not overcook.

4. To serve, heat tortillas inside paper towel for 45 seconds, or until warm. Spoon equal amounts of steak and onion onto each tortilla. Add tomato, lettuce and other garnishes to taste. Roll up and eat.

142 GLAZED BONELESS PORK LOIN
Prep: 10 minutes   Cook: 30 minutes   Serves: 4

2 tablespoons flour
1 large onion, thinly sliced
1 2-pound boneless pork loin
   roast
2 tablespoons dry sherry

2 tablespoons soy sauce
1 tablespoon brown sugar
½ teaspoon salt
½ teaspoon pepper
½ teaspoon ground ginger

1. Cut a 1-inch strip from open end of a regular-size oven cooking bag and reserve. Sprinkle flour in bag. Arrange onion slices in bag. Place pork roast on top of onion.

2. In a small bowl, combine sherry, soy sauce, brown sugar, salt, pepper and ginger. Stir to blend well. Pour over meat. Tie end of bag loosely with reserved strip. Place bag in a shallow baking dish for easy handling.

3. Cook roast on MEDIUM 15 minutes. Turn bag over. If your oven has one, insert temperature probe through bag into center of roast. Continue cooking on MEDIUM about 15 minutes longer, until probe registers 150 to 160 degrees. (Check with an instant-reading thermometer if you don't have a probe, but do not leave in oven.) Turn bag over again. Let roast stand sealed in bag until temperature registers 170 degrees, about 15 minutes.

---

143 CHICKEN TARRAGON
Prep: 10 minutes   Cook: 32 to 38 minutes   Serves: 4

1 3- to 4-pound whole chicken
1 teaspoon Kitchen Bouquet
1 teaspoon vegetable oil
½ teaspoon salt
¼ teaspoon pepper
1 teaspoon tarragon
1 carrot, peeled and cut into 3
   pieces

1 small onion, quartered
1 celery stalk with leaves
6 mushrooms, sliced
¾ teaspoon paprika
1 tablespoon cornstarch
½ cup beef broth

1. Place chicken, breast-side up, in a shallow oval or round baking dish. Brush with mixture of Kitchen Bouquet and oil. Season with salt, pepper and ½ teaspoon tarragon. Arrange carrot, onion, celery and mushrooms around chicken. Cover with waxed paper. Cook on HIGH 15 minutes.

2. Brush chicken with pan juices. Turn over so breast side is down and continue to cook, covered, on HIGH 10 to 13 minutes, 7 minutes per pound. Turn chicken breast-side up and sprinkle with paprika. Cook on DEFROST 5 to 7 minutes, until there is no trace of pink near bones. Transfer chicken to carving board and cover loosely with foil.

3. Strain vegetables and juices through sieve into a 2-cup glass measure. Discard vegetables. Dissolve cornstarch in 2 tablespoons beef broth. Add remaining broth to measure and stir in cornstarch mixture. Cook on HIGH 2 to 3 minutes, until sauce boils and thickens slightly. Season with ½ teaspoon tarragon and additional salt and pepper to taste. Carve chicken and serve with sauce.

144 SWEET-AND-SOUR PORK WITH PEPPERS AND PINEAPPLE

Prep: 10 minutes   Cook: 18 to 25 minutes   Serves: 4 to 6

4 carrots, peeled and thinly
    sliced on the diagonal
3 tablespoons vegetable oil
2 pounds boneless pork loin,
    trimmed of excess fat and
    cut into 2-inch cubes
1 large onion, sliced
1 green bell pepper, cut into
    1-inch squares
1 red bell pepper, cut into
    1-inch squares

1 16-ounce can unsweetened
    pineapple chunks
¼ cup cornstarch
½ cup soy sauce
½ cup (packed) brown sugar
¼ cup white wine vinegar
1 tablespoon Worcestershire
    sauce
¼ teaspoon hot pepper sauce

1. In a 3-quart casserole, combine carrots and oil. Cover and cook on HIGH 5 minutes. Stir in pork, onion and green and red peppers. Cover and cook 3 minutes.

2. Drain pineapple chunks; reserve ½ cup juice. Transfer juice to a medium bowl, add cornstarch and stir until dissolved. Stir in all remaining ingredients to make a sauce.

3. Add sauce and pineapple chunks to pork and vegetables. Stir to mix. Cover and cook on MEDIUM 10 to 17 minutes, stirring twice, until sauce is thickened and pork is tender. Serve over rice or chow mein noodles.

145 STUFFED FLANK STEAK IN ORANGE MARINADE

Prep: 15 minutes   Cook: 25 to 30 minutes   Serves: 4

For best flavor, allow plenty of time for the meat to marinate.

1 1½-pound flank steak
¾ cup orange juice
¼ cup soy sauce
¼ cup dry white wine
2 garlic cloves, crushed
¾ teaspoon pepper
2 tablespoons butter
¼ cup chopped celery

¼ cup chopped onion
¼ cup chopped red or green
    bell pepper
¼ cup dry bread crumbs
¼ cup water
½ teaspoon salt
½ pound fresh mushrooms,
    sliced

1. Score steak lightly in diamond pattern with tip of sharp knife. Place in a 10 × 6 × 2-inch baking dish. Combine orange juice, soy sauce, wine, garlic and ½ teaspoon pepper. Pour over steak. Cover with plastic wrap and refrigerate 4 to 6 hours, or overnight, turning occasionally.

2. In a 4-cup glass measure, combine butter, celery, onion and bell pepper. Cook on HIGH 4 minutes. Stir in bread crumbs, water, salt and ¼ teaspoon pepper.

3. Remove steak from marinade; reserve ¼ cup marinade. Spread stuffing over steak to within 1 inch of all sides. Carefully roll up from one of shorter ends. Tie with string in 3 places. Place seam-side down in a baking dish just large enough to hold steak. Brush with reserved marinade. Place mushrooms over and around steak.

4. Cover with waxed paper. Cook on HIGH 5 minutes. Brush again with reserved marinade. Cover again and cook on MEDIUM 10 minutes. Turn meat over and baste again. Cover and cook on MEDIUM 5 to 10 minutes longer, until meat is tender. Slice and serve with pan drippings and mushrooms.

146   CHICKEN TERIYAKI
Prep: 5 minutes   Cook: 21 to 25 minutes   Serves: 4

This easy, light dish cooks in less than half an hour, but for best flavor, allow a couple of hours for the chicken to marinate.

½ cup soy sauce	2 tablespoons vegetable oil
⅓ cup dry sherry	2 garlic cloves, crushed
½ cup (packed) brown sugar	½ teaspoon ground ginger
¼ cup rice vinegar or white wine vinegar	3 pounds chicken legs, thighs and/or breasts

1. In a large glass or ceramic casserole, combine all of the ingredients except chicken. Mix well to dissolve brown sugar. Add chicken to marinade and turn to coat. Cover and refrigerate for at least 2 hours, or overnight.

2. Remove chicken from marinade. Arrange pieces in a shallow oval or round baking dish, with thickest parts facing outside. Cover with waxed paper. Cook on HIGH 21 to 25 minutes, turning dish if chicken appears to be cooking unevenly.

147   ALMOST FRIED CHICKEN
Prep: 10 minutes   Cook: 31 to 38 minutes   Serves: 4

2 cups corn flakes	½ teaspoon salt
⅓ cup grated Parmesan cheese	¼ teaspoon pepper
½ teaspoon paprika	4 tablespoons butter, melted, or ¼ cup vegetable oil
1 3- to 4-pound chicken, cut into serving pieces	

1. Place corn flakes, Parmesan cheese and paprika in a paper bag. Using a rolling pin, wine bottle or your hands, crush to crumble the flakes coarsely. Shake well. Pour the corn flake coating into a pie plate.

2. Rinse chicken and wipe dry. Season generously with salt and pepper. Dip each piece in melted butter or oil, then dredge in corn flake mixture to coat completely.

3. Arrange chicken pieces in a shallow oval or round baking dish, with thickest parts facing out. Cover with paper towels. Cook on HIGH 21 to 28 minutes (7 minutes per pound). Rotate dish if chicken appears to be cooking unevenly. To be sure chicken is cooked to the bone, reduce power to MEDIUM-LOW or DEFROST and cook 10 minutes longer.

148   STUFFED TURKEY BREAST

Prep: 15 minutes   Cook: 19 to 27 minutes   Serves: 2 to 4

With half a turkey breast you can enjoy a Thanksgiving dinner with all the trimmings whenever you like. And leftovers make great sandwiches.

1 medium onion, chopped	¼ teaspoon thyme leaves
½ cup chopped celery	1 teaspoon salt
1 tablespoon plus 1 teaspoon olive oil	¾ teaspoon pepper
	¼ to ½ cup chicken broth
1 medium zucchini, shredded	½ turkey breast (3½ to 4
½ pound fresh mushrooms, diced	pounds)
1 tablespoon minced parsley	2 teaspoons flour
1½ cups stale bread cubes	1 teaspoon garlic powder
½ teaspoon crushed sage	1 teaspoon paprika

1. In a shallow oval baking dish just large enough to hold turkey, combine onion, celery and 1 tablespoon oil. Cook on HIGH 3 minutes. Stir in zucchini, mushrooms and parsley. Cover with waxed paper and cook 3 minutes. Add bread cubes, sage, thyme, ½ teaspoon salt and ¼ teaspoon pepper; toss to mix. Toss with enough chicken broth to moisten stuffing without making it wet.

2. Mound dressing in center of dish. Place turkey breast over dressing. Rub skin with remaining 1 teaspoon oil. Combine flour, garlic powder, paprika and remaining salt and pepper. Sprinkle over turkey. Cover with waxed paper. Cook on HIGH 21 to 28 minutes, or 7 minutes per pound. Let stand 15 minutes before slicing.

149   PORK RIBS WITH SWEET-AND-SOUR CABBAGE

Prep: 5 minutes   Cook: 40 to 45 minutes   Serves: 4 to 6

3 pounds country-style pork loin ribs, trimmed of fat	1 large onion, chopped
	1 tart apple, peeled, cored and chopped
7 cups water	
1 24-ounce jar sauerkraut, rinsed and drained	1 teaspoon caraway seeds
	¼ teaspoon pepper
1 16-ounce jar sweet and sour red cabbage, liquid reserved	

1. In a 4-quart baking dish, spread out ribs. Add water and cover with lid or vented microwave-safe plastic wrap. Cook on HIGH 20 minutes. Remove ribs from water.

2. In a shallow baking dish, combine sauerkraut and red cabbage with its liquid. Arrange ribs on top, with thickest parts facing outside of dish. Sprinkle onion, apple, caraway seeds and pepper over ribs. Cover and cook on MEDIUM 15 minutes. Check about halfway through and shift slower-cooking ribs to outside of dish.

3. Turn ribs over and test for tenderness with fork. If not quite done, continue to cook, covered, on MEDIUM 5 to 10 minutes. Let stand, covered, for about 10 minutes before serving.

---

150 RASPBERRY-GLAZED CORNISH HENS
Prep: 10 minutes   Cook: 15 to 20 minutes   Serves: 2 or 4

2 **Cornish game hens (about**   2 **teaspoons lemon juice**
   1¼ pounds each)   1 **tablespoon grated orange**
⅓ **cup raspberry preserves**   **zest**

1. Split game hens lengthwise in half. Arrange hen halves, skin-side up, in a 10-inch round, shallow baking dish, or quiche pan, with thickest parts facing outside.

2. In a small bowl, combine raspberry preserves, lemon juice and orange zest. Stir to blend well. Brush glaze over hens. Cover with waxed paper. Cook on HIGH 15 to 20 minutes, or until fork tender. Turn dish if hens appear to be cooking unevenly.

---

151 CHICKEN WITH 40 CLOVES OF GARLIC
Prep: 20 minutes   Cook: 35 minutes   Serves: 4

When garlic cloves are cooked whole along with the chicken, they become buttery soft and mild in taste. Serve this dish with hot crusty bread and encourage family and guests to use the roast garlic as a spread. Or mash the garlic and juices into baked potatoes.

40 **garlic cloves**   ¼ **cup dry white wine**
1½ **cups thinly sliced celery**   ½ **teaspoon paprika**
 1 **medium onion, thinly sliced**   ½ **teaspoon thyme**
 3 **tablespoons olive oil**   ½ **teaspoon salt**
 1 **4-pound chicken, cut into**   ¼ **teaspoon pepper**
    serving pieces   2 **tablespoons flour**

1. In a 4-cup glass measure, place garlic, celery, onion and oil. Cook on HIGH 7 minutes. Meanwhile, arrange chicken in a 13-inch round baking dish, with thickest pieces near outside of dish. Sprinkle with wine and season with paprika, thyme, salt and pepper. Spoon garlic cloves and cooked vegetables along with any juices between pieces of chicken. Cover with fitted cover or with vented microwave-safe plastic wrap.

2. Cook on HIGH 25 to 28 minutes, or 7 minutes per pound, until chicken meat has lost all trace of pink but is still juicy. Turn dish if chicken appears to be cooking unevenly. Spoon drippings over chicken, transfer to a serving platter and cover with aluminum foil to keep warm.

3. Skim fat off drippings in dish. Dissolve flour in 2 tablespoons water and stir into drippings in pan until well blended. Cook on HIGH 2 to 4 minutes, stirring several times, until thickened. Season with additional salt and pepper to taste. Pour over chicken and serve.

152   HONEY-GLAZED TURKEY LEGS
Prep: 5 minutes   Cook: 25 to 29 minutes   Serves: 2 to 4

2 turkey legs (2½ to 3 pounds total)	1 teaspoon grated lemon zest
Salt and pepper	1 teaspoon lemon juice
⅓ cup honey	1 teaspoon cornstarch
	½ teaspoon Kitchen Bouquet

1. Season turkey legs all over with salt and pepper. Place in an oval baking dish, with thickest parts facing outside of dish. Cover with waxed paper. Cook on HIGH 10 minutes. Turn legs over and cook 10 minutes longer.

2. In a small bowl, combine all of the remaining ingredients. Stir to dissolve cornstarch. Cook on HIGH 1½ minutes.

3. Brush turkey legs with half of the glaze. Cover and cook on HIGH 2 minutes. Turn legs over and brush with remaining glaze. Cook 2 minutes longer, or until turkey is tender.

153   POACHED CHICKEN
Prep: 10 minutes   Cook: 30 minutes   Serves: 4

Poaching a chicken in the microwave in an oven cooking bag not only saves time, it saves fuss. There are no pots to clean, and the chicken comes out moist and juicy every time.

1 4-pound whole chicken	1 small parsnip, quartered
Salt and pepper	2 garlic cloves
1 small onion, halved	2 cups water
1 carrot, quartered	1 clove
1 celery top with leaves	1 small bay leaf

1. Rinse chicken well. Season inside and out with salt and pepper to taste. Put whole chicken in a large oven cooking bag set inside a 2-quart casserole. Be sure chicken is breast-side up with the cavity opening facing out. Stuff chicken with onion, carrot, celery, parsnip and garlic. Pour in water. Add clove and bay leaf. Tie top of bag loosely into a bow.

2. Cook chicken on HIGH 15 minutes. Carefully turn bag over so chicken is breast-side down (with bag opening still on top) and cook 15 minutes longer, or a total of 7 minutes per pound. Let chicken cool in bag for 10 minutes. With scissors, cut corner of bag and let juices drain out; reserve juices for soup. Remove chicken and use as desired.

Chapter 8

Fish in a Flash

Its delicacy and high moisture content make seafood ideal for microwave cooking. If you have any doubt, take a pound of shrimp in their shells. Boil half a pound in a pot of water and microwave the other half pound. See if the difference isn't striking. The microwave seals in all the juices and flavor, and it reduces shrinkage considerably, not an insignificant benefit given the cost of fish and shellfish these days.

With only a couple of exceptions, all the recipes in this chapter cook in 10 minutes or less, most of them in much less. And as is typical of microwave cooking in general, a minimum of fat, if any, is needed. So if you are eating fish to eat light, you have a wide range of choices with no compromise on flavor. A number of the recipes here also utilize the sealed parchment cooking that I describe in the introduction to the Chicken in a Hurry chapter on page 49. It works even better with seafood.

If your taste runs to shellfish, try my garlicky Quick and Easy Scampi, Coconut Shrimp, with the lush flavors of the islands, spicy Szechuan Shrimp or elegant Lobster Tails Supreme. Entertain with Coquilles St. Jacques as a first course or with Stuffed Fillet of Sole with Creamy Shrimp Sauce as an applause-winning entrée.

For everyday, enjoy the healthful nutrition of fish simply, with Savory Crumb-Coated Fish Steak, Orange Fish Fillets with Saffron Cream Sauce, Swordfish Teriyaki or Tuna Casserole with Cashews. Get fancy in a flash with Herbed Salmon en Papillote, Brook Trout with Mushrooms and Onions or Sea Scallops with Tomato and Lime.

---

154 SWORDFISH TERIYAKI
Prep: 5 minutes   Cook: 6 to 7 minutes   Serves: 4

2 12-ounce swordfish steaks	1 teaspoon sugar
⅓ cup teriyaki sauce	1 tablespoon vegetable oil
1 garlic clove, crushed	Chopped scallion

1. Rinse fish briefly and pat dry. Set in a small shallow baking dish. In a small bowl, combine teriyaki sauce, garlic, sugar and oil. Stir to dissolve sugar. Pour over fish and let marinate at room temperature, turning once or twice, 15 to 30 minutes.

2. Drain off marinade. Cover dish with waxed paper or parchment. Cook on HIGH 6 to 7 minutes (4 to 5 minutes per pound), just until fish is opaque near bone. Do not overcook. Sprinkle with scallion and serve.

155   SHRIMP AND VEGETABLES CHINESE-STYLE

Prep: 20 minutes   Cook: 4 to 5 minutes   Serves: 4

You can produce a quick and easy Chinese wok-style "stir-fry" in your microwave in minutes—with no oil. Serve with steamed rice.

½ pound fresh bean sprouts
¼ pound fresh snow peas or 1 6-ounce package frozen
1 medium zucchini, cut into thin strips
3 scallions, sliced

1 pound large shrimp, shelled and deveined
2 tablespoons soy sauce
1 teaspoon grated fresh ginger or ¼ teaspoon ground
1 tablespoon dry sherry
½ teaspoon sugar

1. Toss together bean sprouts, snow peas, zucchini and scallions, and arrange in center of a 10-inch round baking dish. Arrange shrimp around the edge of dish with tails facing in (thicker part out).

2. In a small bowl, combine soy sauce, ginger, sherry and sugar. Stir to dissolve sugar. Drizzle over shrimp and vegetables. Cover with waxed paper. Cook on HIGH 4 to 5 minutes, just until shrimp turn pink and curl loosely; do not overcook. Turn dish if shrimp appear to be cooking unevenly. Serve hot, with steamed rice.

156   COCONUT SHRIMP

Prep: 20 minutes   Cook: 5 to 6 minutes   Serves: 2

Enjoy a taste of the islands in the middle of winter. Serve with steamed rice.

⅔ cup canned unsweetened coconut milk
1 tablespoon dry sherry
2 teaspoons cornstarch
1 teaspoon lemon juice
⅛ teaspoon salt
1 teaspoon Hot Chili Oil (p. 85)
2 garlic cloves, minced
2 tablespoons peanut oil

½ pound large shrimp, shelled and deveined
3 ounces fresh shiitake or white button mushrooms, sliced (about 1 cup)
2 tablespoons chopped fresh basil or ½ teaspoon dried
2 tablespoons sliced scallions
1 teaspoon chopped fresh mint or ¼ teaspoon dried

1. In a 2-cup glass measure, combine coconut milk, sherry, cornstarch, lemon juice, salt and ½ teaspoon chili oil. Stir to dissolve cornstarch. Cook on HIGH 1½ minutes, stirring once, until just thickened. Cover coconut sauce to keep warm; set aside.

2. In a 10-inch oval gratin dish or round shallow baking dish, combine garlic, peanut oil and ½ teaspoon chili oil. Cook on HIGH 1 minute. Add shrimp and mushrooms; toss to mix. Cover with waxed paper. Cook 2 minutes.

3. Stir. Add basil, scallions and mint. Continue cooking on HIGH, covered, about 45 seconds, just until shrimp turn pink and curl loosely. Do not over-cook. Pour hot coconut sauce over shrimp and serve.

157   QUICK AND EASY SCAMPI
Prep: 15 minutes   Cook: 5 to 6 minutes   Serves: 2

If you buy your shrimp shelled and deveined, this recipe will take only 5 minutes of preparation. I like to leave the tails on the shrimp for appear-ances. Make in a microwave gratin dish and serve right from the dish.

2 large garlic cloves, minced
2 tablespoons olive oil
3 tablespoons minced parsley
2 tablespoons dry white wine
⅛ teaspoon paprika

¾ pound large shrimp, shelled
    and deveined
1½ tablespoons fresh lemon
    juice
½ teaspoon salt
⅛ teaspoon pepper

1. In gratin or baking dish, combine the garlic and oil. Cook on HIGH 1 minute. Stir in parsley, wine and paprika. Cook 2 minutes longer.

2. Add shrimp and toss to coat. Sprinkle with lemon juice, salt and pepper. Cover with waxed paper and cook on HIGH 2 to 3 minutes, stirring once, just until shrimp turn pink and curl loosely; do not overcook.

158   SHRIMP WITH FETA CHEESE
Prep: 15 minutes   Cook: 4 to 7 minutes   Serves: 3 to 4

A student from Greece gave me this recipe to adapt to the microwave. She said it tasted even better this way. Since the feta is salty, I don't add any extra salt, but taste and season to your own palate.

4 tablespoons butter
2 garlic cloves, minced
¼ cup plus 2 tablespoons
    minced parsley
¼ cup crumbled feta cheese
½ cup bread crumbs
¾ teaspoon oregano

¼ teaspoon pepper
2 tablespoons dry white wine
1½ teaspoons lemon juice
1 pound large shrimp, shelled
    and deveined
Lemon wedges

1. In a shallow baking dish or pie plate, place butter and garlic. Cook on HIGH 1 to 2 minutes, until garlic is slightly softened. Stir in ¼ cup parsley, feta cheese, bread crumbs, oregano, pepper, wine and lemon juice. Blend lightly.

2. Arrange shrimp in dish with tails toward inside. Spoon some of crumb mixture over each shrimp. Cover dish with waxed paper. Cook on HIGH 3 to 5 minutes, just until shrimp turn pink and curl loosely. About halfway through, move any shrimp that are done to center of dish to avoid over-cooking. Sprinkle remaining 2 tablespoons parsley over shrimp and serve hot, with lemon wedges.

159   COQUILLES ST. JACQUES
Prep: 5 minutes   Cook: 10 to 12 minutes   Serves: 2 to 4

The French have been preparing this classic recipe for a long time. My version speeds things up neatly in the microwave. If serving four as a first course, spoon into scallop shells set on small plates for a lovely presentation.

4 **shallots, minced**	1/8 **teaspoon white pepper**
2 **tablespoons unsalted butter**	2 **tablespoons flour**
1 **pound sea scallops**	1/2 **cup heavy cream**
1/3 **cup dry white wine**	**Parsley and lemon wedges**
1/4 **teaspoon salt**	

1. In a 9-inch quiche dish or shallow baking dish, place shallots and butter. Cook on HIGH 2 minutes, or until shallots are soft.

2. Add scallops and toss with butter to coat. Add wine, salt and pepper. Cover with waxed paper. Cook on MEDIUM 6 to 7 minutes, stirring once or twice and moving less-cooked scallops to outside of dish, until scallops are just opaque throughout. Remove with slotted spoon and transfer to a bowl. Cover to keep warm.

3. Dissolve flour in 3 tablespoons of cream. Whisk slowly into juices in dish, blending thoroughly. Whisk in remaining cream. Cook on HIGH 2 to 3 minutes, until thickened. Add scallops and any juices that have accumulated to sauce. Divide among serving plates or scallop shells. Garnish with parsley sprigs and serve with lemon wedges.

160   LOBSTER TAILS SUPREME
Prep: 5 minutes   Cook: 5 to 6 minutes   Serves: 2

2 **8-ounce lobster tails**	**Pinch of paprika**
2 **tablespoons melted butter**	**Drawn Butter (recipe**
1/2 **teaspoon lemon juice**	**follows)**

1. Split each lobster tail through the top shell and carefully pull the meat through the shell in one piece, leaving the small end attached to the shell. Place tails on plate. Combine melted butter, lemon juice and paprika. Brush over lobster.

2. Cover loosely with waxed paper. Cook on HIGH 5 to 6 minutes, just until lobster appears to be cooking unevenly. Serve with Drawn Butter for dipping.

NOTE: To cook 4 lobster tails, allow 9 to 10 minutes

161   DRAWN BUTTER
Prep: 0   Cook: 3 minutes   Makes: 1/2 cup

2 **sticks (1/2 pound) unsalted butter**

1. Put butter into a 2-cup glass measure. Cover with paper towel. Heat on MEDIUM-HIGH 1 to 1 1/2 minutes, until butter is heated through and begins to bubble.

2. Remove from microwave and let stand 3 minutes. Skim foam from top of butter. Slowly pour clear yellow butter into bowl or pitcher. Discard solid white material at bottom of measure. Reheat drawn butter on HIGH 30 to 45 seconds before serving.

---

162 SZECHUAN SHRIMP
Prep: 20 minutes   Cook: 6 to 8 minutes   Serves: 2

Hoisin sauce is available in the Asian food sections of many supermarkets and in Chinese groceries. It will keep almost indefinitely in the refrigerator. Chinese hot oil can be bought bottled, or you can make your own (recipe follows). Serve this tasty dish on a bed of rice with steamed broccoli for a complete meal.

2 tablespoons chopped green
     bell pepper
	1 to 1½ teaspoons Hot Chili
	     Oil (recipe follows)

2 tablespoons chopped onion	¾ pound large shrimp, shelled
1 large garlic clove, minced	and deveined
1 teaspoon minced fresh	2 teaspoons cornstarch
ginger	¼ cup dry sherry
2½ tablespoons peanut oil	2 teaspoons soy sauce
	1 teaspoon hoisin sauce

1. In a 2-quart bowl, combine green pepper, onion, garlic, ginger, peanut oil and ½ teaspoon chili oil. Cook on HIGH 2 minutes. Stir in shrimp. Cover with waxed paper. Cook 2 to 2½ minutes, stirring once, just until shrimp turn pink and begin to curl. Do not overcook. Remove shrimp with a slotted spoon.

2. Dissolve cornstarch in sherry; add to cooking juices along with soy sauce, hoisin sauce and remaining chili oil. Stir to blend. Cook on HIGH 1 minute; stir. Cook for 1 minute longer, or until sauce thickens. Stir shrimp into sauce. Reheat if necessary on HIGH 30 to 60 seconds.

---

163 HOT CHILI OIL
Prep: 5 minutes   Cook: 6½ minutes   Makes: ⅓ to ½ cup

While this homemade condiment is Chinese in character, it will add zest to anything you cook.

¼ cup Asian sesame oil	1 tablespoon minced fresh
¼ cup vegetable oil	ginger
1 teaspoon crushed hot red	4 scallions, cut into ½-inch
pepper	pieces

1. In a 4-cup glass measure, combine sesame and vegetable oils. Cook on HIGH 5 minutes, until very hot. Remove from microwave and immediately stir in hot pepper, ginger and scallions. Cover and cook on HIGH 1½ minutes. Let cool slowly to room temperature.

2. Strain oil; discard solids. Store chili oil in a covered jar in a cool, dark place.

164   SOUTHERN-STYLE CATFISH WITH OKRA AND PEPPER

Prep: 15 minutes   Cook: 5 to 6 minutes   Serves: 2

¼ cup sliced okra	1 garlic clove, minced
1 small tomato, seeded and coarsely chopped	2 4-ounce catfish fillets
	1 teaspoon lemon juice
¼ cup onion, cut into ½-inch dice	¼ teaspoon salt
	⅛ teaspoon thyme leaves
¼ cup green bell pepper, cut into ½-inch dice	⅛ teaspoon cayenne pepper

1. Toss together okra, tomato, onion, bell pepper and garlic. Divide vegetables into 4 equal portions.

2. Tear off two 10 × 14-inch sheets of parchment paper. Fold each in half and trim edges to form a half-moon shape. Open up the parchment and place ¼ of vegetables next to crease on each sheet. Place catfish on vegetables. Season fish with lemon juice, salt, thyme and cayenne. Cover with remaining vegetables. Fold parchment over, fold up edges and crimp to seal.

3. Place packets on plate and cook on HIGH 5 to 5½ minutes, just until fish is opaque throughout.

165   STUFFED FILLET OF SOLE WITH CREAMY SHRIMP SAUCE

Prep: 10 minutes   Cook: 11 to 13 minutes   Serves: 4

An elegant company dish that's pretty and pink. Start with microwaved asparagus served with a vinaigrette, and accompany the fish with rice or new potatoes.

¼ cup thinly sliced scallions	1½ pounds sole or flounder fillets
¼ cup thinly sliced celery	
5 tablespoons unsalted butter	½ cup dry white wine
3 tablespoons chopped parsley	2 tablespoons flour
	1 cup half-and-half or light cream
1½ cups fresh bread crumbs	
½ teaspoon tarragon	1 egg yolk, lightly beaten
½ teaspoon salt	1 cup cooked baby shrimp (drain if using canned)
¼ teaspoon white pepper	

1. In a 4-cup glass measure, combine scallions, celery and 2 tablespoons butter. Cook on HIGH 2 minutes. Blend in parsley, bread crumbs, tarragon, ¼ teaspoon salt and ⅛ teaspoon white pepper.

2. Set fish fillets on counter, skinned side down. Spread bread crumb mixture over fillets. Beginning at thicker end, roll up each fillet and secure with a wooden toothpick. Place in a shallow round or oval baking dish.

3. Pour wine over fish. Cover with waxed paper. Cook on HIGH 5 to 6 minutes, just until fish becomes opaque throughout. Turn dish if fish appears to be cooking unevenly. Carefully remove fish to a platter and cover with foil to keep warm. Strain and reserve juices in dish.

4. In a 4-cup glass measure, heat the remaining 3 tablespoons butter on HIGH 45 seconds, until melted. Stir in flour, half-and-half and remaining ¼ teaspoon salt and ⅛ teaspoon white pepper. Cook 1½ minutes. In a small bowl, gradually whisk about ½ cup sauce into egg yolk. Whisk egg yolk mixture back into remaining sauce. Add shrimp and reserved cooking juices. Cook on HIGH 1 to 2 minutes, stirring once, until sauce thickens. For a thicker sauce, cook on MEDIUM 1 minute longer. Pour sauce over fish and serve at once.

---

166   SEA BASS PROVENCALE
Prep: 15 minutes   Cook: 8 to 10 minutes   Serves: 4

3 tablespoons extra-virgin
   olive oil
2 garlic cloves, minced
2 shallots, minced
1½ pounds thick sea bass fillets,
   cut into 2-inch chunks
1 teaspoon lemon juice

1 large ripe tomato, peeled
   seeded and chopped
¾ teaspoon salt
¼ teaspoon pepper
¼ cup chopped parsley
   Lemon slices, for garnish

1. In a shallow baking dish, combine oil, garlic and shallots. Cook on HIGH 2 minutes. Add fish chunks and toss to coat with oil. Sprinkle on lemon juice. Cover with waxed paper.

2. Cook on MEDIUM 3 minutes. Add tomato, salt, pepper and 3 table-spoons parsley. Toss gently to mix. Cover again and continue to cook 3 to 5 minutes, just until fish is opaque throughout. Do not overcook. Sprinkle remaining parsley on top and garnish with lemon slices.

---

167   SAVORY CRUMB-COATED FISH STEAK
Prep: 5 minutes   Cook: 2½ to 3½ minutes   Serves: 1

Treat yourself when you're eating alone. Or multiply, adding 2 to 3 minutes for each additional serving.

1 teaspoon butter or
   margarine
2 tablespoons seasoned bread
   crumbs

4 to 6 ounces fish steak, cut 1
   inch thick
   Lemon wedges

1. Place butter on a dinner plate. Cook on HIGH 30 seconds, until melted. Brush fish with butter. Sprinkle 1 tablespoon bread crumbs over each side of fish. Pat gently to help crumbs adhere.

2. Place fish diagonally across a microwave paper towel. Fold 3 corners toward center, covering fish like an envelope. Fold remaining corner over other 3 to enclose fish. Place folded-side down on plate. Cook on MEDIUM-HIGH 2 to 3 minutes, until fish is opaque throughout (time will depend on type and exact weight of fish). Let stand 2 minutes before unwrapping. Serve hot, with lemon wedges.

168 HALIBUT WITH GREEN CHILE SALSA
Prep: 10 minutes   Cook: 5½ to 6 minutes   Serves: 3 to 4

½ large sweet onion, thinly
    sliced
1½ pounds halibut or other
    firm-fleshed white fish,
    cut 1 inch thick
    Salt and pepper

1 8-ounce can green chile salsa
1 medium tomato, coarsely
    chopped
1 tablespoon chopped cilantro
1 2-ounce can sliced black
    olives, drained

1. In a shallow baking dish just large enough to hold fish, arrange a single layer of sliced onion. Place fish on top. Season lightly with salt and pepper. Spoon salsa over fish. Sprinkle tomato and cilantro on top.

2. Cover with waxed paper and cook on HIGH 5½ to 6 minutes, or until fish is just barely opaque throughout. Top fish with olive slices.

169 BROOK TROUT WITH MUSHROOMS AND ONIONS
Prep: 10 minutes   Cook: 8 to 9 minutes   Serves: 2

1 small onion, thinly sliced
2 tablespoons extra-virgin
    olive oil
2 tablespoons chopped fresh
    parsley

6 mushrooms, sliced
2 8-ounce trout or 1 1-pound
    trout
1 small lemon, thinly sliced

1. In a shallow oval baking dish just large enough to hold the fish, combine the onion and oil. Toss to moisten onion. Cook on HIGH 4 minutes.

2. Reserve ½ tablespoon parsley. Combine onions, mushrooms and remaining parsley. Spoon some into cavities of trout. Place trout in baking dish and spoon remaining onions and mushrooms over and around fish. Overlap lemon slices on top of fish. Sprinkle with reserved parsley.

3. Cover loosely with waxed paper and cook on HIGH 4 to 5 minutes, just until fish turns opaque. Divide trout between 2 serving plates and spoon some of the mushrooms and onions over each portion.

170 FISH STEAK WITH FRESH TOMATO AND BASIL
Prep: 10 minutes   Cook: 3 to 4 minutes   Serves: 2

1 ¾-pound fish steak, such as
    swordfish, halibut, cod,
    cut 1½ inches thick
2 plum tomatoes, cut into
    wedges
    Salt and pepper

1½ teaspoons extra-virgin olive
    oil
½ lemon, thinly sliced
2 tablespoons minced fresh
    basil or parsley

1. Place fish steak in a small shallow baking dish. Arrange tomato wedges around fish. Season fish and tomatoes generously with salt and pepper and drizzle with olive oil. Top fish with lemon slices and basil.

2. Cover dish with parchment or waxed paper. Cook on HIGH 3 to 4 minutes, just until fish is barely opaque next to bone. Let stand, covered, for 2 minutes before serving.

---

171 HERBED SALMON EN PAPILLOTE
Prep: 15 minutes   Cook: 3 to 4 minutes   Serves: 2

If you don't have parchment, make this in a small covered casserole just large enough to hold the fish.

1 medium carrot, cut into thin 3-inch strips	2 teaspoons minced fresh dill or 1 teaspoon dried
1 celery stalk, cut into thin 3-inch strips	4 fresh sorrel leaves, shredded (optional)
1 small onion, thinly sliced	3 tablespoons sliced scallion
2 4- to 5-ounce salmon fillets	2 tablespoons chopped parsley
Salt and pepper	2 teaspoons melted butter

1. Tear off two 10 × 14-inch sheets of parchment. Fold in half and trim edges to form a half-moon shape. Open up paper and butter.

2. Place half the carrot, celery and onion to one side of crease on each sheet of buttered parchment. Top with salmon fillet. Season with salt and pepper to taste. Sprinkle dill, sorrel, scallion and parsley over salmon. Drizzle 1 teaspoon melted butter over each.

3. Fold over paper, fold up edges and crimp to seal. Place on plate and cook on HIGH 3 to 4 minutes, or until salmon is just opaque throughout. Do not overcook. Serve in parchment, cutting open top to show fish.

---

172 SEA SCALLOPS WITH TOMATO AND LIME
Prep: 10 minutes   Cook: 8 to 9 minutes   Serves: 4

2 shallots, minced	½ teaspoon pepper
2 garlic cloves, minced	1 large ripe tomato, peeled, seeded and chopped
3 tablespoons olive oil	¼ cup chopped cilantro or parsley
1½ pounds sea scallops	Lime slices, for garnish
2 teaspoons lime juice	
½ teaspoon salt	

1. Place shallots, garlic and oil in a shallow round or oval baking dish. Cook on HIGH 2 minutes, stirring once.

2. Stir in scallops and lime juice. Cover with waxed paper or parchment. Cook on MEDIUM 3 minutes. Stir in salt, pepper, tomato and half of chopped cilantro. Cook 3 to 4 minutes, until scallops are opaque throughout; do not overcook. Garnish with lime slices and remaining cilantro.

173 TUNA CASSEROLE WITH CASHEWS
Prep: 10 minutes   Cook: 7 to 10 minutes   Serves: 4

1 cup thinly sliced celery	½ cup frozen peas
1 cup chopped onion	1 10¾-ounce can condensed
1 tablespoon butter or	cream of mushroom
margarine	soup, undiluted
1 7-ounce can tuna, drained	½ cup coarsely chopped
and flaked	cashews

1. In a 1-quart casserole, combine celery, onion and butter. Cook, uncovered, on HIGH 4 to 5 minutes, until vegetables are softened.

2. Add tuna, frozen peas, mushroom soup and cashews. Cover and cook 3 to 5 minutes, or until piping hot. Serve over rice or chow mein noodles.

174 ORANGE FISH FILLETS WITH SAFFRON CREAM SAUCE
Prep: 5 minutes   Cook: 4 to 5 minutes   Serves: 4

Orange zest is the colored part of the rind. Remove it with a swivel-bladed vegetable peeler and then mince. You can use any firm-fleshed white fish fillet for this recipe, such as sea bass, halibut, cod, red snapper.

4 4- to 5-ounce fish fillets	Saffron Cream Sauce (recipe
Salt and pepper	follows)
4 teaspoons minced orange	Orange slices, for garnish
zest	

1. Place fish in a baking dish just large enough to hold fillets in a single layer. Season lightly with salt and pepper. Sprinkle 1 teaspoon orange zest over each fillet.

2. Cover with waxed paper. Cook on HIGH 4 to 5 minutes, just until fish turns opaque. Rotate dish if fish appears to be cooking unevenly, but do not overcook. Transfer fillets to warmed serving plates and spoon Saffron Cream Sauce on top. Garnish with orange slices.

175 SAFFRON CREAM SAUCE
Prep: 5 minutes   Cook: 10 to 11 minutes   Makes: about ¾ cup

¼ cup fish stock or bottled	Small pinch of saffron
clam juice	threads
¼ cup dry white wine	2 tablespoons butter
1 tablespoon white wine	2 tablespoons flour
vinegar	2 tablespoons heavy cream
1 teaspoon minced shallot or	Salt and pepper
white of scallion	

1. In a 4-cup glass measure, combine fish stock, wine, vinegar and shallot. Crumble saffron into stock mixture. Cook on HIGH 7 minutes, stirring twice.

2. In a 1-cup glass measure, cook butter on HIGH 30 seconds, or until melted. Whisk in flour until blended and smooth. Blend in cream. Whisk into stock mixture. Cook sauce on HIGH 2 to 3 minutes, stirring once or twice, until hot and thickened. Season with salt and pepper to taste.

---

176 TROUT FILLETS WITH THYME AND SHALLOTS IN PARCHMENT

Prep: 15 minutes   Cook: 4 to 6 minutes   Serves: 2

I am partial to parchment because not only does it eliminate pots and pans, but it seals in juices, steams perfectly and opens up in a beautiful presentation on the plate. If you do not have parchment, this recipe can be cooked in a covered shallow baking dish just large enough to hold the fish.

2 tablespoons butter	Pinch of salt and pepper
2 tablespoons minced shallot or onion	2 4-ounce trout fillets
1 teaspoon lemon juice	2 large mushrooms, sliced
½ teaspoon thyme	1 tablespoon sliced scallion

1. In a 2-cup glass measure, combine butter, shallot, lemon juice, thyme, salt and pepper. Cook on MEDIUM 2 minutes. Set herb butter aside.

2. Tear off two 10 × 14-inch sheets of parchment. Fold in half and trim edges to form half-moon shape. Open paper and set trout fillet to one side of crease. Arrange mushrooms and scallion over fish. Pour half the herb butter over each fillet. Fold over paper, fold edges and crimp to seal.

3. Set packets on plate and cook on HIGH 2½ to 3½ minutes, or until fish is just opaque throughout. Serve at once.

---

177 CREAMY CURRIED TUNA IN PATTY SHELLS

Prep: 5 minutes   Cook: 7 to 9 minutes   Serves: 6

Puff pastry patty shells are available in frozen food sections of most supermarkets. Bake according to package directions. Or serve over rice.

½ cup chopped celery	¾ cup half-and-half or light cream
½ cup chopped carrot	
⅓ cup chopped scallions	2 6½- to 7-ounce cans solid white tuna
2 tablespoons butter	
2 teaspoons curry powder	6 baked puff pastry patty shells
1½ tablespoons flour	
½ cup chicken broth	

1. In a 1-quart bowl, combine celery, carrot, scallions and butter. Cover and cook on HIGH 3 to 4 minutes, until tender. Stir in curry powder and flour, blending well. Gradually stir in broth and half-and-half. Cover and cook on HIGH 3 to 4 minutes, until slightly thickened, stirring twice.

2. Add tuna, breaking up larger pieces with a fork. Cook 1 minute, until hot. Spoon curried tuna into individual patty shells on serving plates. Spoon remainder around pastry.

178   CODFISH ORIENTALE
Prep: 5 minutes   Cook: 4 to 5 minutes   Serves: 1 to 2

1   garlic clove, crushed
1   teaspoon grated fresh ginger
1   teaspoon vegetable oil
½   pound cod or other firm-
      fleshed white fish fillet
1   tablespoon sake or dry
      sherry

1   teaspoon soy sauce
½   teaspoon honey
⅛   teaspoon pepper
1   tablespoon thinly sliced
      scallion green

1. In a 2-cup glass measure, combine garlic, ginger and oil. Cook on HIGH 45 seconds. Let cool slightly.

2. Place fish in a shallow glass dish. Stir sake, soy sauce, honey and pepper into garlic-ginger mixture. Pour this marinade over fish and refrigerate for at least 30 minutes and up to 3 hours, turning fish several times.

3. Tear off a 10 × 14-inch sheet of parchment. Fold in half and trim edges to form half-moon shape. Open up parchment and place fish to one side of crease. Sprinkle any bits of garlic and ginger from marinade over fish. Fold parchment over to cover, fold up edges and crimp to seal. Place packet in a small, shallow baking dish. Cook on HIGH 2½ to 3 minutes, just until fish turns opaque. Tear open, sprinkle scallion green over fish and serve.

NOTE: Add 2 minutes of cooking time for each 4 ounces of fish added.

Chapter 9

Presto—Pasta, Rice and Grains

We're all learning the benefits of eating more complex carbohydrates and whole grains. And if pasta isn't a national passion, I don't know what is. It certainly appears with frequent regularity at my house! Here the microwave plays a slightly different role, but it's still a handy tool to have around.

When cooking ordinary rice, there's not a lot of time saved in the microwave, but it is no small matter that there is no sticking or risk of burning and no worry about a mess boiling up all over the stove. If you make risotto, however, you save not only time, but the effort of constant stirring.

Most pasta recipes work best with the pasta prepared conventionally in a large pot of boiling water on a stovetop. While the pasta is cooking, however, you can whip up the sauce in the microwave in mere minutes. And for total convenience, I've devised several recipes that do cook the pasta right along with the sauce in the oven.

Side dishes will never be boring with this assortment of recipes. Having rice? Choose from a Simple Rice Pilaf, Turkish Rice with Walnuts and Raisins or Barley Rice Casserole. Want something different? How about Grits with Mushrooms and Parmesan Cheese or a quick Risotto Rapido. Serve pasta at least once a week at your house? You'll never get bored with all these dishes to choose from, including Pasta with Tunafish Sauce, Linguine with White Clam Sauce, One-Pot Macaroni and Beef with Corn and Chiles and Fettuccine Alfredo.

---

179 SIMPLY RICE
Prep: 2 minutes   Cook: 12 minutes   Serves: 4

To cook rice in the microwave, use a 3- to 4-quart casserole with a cover. I like converted rice best. It can wait for you or be reheated without turning sticky.

1 cup converted rice	**½ teaspoon salt**
2 cups water	

1. In a 4-quart casserole, combine rice, water and salt. Cover and cook on HIGH 12 minutes.

2. Let stand, covered, 5 minutes, until all water is absorbed, before serving.

NOTE: To reheat, add 2 tablespoons water for each cup of cooked rice. Cover and cook on HIGH 1 to 2 minutes, until hot.

180   SIMPLE RICE PILAF
Prep: 5 minutes   Cook: 15 minutes   Serves: 4

1 small onion, minced
2 tablespoons butter
¼ teaspoon thyme

1 cup converted rice
2 cups canned chicken broth
1 bay leaf

1. In a 4-quart casserole, combine onion and butter. Cook on HIGH 3 minutes. Stir in thyme, rice and chicken broth. Tuck bay leaf in center.

2. Cover with lid and cook on HIGH 12 minutes. Let stand, covered, 5 minutes, until all liquid is absorbed. Discard bay leaf and serve.

181   TURKISH RICE WITH WALNUTS AND RAISINS
Prep: 5 minutes   Cook: 17 to 19 minutes   Serves: 4 to 6

1 large onion, chopped
3 tablespoons butter
¼ cup coarsely chopped
  walnuts
1 cup long-grain white rice
¼ cup raisins

½ teaspoon salt
¼ teaspoon pepper
¼ teaspoon ground sage
⅛ teaspoon ground allspice
2 cups boiling beef stock or
  canned broth

1. In a 4-quart casserole, cook onion with butter on HIGH 4 minutes. Stir in walnuts and rice. Cook 2 minutes, stirring once.

2. Add raisins, salt, pepper, sage, allspice and stock. Stir to blend. Cover and cook on HIGH 12 minutes. Let stand, covered, 5 minutes, or until liquid is absorbed.

182   RICE WITH MUSHROOMS AND PIMIENTOS
Prep: 5 minutes   Cook: 20 to 22 minutes   Serves: 4 to 6

I like this colorful side dish cold as well as hot. If you plan to serve it chilled, substitute an equal amount of olive oil for the butter.

½ pound fresh mushrooms,
  stems chopped, caps
  thinly sliced
1 large onion, chopped
3 tablespoons butter
2 cups chicken stock or
  canned broth

½ teaspoon salt
¼ teaspoon pepper
1 cup long-grain white rice
1 4-ounce jar whole
  pimientos, drained and
  diced

1. In a 4-quart casserole, combined chopped mushroom stems, onion and butter. Cook on HIGH 3 minutes.

2. Add broth, salt, pepper and rice. Cover and cook on HIGH 10 minutes. Stir in mushroom slices. Cover and cook 2 minutes. Let stand, covered, 5 to 7 minutes, until all liquid is absorbed. Stir in pimientos. Serve hot.

183 CREAMY PASTA WITH EGGPLANT AND TOMATOES

Prep: 10 minutes   Cook: 17 minutes   Serves: 3 to 4

2 garlic cloves, minced
2 tablespoons olive oil
1 small eggplant (about ¾ pound), cut into 1-inch cubes
4 medium tomatoes, peeled, seeded and cut into 8 wedges each
½ teaspoon basil

3 tablespoons butter, softened
3 tablespoons flour
1½ cups milk
½ teaspoon salt
¼ teaspoon pepper
½ pound penne or shells
1 cup shredded mozzarella cheese

1. In a 2-quart glass measure or bowl, cook garlic and oil on HIGH 3 minutes. Stir in eggplant cubes. Cover and cook on HIGH 6 minutes. Stir in tomatoes and basil and continue to cook, covered, 2 minutes. Set aside, covered.

2. In a small bowl, blend together butter and flour to make a smooth paste. In a 2-quart glass measure or bowl, heat milk on HIGH 2 minutes. Whisk in butter paste. Season with salt and pepper. Cook on HIGH 4 minutes, whisking twice, until thickened.

3. Meanwhile, cook penne in a large pot of boiling salted water according to package directions. Drain and transfer to a large shallow serving bowl. Stir cheese into hot cream sauce until melted. Add eggplant mixture and stir to blend. Pour over pasta, toss and serve.

184 PASTA WITH TUNAFISH SAUCE

Prep: 5 minutes   Cook: 18 minutes   Serves: 4

2 tablespoons olive oil
3 flat anchovy fillets
4 garlic cloves, minced
1 28-ounce can crushed tomatoes
2 6½-ounce cans tuna packed in olive oil, preferably imported from Italy

1 pound spaghetti
3 tablespoons chopped parsley
1½ tablespoons drained capers

1. In a 2-quart glass measure or bowl, heat oil on HIGH 1 minute. Add anchovies and garlic. Cook 2 minutes, stirring once. Stir in crushed tomatoes. Cover with waxed paper and cook 10 minutes, stirring once.

2. Drain tuna, reserving oil; flake tuna. Add tuna and oil to sauce. Cover and cook on HIGH 5 minutes.

3. While sauce is being prepared, cook spaghetti in a large pot of boiling salted water according to package directions. Drain and place in a large, shallow serving bowl. Pour hot tuna sauce over spaghetti, add parsley and capers, toss and serve.

185 JALAPENO CHEESE CORN BREAD
Prep: 10 minutes   Cook: 16 to 17 minutes   Serves: 8 to 10

4 tablespoons butter
1 cup yellow cornmeal
1 cup all-purpose flour
1 tablespoon baking powder
2 tablespoons sugar
½ teaspoon salt

2 eggs
⅔ cup milk
1 to 2 tablespoons minced
seeded jalapeño peppers
¾ cup shredded Cheddar
cheese

1. Put butter in a 1-cup glass measure and cook on HIGH 1 minute, or until melted. Let cool slightly.

2. In a medium bowl, combine cornmeal, flour, baking powder, sugar and salt. Whisk gently to blend. In another bowl, beat eggs lightly. Whisk in milk and melted butter. Add liquid to dry ingredients and mix until just barely blended. Add jalapeños and ½ cup cheese; mix to blend.

3. Turn batter into a 6-cup ring mold or 8-inch round cake pan with a glass in the center. Cook on MEDIUM 14 minutes. Sprinkle remaining ¼ cup cheese over corn bread and cook 1 to 2 minutes longer, until cheese is melted, corn bread has begun to pull away from outside of pan and a toothpick inserted in the center comes out clean. Set pan on a solid, flat heatproof surface and let stand for 10 minutes before unmolding.

186 SOUTHERN-STYLE GRITS
Prep: 5 minutes   Cook: 23 minutes   Serves: 4 to 6

1 cup quick-cooking grits
¾ teaspoon salt
2 cups hot water
1 cup milk

1½ cups shredded sharp
Cheddar cheese
3 tablespoons butter

1. In a 3-quart casserole, combine grits, salt and hot water. Cook on HIGH 3 minutes, stirring once. Stir in milk. Cook on MEDIUM 5 minutes.

2. Stir in 1 cup cheese. Cover and cook on MEDIUM 12 minutes, stirring after 5 minutes. Sprinkle remaining ½ cup cheese on top and cook, uncovered, on HIGH 3 minutes, just until cheese melts. Stir in butter.

187 BARLEY RICE CASSEROLE
Prep: 10 minutes   Cook: 40 minutes   Serves: 6 to 8

½ pound fresh mushrooms,
sliced
2 celery stalks, chopped
1 medium onion, chopped
1 stick butter

1 cup long-grain white rice
1 cup barley
2 10½-ounce cans beef broth
1½ cups water
Salt and pepper

1. In a 3-quart casserole, combine mushrooms, celery, onion and butter. Cover and cook on HIGH 5 minutes, stirring once.

2. Add rice and barley. Stir until well coated. Add broth and water. Cover and cook on HIGH 25 minutes. Let stand, covered, 10 minutes, until remaining liquid is absorbed. Season with salt and pepper to taste.

188 TWO-GRAIN SALAD WITH GREEN BEANS AND PINE NUTS
Prep: 10 minutes   Cook: 16 to 19 minutes   Serves: 4

½ cup barley
1½ cups chicken stock or
   canned broth
½ cup bulgur
½ pound green beans, cut into
   ¾-inch pieces
¼ cup pine nuts

1 teaspoon butter
2 tablespoons lemon juice
½ teaspoon Dijon mustard
½ teaspoon salt
½ teaspoon pepper
¼ cup extra-virgin olive oil

1. In a 3-quart casserole, place barley and stock. Cover and cook on HIGH 6 minutes. Stir in bulgur and continue to cook, covered, 5 to 6 minutes, until liquid is absorbed. Set aside.

2. Wash green beans and leave wet. Wrap well in microwave-safe plastic wrap. Place on plate. Cook on HIGH 4 to 5 minutes, until crisp-tender.

3. Place pine nuts and butter in a 1-cup glass measure. Cook on HIGH 1 to 2 minutes, stirring every 30 seconds, until toasted.

4. In a small bowl, whisk together lemon juice, mustard, salt and pepper. Gradually whisk in oil to make dressing. Add green beans and pine nuts to grains. Toss lightly to mix. Add dressing and toss to coat. Serve slightly chilled or at room temperature.

189 EASY PASTA WITH ZUCCHINI AND MUSHROOMS
Prep: 10 minutes   Cook: 7 minutes   Serves: 2

Heating convenience products in the glass jars they come in saves lots of dish washing. Just be sure to remove metal caps before placing in the microwave, and use pot holders to remove jars, because they do get hot.

2 small zucchini, thinly sliced
6 fresh mushrooms, sliced
½ teaspoon marjoram
   Salt and pepper

1 15-ounce glass jar pasta in
   tomato sauce
¼ cup grated Parmesan cheese

1. Arrange zucchini and mushroom slices in center of 2 microwave-safe dinner plates. Sprinkle with marjoram and season lightly with salt and pepper. Cover with microwave-safe plastic wrap. Cook each plate on HIGH 2 minutes. Set aside without unwrapping.

2. Remove metal lid from jar of pasta. Cover with paper towel to absorb splatter. Cook on HIGH 3 minutes, stirring once, until hot. Remove jar carefully using pot holders. Add half the Parmesan cheese and stir. Spoon half the pasta over each plate of vegetables. Sprinkle each with 1 tablespoon Parmesan cheese and serve.

190   RISOTTO RAPIDO
Prep: 10 minutes   Cook: 22 to 24 minutes   Serves: 4

2 cups chicken or beef stock or
     canned broth
3 tablespoons olive oil
1 medium onion, finely
     chopped

1 garlic clove, minced
¾ cup Arborio rice
½ cup grated Parmesan cheese

1. In a 4-cup glass measure, cook broth on HIGH 3 minutes. Set aside.

2. In a 3-quart casserole, cook oil on HIGH 2 minutes. Stir in onion and garlic. Cook on HIGH 3 minutes.

3. Stir in rice until coated with oil. Cook on HIGH 4 minutes. Stir in hot stock. Cook, uncovered, on HIGH 10 to 12 minutes, until liquid is almost absorbed, but a saucy consistency remains. Cover and let stand until most of liquid is absorbed and rice is creamy, about 5 minutes. Stir in cheese and serve.

191   SAFFRON RISOTTO WITH MUSHROOMS
Prep: 10 minutes   Cook: 24 to 28 minutes   Serves: 4

3 tablespoons olive oil
1 small onion, finely chopped
1 garlic clove, minced
¾ cup Arborio rice
¼ teaspoon saffron threads,
     crushed

2 cups hot chicken stock or
     canned broth
½ pound fresh mushrooms,
     sliced
1 tablespoon butter
   Salt and pepper

1. In a 3-quart casserole, cook oil on HIGH 1 minute, until hot. Stir in onion and garlic and cook 2 minutes.

2. Add rice and stir until grains are coated. Cook on HIGH 4 minutes. Blend saffron with hot stock and stir into rice. Cook, uncovered, on HIGH 5 minutes; stir. Continue to cook 5 to 7 minutes, until most of liquid is absorbed but a saucy consistency remains. Cover and let stand until liquid is absorbed and rice is creamy, about 5 minutes.

3. While rice is standing, put mushrooms in a bowl with butter. Cook on HIGH 3 minutes. Stir mushrooms into rice and season with salt and pepper to taste.

192   RICE MUSHROOM PILAF
Prep: 10 minutes   Cook: 20 to 21 minutes   Serves: 4

2 cup canned beef broth
2 tablespoons butter
1 medium onion, chopped

1 cup long-grain white rice
¼ pound mushrooms, sliced

1. In a 4-cup glass measure, cook broth on HIGH 4 minutes, or until hot. Set aside.

2. In a 4-quart casserole, melt butter on HIGH 1 minute. Stir in onion and rice. Cook on HIGH 3 to 4 minutes, stirring once or twice, until rice is lightly toasted.

3. Stir in mushrooms and hot broth. Cover and cook on HIGH 12 minutes. Let stand, covered, 5 minutes, until all liquid is absorbed.

---

193 ARTICHOKE-CRAB FETTUCCINE WITH MUSHROOMS
Prep: 10 minutes   Cook: 6 to 9 minutes   Serves: 3 to 4

½ **pound fettuccine**	2 **tablespoons butter**
6 **ounces canned crabmeat**	¾ **cup heavy cream**
1 **8½-ounce can artichoke**	5 **ounces Bel Paese cheese,**
hearts in brine	**finely diced**
¼ **pound fresh mushrooms,**	**Salt and pepper**
sliced	½ **cup grated Parmesan cheese**

1. Cook pasta in a large pot of boiling salted water on top of stove according to package directions. Meanwhile, drain crabmeat. Pick over to remove any bits of cartilage; set aside. Drain artichokes and cut into quarters.

2. In a 2-quart glass measure or bowl, combine mushrooms and butter. Cook on HIGH 2 minutes. Add artichoke hearts, crabmeat and cream. Stir gently to mix. Cook on MEDIUM 3 to 5 minutes, until dish simmers for 2 to 3 minutes.

3. Stir in Bel Paese cheese. Cook on MEDIUM 1 to 2 minutes, until melted. Season with salt and pepper to taste. Drain fettuccine and transfer to a large, shallow serving bowl. Pour hot sauce over pasta and toss. Top with Parmesan cheese. Serve at once.

---

194 PASTA WITH PEAS AND RICOTTA
Prep: 10 minutes   Cook: 12 to 13 minutes   Serves: 6 to 8

1 **pound medium pasta shells**	¼ **pound shredded Fontinella**
1 **10-ounce package frozen**	**or Provolone cheese**
peas	**(1 cup)**
¾ **pound sliced bacon**	½ **teaspoon salt**
1 **pound ricotta cheese**	¼ **teaspoon pepper**

1. Cook pasta in a large pot of boiling salted water on top of stove as directed on package. Meanwhile, put frozen peas in a colander and rinse under running water until ice crystals melt. Drain well. Place bacon slices between paper towels and cook on HIGH about 30 seconds per slice, until crisp. Set aside.

2. Combine ricotta and Fontinella cheese in a 2-quart bowl. Cook on MEDIUM until cheeses melt, 5 to 6 minutes, stirring once. Crumble bacon into cheese mixture. Add peas and season with salt and pepper. Cook on HIGH 1 minute to heat through. Drain pasta and transfer to a large serving bowl. Pour cheese sauce over pasta, toss and serve.

195   CHINESE "FRIED" RICE
Prep: 10 minutes   Cook: 13 minutes   Serves: 6 to 8

Here's my favorite recipe for leftover rice. This dish tastes so good, you may want to make some just for the occasion.

3 **tablespoons vegetable oil**	1 **tablespoon water**
3 **cups cooked converted rice**	¼ **teaspoon sugar**
1½ **tablespoons soy sauce**	½ **pound mushrooms, sliced**
3 **eggs**	¼ **cup sliced scallions**

1. In a 3-quart casserole, heat oil on HIGH 1 minute. Stir in rice. Cook on HIGH 5 minutes, stirring twice. Stir in soy sauce.

2. In a small bowl, beat eggs with water and sugar. Pour into center of rice. Cover with lid and cook on MEDIUM-HIGH 5 minutes, stirring once. Stir in mushrooms and continue to cook, covered, 2 minutes. Stir in scallions and serve.

196   SAFFRON RICE
Prep: 5 minutes   Cook: 12 minutes   Serves: 4 to 6

1 **cup long-grain white rice**	⅛ **teaspoon pepper**
1 **large onion, chopped**	¼ **teaspoon saffron threads,**
2 **cups chicken stock or water**	**crumbled**
½ **teaspoon salt**	

1. In a 4-quart casserole, combine rice, onion, stock, salt, pepper and saffron. Cover and cook on HIGH 12 minutes.

2. Set aside, covered, and let stand 5 minutes, until all liquid is absorbed.

197   TOASTED RICE WITH WILD MUSHROOMS
Prep: 10 minutes   Cook: 23 to 24 minutes   Serves: 4 to 6

2 **cups canned chicken broth**	½ **pound fresh shiitake**
1 **cup long-grain white rice**	**mushrooms, stemmed,**
7 **tablespoons butter**	**caps sliced**
1 **small onion, chopped**	**Salt and pepper**
1 **garlic clove, minced**	

1. In a 2-cup glass measure, cook broth on HIGH 2 minutes, or until hot. Set aside.

2. In a 4-quart casserole, combine rice and 4 tablespoons butter. Cook on HIGH 1 minute. Stir and cook 1 minute longer. Stir in onion. Continue to cook, stirring once or twice, until rice is lightly browned, about 5 minutes. Add hot broth to rice. Cover with lid and cook on HIGH 12 minutes. Let stand, covered, 5 minutes.

3. While rice is standing, combine garlic, sliced shiitakes, and remaining 3 tablespoons butter in shallow baking dish. Cook on HIGH 2 to 3 minutes, just until mushrooms are tender. Stir into rice and season with salt and pepper to taste.

198 MACARONI AND CHEESE
Prep: 10 minutes   Cook: 25 to 29 minutes   Serves: 3 to 4

The trick to this recipe is to prepare it in advance and refrigerate it for at least 4 hours, or overnight, to allow the flavors to blend and the macaroni to soften. If you prepare the dish at the last moment, cook it 30 to 35 minutes on MEDIUM in Step 3.

3 tablespoons butter	2 cups shredded Cheddar
3 tablespoons flour	cheese (about ½ pound)
1 teaspoon dry mustard	½ pound elbow macaroni
1 teaspoon salt	½ cup fresh bread crumbs
½ teaspoon pepper	½ teaspoon paprika
2½ cups milk	

1. Place 2 tablespoons butter in a round 2-quart baking dish. Cook on HIGH 1 minute until melted. Blend in flour, mustard, salt and pepper until smooth. Slowly whisk in milk. Cook on HIGH 7 to 9 minutes, stirring several times, until mixture thickens slightly. Add 1½ cups cheese and stir until melted. Stir in macaroni. Let cool slightly. Cover and refrigerate at least 4 hours, or overnight.

2. In a 1-cup glass measure toss bread crumbs and paprika. Add remaining 1 tablespoon butter and cook on HIGH 1½ to 2 minutes, stirring once, until lightly toasted.

3. About 15 minutes before serving, place covered baking dish with macaroni and cheese in microwave. Cook on HIGH 5 minutes; stir. Change power level to MEDIUM and cook, covered, 8 to 10 minutes, until dish is hot and macaroni is tender. Uncover and sprinkle remaining ½ cup cheese over macaroni. Top with toasted bread crumbs. Cook on HIGH 2 minutes, until cheese melts.

199 CARAWAY NOODLES WITH CABBAGE
Prep: 15 minutes   Cook: 17 minutes   Serves: 6 to 8

2 medium onions, sliced	2 teaspoons caraway seeds
2 garlic cloves, minced	1 teaspoon salt
4 tablespoons butter	½ teaspoon pepper
½ cup chicken broth	1 8-ounce package wide egg
1 small head green cabbage,	noodles
shredded	1 cup sour cream

1. In a 4-quart casserole or bowl, combine onion, garlic and butter. Cook on HIGH 6 minutes. Add chicken broth. Stir in cabbage. Season with caraway seeds, salt and pepper. Toss to blend well. Cover and cook 10 minutes.

2. Meanwhile, cook noodles on top of stove in a large pot of boiling salted water until tender, about 10 minutes. Drain at once. Add noodles to hot cabbage. Toss to mix. Stir in sour cream. Cook on MEDIUM 30 to 60 seconds, or until just heated through. Serve hot.

200 MANICOTTI WITH COTTAGE CHEESE AND MOZZARELLA

Prep: 20 minutes   Cook: 16 to 19 minutes   Serves: 4 to 6

1 5-ounce package manicotti shells (12 pieces)
1 8-ounce package cream cheese, at room temperature
1 cup cottage cheese
¼ pound mozzarella cheese, finely diced (1 cup)
2 eggs

2 tablespoons chopped parsley
½ teaspoon salt
⅛ teaspoon pepper
⅛ teaspoon nutmeg
2½ cups spaghetti sauce, preferably homemade
½ cup grated Parmesan cheese

1. In a large pot of boiling salted water, cook manicotti on top of stove according to package directions until barely tender; drain.

2. Meanwhile, in a medium bowl, blend cream cheese until smooth. Mix in cottage cheese. Stir in mozzarella, eggs, parsley, salt, pepper and nutmeg. Using a blunt knife to help, fill each manicotti shell with about ¼ cup cheese filling.

3. Cover bottom of a 10-inch square baking dish with half the spaghetti sauce. Arrange filled manicotti in dish. Pour remaining sauce over top. Cover with parchment or waxed paper. Cook on MEDIUM-HIGH 15 to 17 minutes, until hot and bubbly. Sprinkle Parmesan cheese on top and cook 1 to 2 minutes longer, until melted.

201 NOODLE PUDDING CASSEROLE

Prep: 5 minutes   Cook: 15 to 16 minutes   Serves: 4 to 6

Serve this as a meatless main dish or as a protein-rich side dish with roast chicken or meat.

5 tablespoons butter
3 eggs
12 ounces cottage cheese
2½ cups milk
1 cup sour cream
½ teaspoon salt

⅛ teaspoon white pepper
1 8-ounce package egg noodles, about ½ inch wide
½ cup fresh bread crumbs
¼ teaspoon paprika

1. In a 1-cup glass measure, heat 4 tablespoons butter on HIGH 1 minute, or until melted.

2. In a 2½-quart soufflé dish or casserole, beat eggs lightly. Blend in cottage cheese, milk, sour cream, melted butter, salt and white pepper. Stir in noodles. Cover with a plate and cook on HIGH 10 minutes. Stir noodles so they are completely covered by sauce. Continue to cook, covered, 3 minutes, or until liquid is absorbed. Set aside without removing cover.

3. In same 1-cup measure, place bread crumbs with remaining 1 tablespoon butter. Cook on HIGH 1 to 2 minutes, stirring once or twice, until bread is lightly browned. Sprinkle bread crumbs over noodles and top with a light dusting of paprika. Serve hot, with additional sour cream on the side.

202   GARLIC BREAD WITH PARMESAN CHEESE

Prep: 5 minutes   Cook: 1 minute   Serves: 6 to 8

1 stick butter or margarine,
     softened
3 garlic cloves, crushed
     through a press, or 1
     teaspoon garlic powder

1 1-pound loaf of French or
     Italian bread
½ cup grated Parmesan cheese
     Paprika

1. In a small bowl, combine butter and garlic; blend well. Cut loaf of bread into 2-inch-thick slices without cutting all the way through. Spread both sides of slices with garlic butter. Sprinkle with cheese and paprika.

2. Place loaf on double layer of paper towels; set on a microwave rack if you have one. Cook on MEDIUM 1 minute, or until heated through.

203   THELMA'S GARLIC BREAD

Prep: 5 minutes   Cook: 1 to 2 minutes   Serves: 6 to 8

½ cup mayonnaise
¼ cup grated Parmesan cheese
3 garlic cloves, crushed
     through a press, or 1
     teaspoon garlic powder

1 1-pound long loaf of French
     or sourdough bread
     Paprika

1. In a small bowl, combine mayonnaise, cheese and garlic. Blend well. Slice the loaf of bread in half lengthwise. Spread the garlic mixture generously over both halves of the bread. Sprinkle lightly with paprika.

2. Place each half of the loaf on paper towels, on a microwave rack if you have one. Heat on MEDIUM 1 to 2 minutes, just until heated through. Cut bread into thick slices and serve hot.

204   WILD RICE WITH CHESTNUTS

Prep: 5 minutes   Cook: 22 minutes   Serves: 4 to 6

This is a great side dish for Cornish game hens, chicken or veal. It also makes an excellent stuffing (see Chicken Thighs Stuffed with Wild Rice and Chestnuts, page 70).

2 tablespoons minced shallots
     or onion
2 tablespoons butter
1 8-ounce can chestnuts,
     coarsely chopped

⅔ cup wild rice
1½ cups chicken stock or
     canned broth
     Salt and pepper

1. In a 3-quart casserole, combine shallots and butter. Cover with lid and cook on HIGH 2 minutes. Stir in chestnuts. Cover and cook 3 minutes.

2. Stir in rice and chicken stock. Cover and cook on HIGH 17 minutes. Let stand, covered, 10 minutes, until liquid is completely absorbed. Season with salt and pepper to taste.

205   ITALIAN SEASONED BREAD CRUMBS WITH PARMESAN CHEESE

Prep: 5 minutes   Cook: 2 to 4 minutes   Makes: ½ cup

Here's an instant topping for casseroles, vegetables and fish. I make crumbs anytime I have old bread and freeze them in an airtight container.

1 slice of firm-textured white
   or egg bread
1 tablespoon butter
2 tablespoons grated
   Parmesan cheese

¼ teaspoon oregano
¼ teaspoon basil
¼ teaspoon garlic salt
¼ teaspoon pepper

1. Tear bread into pieces and drop into blender or food processor. Process to crumbs.

2. Place crumbs in a 2-cup glass measure. Put butter on top. Cook on HIGH 2 to 4 minutes, stirring once, until lightly browned. Immediately add all remaining ingredients and toss to mix.

206   DOGGIE DOUGHNUTS

Prep: 10 minutes   Cook: 10 minutes   Makes: about 20

It's fun cooking for your dog. And you have the assurance of knowing just what's going into his healthy treats. Isn't it funny that dogs like garlic too?

2 cups whole wheat flour
1 egg, lightly beaten
⅔ cup beef or chicken broth

3 tablespoons oatmeal
1 teaspoon garlic powder

1. Place flour in a bowl. Add egg and broth and mix well. Blend in oatmeal and garlic powder. Roll dough into a ball. Roll out on a lightly floured surface to a round about ½ inch thick. Cut with small doughnut cutters into rings. Gather up scraps, roll out again and cut out more rings. Shape last bits by hand. (There should be no waste.)

2. Arrange rings on a shallow baking dish or on a sheet of parchment paper in a single layer. Cook on HIGH 10 minutes, or until firm. Let cool until hardened. Store in covered container when dog is not looking.

207   GRITS WITH MUSHROOMS AND PARMESAN CHEESE

Prep: 5 minutes   Cook: 17 minutes   Serves: 4

1 large onion, chopped
3 tablespoons butter
½ pound mushrooms, sliced
1¼ cups chicken stock or
   canned broth

1¼ cups milk
½ cup quick-cooking grits
   Salt, pepper and hot pepper
   sauce
¼ cup grated Parmesan cheese

1. In a 4-cup glass measure, cook onion and butter on HIGH 4 minutes, stirring once. Stir in mushrooms and cook 2 minutes. Stir and set aside.

2. In a 4-quart casserole, combine stock and milk. Cover with lid and cook on HIGH 5 minutes, or until boiling. Stir in grits. Cover and cook 3 minutes; stir. Continue to cook 3 minutes longer. At this point, grits should have absorbed most of liquid. (Like rice, grits will continue to absorb moisture upon standing.)

3. Season grits with salt, pepper and hot sauce to taste. Stir in onion-mushroom mixture and Parmesan cheese. Serve at once.

---

208   SPAGHETTI WITH RED CLAM SAUCE
Prep: 5 minutes   Cook: 18 to 20 minutes   Serves: 4 to 6

2 large onions, chopped	½ teaspoon salt
3 tablespoons olive oil	⅛ teaspoon black pepper
2 garlic cloves, minced	⅛ to ¼ teaspoon crushed hot
1 28-ounce can peeled plum	red pepper, to taste
tomatoes, coarsely	1 10-ounce can whole clams,
chopped, liquid reserved	drained
½ cup dry white wine	1 pound spaghetti
½ teaspoon oregano	

1. In a 2-quart casserole, cook onions in oil on HIGH for 5 minutes. Stir in garlic and cook 1 minute. Stir in tomatoes with liquid, wine, oregano, salt, black pepper and hot pepper. Cover and cook 7 minutes.

2. Cook spaghetti in large pot of boiling salted water on top of stove according to package directions. Meanwhile, stir clams into sauce, cover and cook on MEDIUM-HIGH 5 to 7 minutes, until heated through. Serve over drained hot spaghetti.

---

209   LINGUINE WITH WHITE CLAM SAUCE
Prep: 10 minutes   Cook: 10 to 12 minutes   Serves: 4 to 6

1 medium onion, finely	¼ teaspoon white pepper
chopped	Pinch of cayenne pepper
3 garlic cloves, minced	1 10-ounce can whole baby
2 tablespoons butter	clams, liquid reserved
3 tablespoons flour	1 6½-ounce can minced clams,
½ cup milk	liquid reserved
½ cup bottled clam juice	1 pound linguine
¼ cup dry white wine	¼ cup minced parsley
½ teaspoon thyme leaves	

1. In a 2-quart glass measure or bowl, combine onion, garlic and butter. Cook on HIGH 3 minutes. Stir in flour until well blended. Stir in milk, clam juice, wine, thyme, white pepper, cayenne and whole and minced clams with liquid. Cover with waxed paper. Cook on HIGH 7 to 9 minutes, stirring every 3 minutes, until sauce thickens slightly.

2. Meanwhile, cook linguine in a large pot of boiling salted water on top of stove according to package directions. Drain and transfer to a large, shallow serving bowl. Pour sauce over pasta, add parsley and toss.

210   SPAGHETTI CASSEROLE
Prep: 15 minutes   Cook: 25 minutes   Serves: 4

1 pound lean ground beef	1½ cups tomato juice
1 large onion, chopped	1 teaspoon sugar
1 celery rib, chopped	1 teaspoon Italian seasoning
8 ounces thin spaghetti, broken into pieces	½ teaspoon salt
1 28-ounce can peeled plum tomatoes, coarsely chopped, liquid reserved	½ cup grated Parmesan cheese

1. In a 3-quart casserole, place meat, onion and celery. Cook on HIGH 5 minutes, stirring once to break up any lumps. Pour off fat.

2. Stir in spaghetti, tomatoes with liquid, tomato juice, sugar, Italian seasoning and salt. Cover with lid and cook on HIGH 5 minutes.

3. Stir in ¼ cup Parmesan cheese. Cover and cook on HIGH 15 minutes, or until pasta is tender but still firm. Let stand, covered, for 10 minutes. Sprinkle remaining cheese over top and serve.

211   FETTUCCINE ALFREDO
Prep: 5 minutes   Cook: 5 to 6 minutes   Serves: 4

¾ pound fettuccine	⅛ teaspoon white pepper
4 tablespoons butter	Dash of cayenne pepper
3 tablespoons flour	1½ cups grated Parmesan cheese
2 cups milk	
¼ teaspoon salt	

1. Cook fettuccine in a large pot of boiling salted water on top of stove according to package directions. Meanwhile, in a 2-quart glass measure or bowl, cook butter on HIGH 1 minute, or until melted. Stir in flour and blend well. Stir in milk, salt, white pepper and cayenne. Cook on HIGH 4 to 5 minutes, or until thickened, stirring twice.

2. Drain pasta. Stir 1 cup Parmesan cheese into hot sauce until melted. Pour over pasta, toss and serve, with the remaining cheese on the side.

212   BUTTERMILK CORN BREAD
Prep: 10 minutes   Cook: 15 to 16 minutes   Serves: 8 to 10

For best results in texture, use a ring mold. Or set an empty glass in the center of a round cake pan.

4 tablespoons butter	½ teaspoon salt
1 cup yellow cornmeal	⅔ cup buttermilk
1 cup flour	2 eggs, lightly beaten
3 teaspoons baking powder	1 7-ounce can corn kernels, drained
3 tablespoons sugar	

1. Put butter in a 1-cup glass measure and cook on HIGH 1 minute, or until melted. Let cool slightly.

2. In a medium bowl, combine cornmeal, flour, baking powder, sugar and salt. Whisk gently to blend. In a small bowl, whisk together buttermilk and eggs. Add liquid to dry ingredients. Add melted butter. Mix just until barely blended. Add corn and stir to mix.

3. Turn batter into a 6-cup ring mold or an 8-inch round cake pan with a glass in the center. Cook on MEDIUM 14 to 15 minutes, or until corn bread begins to pull away from outside of pan and a toothpick inserted in the center comes out clean. Set pan on a solid, flat heatproof surface and let stand for 10 minutes before unmolding.

213 ONE-POT MACARONI AND BEEF WITH CORN AND CHILES

Prep: 10 minutes   Cook: 42 to 47 minutes   Serves: 4 to 6

1 pound lean ground beef
1 cup finely chopped onion
1 cup uncooked elbow
   macaroni
1 14-ounce can peeled plum
   tomatoes, coarsely
   chopped, liquid reserved
1 cup spaghetti sauce

1 7-ounce can corn kernels,
   liquid reserved
1 4-ounce can diced green
   chiles
1 teaspoon salt
½ teaspoon chili powder
¼ teaspoon pepper

1. In a 2-quart casserole, crumble beef. Add onion. Cook on HIGH 5 minutes, stirring once. Drain off any excess fat.

2. Stir in macaroni, tomatoes with liquid, spaghetti sauce, corn with liquid, chiles, salt, chili powder and pepper. Cover and cook on HIGH 7 minutes. Stir. Cook on MEDIUM 30 to 35 minutes, or until macaroni is tender. Let stand, covered, 10 minutes before serving.

214 BEEF AND MACARONI CASSEROLE ITALIAN-STYLE

Prep: 10 minutes   Cook: 23 to 24 minutes   Serves: 6

1 pound lean ground beef
1 onion, chopped
1 green bell pepper, chopped
1 garlic clove, minced
1 32-ounce jar thick spaghetti
   sauce

1½ cups uncooked elbow
   macaroni
1 teaspoon oregano
1½ cups shredded mozzarella
   cheese

1. Crumble beef into a 3-quart casserole. Cook on HIGH 3 minutes. Stir to break up any lumps. Stir in onion, green pepper and garlic. Cook 3 minutes longer.

2. Stir in spaghetti sauce, macaroni and oregano. Reserve 2 tablespoons cheese; stir in remainder. Cover and cook on MEDIUM 15 minutes. Stir and sprinkle reserved cheese over top. Cook 2 to 3 minutes, until melted. Let stand, covered, for 5 minutes before serving.

215 SWEET NOODLE PUDDING WITH APPLE
Prep: 10 minutes   Cook: 12 to 14 minutes   Serves: 4 to 6

4 tablespoons butter	1 large tart green apple,
3 eggs	peeled, cored and
12 ounces cottage cheese	coarsely chopped
2½ cups milk	½ cup golden raisins
1 cup sour cream	1 teaspoon cinnamon
1 8-ounce package egg	1 teaspoon vanilla extract
noodles, about ½ inch	½ cup graham cracker crumbs
wide	

1. In a 1-cup glass measure, heat butter on HIGH 1 minute, or until melted.

2. In a 2½-quart soufflé dish or casserole, beat eggs lightly. Blend in cottage cheese, milk, sour cream and melted butter. Add noodles, apple, raisins, cinnamon and vanilla. Stir to mix. Cover with a plate and cook on HIGH 10 minutes. Stir noodles until they are completely covered with sauce. Sprinkle graham cracker crumbs over top. Continue to cook, covered, 3 minutes longer, or until liquid is absorbed.

3. Serve hot, with additional sour cream on the side.

Chapter 10

A Way with Vegetables

If you bought a microwave oven and then used it for nothing more than cooking vegetables, I am sure you would feel you'd made an excellent investment. This is where the technology really shows off. Vegetables turn out crisp and brightly colored. Flavors are intense, and valuable vitamins are preserved. Nothing is rinsed away in water. When it comes to cooking vegetables, the microwave really is a star.

Since most of us are eating more vegetables these days, I've tried to include a tasty variety of recipes that offers a range of choices. There are dishes that stand on their own, like Vegetable Pie with Parmesan Cornmeal Crust, Wilted Chef's Salad with Caesar Dressing and Eggplant Parmesan. There are easy side dishes, such as Sesame Spinach, Ratatouille with Mushrooms and Orange Carrots with Fresh Mint. Choose from less common vegetables, such as Artichokes Italian-Style and Braised Belgian Endive, or give new life to dependable standbys, with recipes like Maple Butter Squash, Broccoli with Dill Sauce and holiday Sweet Potatoes with Pineapple Rings. I've even included an easy microwave technique for making your own baby food—quickly and safely—so you know exactly what's in it.

216 BROCCOLI WITH DILL SAUCE
Prep: 5 minutes   Cook: 6 to 8 minutes   Serves: 4

1 bunch broccoli, trimmed	¼ teaspoon salt
2 tablespoons half-and-half or	Dash of pepper
light cream	1 tablespoon butter
½ teaspoon dried dill	

1. Peel broccoli stems by grasping skin at bottom with edge of paring knife and pulling; it should come right off to the top in strips. Slice thick stalks in half lengthwise. Wrap broccoli in double thickness of paper towels. Moisten packet under faucet; allow excess water to run off. Set on a plate. Cook on HIGH 5 to 7 minutes, until just tender. Let stand wrapped in hot towel while you make sauce.

2. In a 1-cup glass measure, combine half-and-half with dill, salt, pepper and butter. Cook on HIGH 1 minute, or until sauce comes to a boil. Unwrap broccoli and place in a serving dish. Pour hot sauce over top and serve.

217 VEGETABLE PIE WITH PARMESAN CORNMEAL CRUST

Prep: 20 minutes   Cook: 22 to 25 minutes   Serves: 6

Serve for lunch or a first course as you would a quiche.

2 tablespoons olive oil	¼ teaspoon salt
1 small eggplant, cut into 1-inch cubes	⅛ teaspoon pepper
½ cup sliced scallions	1 cup evaporated milk
1 small green bell pepper	2 eggs
10 fresh mushrooms, sliced	Parmesan Cornmeal Crust (recipe follows)
½ cup corn kernels—fresh, frozen or canned	2 small tomatoes, sliced ¼ inch thick

1. In a 4-cup glass measure, heat oil on HIGH 1 minute. Stir in eggplant and scallions. Cover and cook 2 minutes; stir. Continue to cook 3 to 5 minutes longer, until eggplant is soft and tender.

2. Cut three ¼-inch-thick slices off bell pepper; set pepper rings aside. Chop remaining pepper and stir into eggplant. Stir in mushrooms. Cover and cook on HIGH 2 minutes. Stir in corn, salt and pepper; set aside.

3. In a 2-cup glass measure, cook milk on HIGH 1 minute, or until hot. Lightly beat eggs in medium bowl. Gradually whisk in ½ cup hot milk. Whisk in remaining milk.

4. Spread vegetables in cooked Parmesan Cornmeal Crust. Pour egg mixture over vegetables. Arrange pepper rings and tomato slices decoratively on top. Cook on MEDIUM 10 minutes, turning if pie appears to be cooking unevenly. Change power level to MEDIUM-HIGH and cook 3 to 4 minutes, just until center is barely set. Place pie plate on flat heat-resistant surface for 10 minutes to allow filling to set up before cutting.

218 PARMESAN CORNMEAL CRUST

Prep: 10 minutes   Cook: 6 to 7 minutes   Makes: 1 9-inch single pie shell

1 cup flour	½ teaspoon salt
2 tablespoons yellow cornmeal	Dash of cayenne pepper
2 tablespoons grated Parmesan cheese	⅓ cup vegetable shortening
	3 to 4 tablespoons ice water
	1 egg, beaten

1. In a food processor, combine flour, cornmeal, cheese, salt and cayenne. Pulse to mix. Add shortening in pieces and pulse until mixture resembles coarse meal. Add water and pulse just until dough begins to mass together; do not overprocess. Turn out dough and gather into a ball. Wrap and refrigerate for about 20 minutes.

2. Flatten dough into a disk; smooth out any cracks around the edge. On a lightly floured surface, roll out dough into a ⅛-inch-thick round. Place in a 9-inch pie plate or quiche dish, pressing against sides and bottom without stretching dough. Fold down sides and press to fit contour of dish. Pierce bottom and sides all over with fork.

3. Brush entire surface of dough with egg. Bake on HIGH 6 to 7 minutes, until crust appears slightly crisp. Turn dish if crust seems to be cooking unevenly.

---

219 VEGETABLE MEDLEY SALAD WITH BLUE CHEESE AND DILL
Prep: 20 minutes   Cook: 7 to 9 minutes   Serves: 4 to 6

1 head cauliflower	⅓ cup olive oil
1 bunch broccoli	2 tablespoons red wine
1 green or red bell pepper, cut	vinegar
into thin strips	2 tablespoons minced fresh
1 large zucchini, cut into thin	dill or 1 teaspoon dried
strips	½ teaspoon salt
1 small red onion, sliced	¼ teaspoon pepper
2 ounces crumbled blue	
cheese	

1. Divide cauliflower into 1-inch florets. Cut tops of broccoli into 1-inch florets. Peel stalks and thinly slice. Wrap cauliflower and broccoli in separate bundles in several paper towels. Moisten towels under faucet until wet; allow excess moisture to run off. Place on plate. Cook together on HIGH 7 to 9 minutes, until vegetables are just tender. Set aside to cool.

2. In a large bowl, combine cauliflower and broccoli with bell pepper, zucchini, red onion and blue cheese. Toss to mix.

3. In a small bowl, whisk together oil, vinegar, dill, salt and pepper. Pour over salad and toss. Cover and refrigerate for at least 2 hours, tossing occasionally, before serving.

---

220 CORN CUSTARD WITH BELL PEPPER
Prep: 5 minutes   Cook: 12 to 14 minutes   Serves: 6

1 red or green bell pepper,	2 eggs, lightly beaten
chopped	1 17-ounce can cream-style
2 tablespoons butter	corn
2 tablespoons flour	¾ cup shredded Cheddar
½ teaspoon baking powder	cheese
¼ cup milk or cream	

1. In a 4-cup glass measure, combine bell pepper and butter. Cook on HIGH 2 minutes. Sprinkle in flour and baking powder; stir until blended. Stir in milk, eggs, corn and cheese.

2. Pour custard into an 8-inch round baking dish. Elevate dish on rack if you have one. Cover with waxed paper. Cook on MEDIUM 10 to 12 minutes, until center is almost set. Turn dish if custard appears to be cooking unevenly. Transfer to a flat heatproof surface and let stand about 5 minutes before serving, to allow custard to finish setting up.

221   SPINACH TIMBALES WITH FRESH TOMATO SAUCE

Prep: 15 minutes   Cook: 10 to 12 minutes   Serves: 4

Here's an attractive dish for a dinner party. It goes well with roast beef or leg of lamb. If you do not have microwave-safe ramekins, use small glass custard cups.

1 10-ounce package frozen chopped spinach	1 whole egg
½ cup shredded Monterey jack cheese	1 egg yolk
	¼ cup heavy cream
¼ cup minced shallots or onion	½ teaspoon salt
	¼ teaspoon pepper
1 garlic clove, minced	Fresh Tomato Sauce (recipe
1 tablespoon lemon juice	follows)

1. Place package of spinach on a plate. Cook on HIGH 3 minutes. Let stand a few minutes. Remove spinach from package; squeeze dry.

2. In a medium bowl, blend together spinach, cheese, shallots, garlic and lemon juice. In a small bowl, whisk together whole egg, egg yolk, cream, salt and pepper. Add to spinach and blend well.

3. Spoon spinach mixture into 4 buttered 6-ounce ramekins or custard cups. Arrange ramekins in a circle on a round plate. Cook on MEDIUM 7 to 9 minutes, or until mixture begins to pull away slightly from sides. Unmold and spoon tomato sauce around timbales. Serve hot or cold.

222   FRESH TOMATO SAUCE

Prep: 10 minutes   Cook: 3 minutes   Makes: about 1 cup

2 medium tomatoes, peeled, seeded and chopped	¼ teaspoon salt
	⅛ teaspoon pepper
1 large garlic clove, minced	3 tablespoons heavy cream
Pinch each basil and sugar	2 tablespoons dry white wine

1. In a 4-cup glass measure, combine tomatoes, garlic, basil, sugar, salt and pepper. Cover with waxed paper. Cook on HIGH 3 minutes. Let cool slightly.

2. In a blender or food processor, puree tomato mixture until smooth. Blend in cream and wine.

223 CAULIFLOWER MARINATED IN WINE AND OLIVE OIL

Prep: 5 minutes   Cook: 7 to 10 minutes   Serves: 6

1 **large head cauliflower,**
  separated into florets
2 **garlic cloves, minced**
⅓ **cup olive oil**
2 **tablespoons dry white wine**
  or white wine vinegar

1 **tablespoon lemon juice**
¼ **teaspoon salt**
⅛ **teaspoon white pepper**
½ **teaspoon Italian seasoning**

1. Place cauliflower florets in a shallow baking dish or on a plate. Moisten a double sheet of paper towel under faucet and place over cauliflower, tucking ends underneath. Cook on HIGH 4 to 7 minutes, or until tender but still firm. Let cool in towel. Unwrap cauliflower, drain and transfer to bowl.

2. In a 1-cup glass measure, cook garlic with olive oil on HIGH 1½ to 2 minutes, until golden. Stir in wine, lemon juice, salt, pepper and Italian seasoning. Pour dressing over warm cauliflower. Toss lightly to coat. Marinate at room temperature for at least 1 hour, tossing occasionally, before serving.

224 BRAISED BELGIAN ENDIVE

Prep: 5 minutes   Cook: 5 to 6 minutes   Serves: 4

4 **heads Belgian endive, ends**
  trimmed
¼ **cup canned chicken broth**

4 **teaspoons butter**
⅛ **teaspoon nutmeg**
Salt and pepper

1. In a small shallow baking dish, place endive, broth and butter. Sprinkle with nutmeg. Cover with microwave-safe plastic wrap.

2. Cook on HIGH 4 minutes. Remove wrap and turn endive over. Cook, uncovered, 1 to 2 minutes, until fork tender. Season with salt and pepper to taste.

225 PERFECT ASPARAGUS

Prep: 15 minutes   Cook: 5 to 6 minutes   Serves: 4

1 **pound fresh asparagus**
3 **tablespoons melted butter**

1 **tablespoon lemon juice**
Salt and pepper

1. Snap off tough bottoms of stalks. With a swivel-bladed vegetable peeler, peel bottom ⅔ of stalks. Wash well and do not drain. Divide in half and place in oval baking dish with tips facing inside of dish. Cover dish with microwave-safe plastic wrap.

2. Cook on HIGH 5 to 6 minutes. Let stand, covered, 2 minutes. Drain asparagus and transfer to a serving dish. Combine melted butter with lemon juice. Drizzle over hot asparagus and season with salt and pepper to taste.

226   SWEET POTATOES WITH PINEAPPLE RINGS
Prep: 10 minutes   Cook: 7 to 10 minutes   Serves: 8

1   teaspoon cornstarch
½   cup orange juice
2   cups cooked, mashed sweet potatoes
⅔   cup (packed) brown sugar
4   tablespoons butter, melted
1¼   teaspoons pumpkin pie spice

1   teaspoon grated orange zest
¼   cup chopped pecans
⅓   cup raisins
1   20-ounce can pineapple rings
¾   cup miniature marshmallows

1. In a medium bowl, dissolve cornstarch in orange juice. Stir in sweet potatoes, brown sugar, butter, 1 teaspoon pumpkin pie spice, orange zest, pecans and raisins. Mix well.

2. In a 12-inch shallow round baking dish, arrange pineapple rings in a single layer. Top each pineapple ring with ⅓ cup sweet potato mixture. Cook on HIGH 5 to 7 minutes, or until potatoes are hot. Scatter marshmallows over sweet potatoes and sprinkle on remaining ¼ teaspoon pumpkin pie spice. Cook on HIGH 2 to 3 minutes, until marshmallows puff and begin to melt. Serve hot.

227   WRAPPED GREEN BEANS
Prep: 10 minutes   Cook: 5 to 7 minutes   Serves: 4

Green beans cook best when clustered together.

1   pound green beans

1. Wash beans; remove stem ends and strings. Do not dry. Divide wet beans in half and wrap each bunch in microwave-safe plastic wrap. Place on plate.

2. Cook on HIGH 5 to 7 minutes, depending on your preference for crispness. Let sit for 2 minutes before unwrapping. Package will be extremely hot.

228   CLASSIC GREEN BEANS
Prep: 10 minutes   Cook: 5 to 7 minutes   Serves: 4

1   pound green beans
1   tablespoon butter
1   teaspoon lemon juice

¼   teaspoon salt
⅛   teaspoon pepper

1. Place beans in the smallest possible casserole that is just large enough to hold them. Add ¼ cup water, cover with lid and cook on HIGH 5 to 7 minutes, depending on your preference for crispness.

2. Drain beans and dump into a heated serving bowl. Toss with butter, lemon juice, salt and pepper.

229   BROCCOLI ITALIAN-STYLE
Prep: 5 minutes   Cook: 5 to 7 minutes   Serves: 4

1 bunch broccoli, trimmed
3 tablespoons extra-virgin
   olive oil
1 tablespoon fresh lemon
   juice

½ teaspoon salt
½ teaspoon pepper

1. Peel broccoli stalks in strips by grasping skin at bottom between thumb and paring knife and pulling up. Slice any thick stalks in half lengthwise. Wrap broccoli in double thickness of paper towels. Moisten towels under faucet until wet; allow excess water to run off. Set packet on plate.

2. Cook on HIGH 5 to 7 minutes, until just tender. Let stand, wrapped in towel, 3 to 4 minutes. Unwrap broccoli and transfer to a serving dish. In a small bowl, whisk together olive oil, lemon juice, salt and pepper. Drizzle over broccoli. Serve hot or at room temperature.

230   CHAMPAGNE CARROTS
Prep: 10 minutes   Cook: 5 minutes   Serves: 4

½ pound carrots, peeled and
   sliced on the diagonal
   about ¼ inch thick
¼ cup champagne or dry white
   wine

2 teaspoons butter
1 teaspoon minced fresh dill
   or ½ teaspoon dried
Salt and pepper
1 tablespoon chopped parsley

1. Put carrots in a small casserole just large enough to hold them. Add champagne, butter and dill. Cover with lid and cook on HIGH 5 minutes.

2. Season with salt and pepper to taste. Garnish with chopped parsley.

231   ORANGE CARROTS WITH FRESH MINT
Prep: 10 minutes   Cook: 6 to 9 minutes   Serves: 4

2 cups diagonally sliced
   carrots
3 tablespoons water
¼ cup orange juice, preferably
   fresh
2 tablespoons grated orange
   zest

1 teaspoon cornstarch
½ teaspoon sugar
⅛ teaspoon salt
1 tablespoon chopped fresh
   mint

1. Put carrots in a small casserole just large enough to hold them. Add water. Cover with lid and cook on HIGH 5 to 7 minutes, stirring once, until just tender. Drain and return to casserole.

2. In a 2-cup glass measure, combine orange juice, orange zest, cornstarch, sugar and salt. Stir to dissolve cornstarch and sugar. Add to carrots. Cook, uncovered, on HIGH 1 to 2 minutes, until thickened. Transfer to a serving dish and sprinkle mint on top.

232   SPINACH MUSHROOM SALAD
Prep: 10 minutes   Cook: 3 to 5 minutes   Serves: 4

Crisping the bacon in the microwave is fast and neat. Cooking whole slices between paper towels absorbs all the fat. Here the bacon is diced and cooked in a glass measure to collect the drippings for the dressing.

6 slices lean bacon, diced
¼ cup fresh lemon juice
2 tablespoons water
½ teaspoon dry mustard
¼ teaspoon pepper
4 scallions, thinly sliced

1 pound fresh spinach, stemmed, rinsed and dried
½ pound fresh mushrooms, sliced
1 hard-cooked egg, grated

1. Place bacon in a 4-cup glass measure. Cover with paper towel. Cook on HIGH 2 to 3 minutes, stirring once, until bacon is crisp. Remove bacon with slotted spoon and drain on paper towel. Add lemon juice, water, mustard and pepper to bacon drippings. Blend dressing well.

2. In a large salad bowl, combine scallions, spinach and mushrooms. Stir dressing and cook on HIGH 1 to 2 minutes, until boiling. Pour over salad and toss lightly. Sprinkle bacon and grated egg on top and serve at once.

233   SESAME SPINACH
Prep: 10 minutes   Cook: 3 to 5 minutes   Serves: 4 to 6

2 teaspoons sesame seeds
1 tablespoon vegetable oil
1 large bunch fresh spinach
   (10 to 12 ounces)
2 tablespoons soy sauce
2 scallions, chopped

1½ teaspoons Asian sesame oil
1 tablespoon rice wine vinegar
1 teaspoon sugar
⅛ teaspoon ground ginger

1. Place sesame seeds in a 1-cup glass measure. Stir in 1 teaspoon vegetable oil. Cook on HIGH 1 to 2 minutes, stirring once, until lightly toasted.

2. Remove tough stems from spinach; rinse leaves well. Place spinach with water clinging to leaves in 2-quart bowl. Cover and cook on HIGH 2 to 3 minutes, just until steaming but still bright green. Drain off liquid.

3. In a small bowl, combine soy sauce, scallions, sesame oil, vinegar, sugar, ginger, toasted sesame seeds and remaining 2 teaspoons vegetable oil. Mix well. Pour over spinach and toss. Serve hot or cold.

234   SWEET-AND-SOUR RED CABBAGE
Prep: 15 minutes   Cook: 10 to 15 minutes   Serves: 6

1 1½-pound red cabbage
1 tart apple
1 tablespoon butter
3 tablespoons sugar

⅓ cup red wine vinegar or cider vinegar
¾ teaspoon salt

1. Shred cabbage on grater or in food processor. Put into a 3-quart casserole.

Peel, core and dice apple. Add to cabbage. Add butter. Stir in sugar, vinegar and salt.

2. Cover casserole with lid and cook on HIGH 10 to 15 minutes, stirring once, until tender but not mushy.

---

235 SWEET-AND-SOUR CABBAGE WITH CHESTNUTS AND BACON
Prep: 15 minutes   Cook: 18 to 21 minutes   Serves: 4 to 6

6 slices of bacon, diced
1 medium onion, thinly sliced
2 tablespoons vegetable oil
1 1½-pound red cabbage, shredded
1 tart apple, peeled, cored and diced

⅓ cup red wine vinegar
3 tablespoons brown sugar
¼ teaspoon salt
½ teaspoon pepper
1 8-ounce can chestnuts

1. Place bacon in a 3-quart casserole. Cover with paper towel. Cook on HIGH 2 to 3 minutes, stirring once, until crisp. Remove bacon with slotted spoon and set aside. Pour off all but 2 tablespoons bacon drippings.

2. Add onion to bacon drippings; stir to coat. Cook on HIGH 3 minutes. Add oil, cabbage, apple, vinegar, brown sugar, salt and pepper. Toss to mix. Cover with lid and cook on HIGH 10 minutes, stirring twice.

3. Add bacon and chestnuts and toss. Cover and cook on HIGH 3 to 5 minutes, until chestnuts are hot and cabbage is tender.

---

236 ITALIAN VEGETABLES IN CREAM SAUCE WITH CHEESE
Prep: 5 minutes   Cook: 9 to 11 minutes   Serves: 4

1 16-ounce package frozen mixed Italian vegetables
3 tablespoons butter
3 tablespoons flour
½ teaspoon Italian seasoning

½ teaspoon salt
¼ teaspoon pepper
⅔ cup milk
½ cup shredded Monterey jack or Provolone cheese

1. Remove vegetables from package and place in a shallow oval or round serving dish just large enough to hold them. Sprinkle with 3 tablespoons water. Cover with double layer of wet paper towels. Cook on HIGH 5 to 6 minutes, until crisp-tender.

2. Put butter in a 2-cup bowl and cook on HIGH 1 minute, or until melted. Blend in flour, Italian seasoning, salt and pepper until smooth. Gradually whisk in milk. Cook, uncovered, on HIGH 2 to 3 minutes, stirring several times, until sauce boils and thickens.

3. Uncover vegetables and drain well. Return to serving dish. Pour hot cream sauce over vegetables and sprinkle cheese on top. Cook, uncovered, on HIGH 1 to 1½ minutes, until cheese melts.

237   BASIL VEGETABLE TOSS
Prep: 10 minutes   Cook: 8 minutes   Serves: 4

1 small onion, thinly sliced
2 tablespoons olive oil
1 medium zucchini, sliced
1 small red bell pepper, cut
   into 1-inch squares
1 small green bell pepper, cut
   into 1-inch squares
½ pound fresh mushrooms,
   sliced

¼ teaspoon salt
¼ teaspoon pepper
3 tablespoons minced fresh
   basil or parsley
3 tablespoons grated
   Parmesan cheese
   (optional but desirable)

1. In a small casserole, place onion and oil. Cook on HIGH 4 minutes. Stir in zucchini and bell peppers. Cover and continue to cook 2 minutes, until slightly tender.

2. Stir in mushrooms, salt and pepper. Cover and cook on HIGH 2 minutes, or until mushrooms are just tender. Add basil and toss. Serve with a sprinkling of Parmesan cheese if desired.

238   PERFECT CARROTS
Prep: 10 minutes   Cook: 6 to 7 minutes   Serves: 4

1 pound carrots, peeled   2 tablespoons water

1. Slice carrots crosswise on the diagonal about ¼ inch thick. Place in a small bowl or casserole, just large enough to hold them.

2. Add water. Cover and cook on HIGH 6 to 7 minutes, until just tender.

239   BROCCOLI RING WITH CHEDDAR CHEESE
Prep: 10 minutes   Cook: 14 to 16 minutes   Serves: 6

While this can be made in a small casserole, this recipe turns out best when prepared in a ring mold. For a nice touch, fill the center with cherry tomatoes.

1 tablespoon butter, softened
2 10-ounce packages frozen
   chopped broccoli
2 cups shredded sharp
   Cheddar cheese

¼ cup flour
2 garlic cloves, minced
½ teaspoon salt
¼ teaspoon pepper
4 eggs, well beaten

1. Use butter to generously coat inside of a 6-cup ring mold. Place boxes of frozen broccoli on plate. Cook on HIGH 6 minutes. Let stand 5 minutes to finish thawing. Drain well in colander.

2. In a large bowl, combine broccoli, cheese, flour, garlic, salt and pepper. Add beaten eggs and mix well. Spoon mixture into buttered mold. Cook, uncovered, on HIGH 8 to 10 minutes, until custard appears set around edges; turn dish if ring appears to be cooking unevenly. Let stand for 5 minutes. Run a knife around the edges to loosen. Unmold onto a serving plate.

240 SPAGHETTI SQUASH WITH TOMATOES, ZUCCHINI AND PEPPERS

Prep: 10 minutes   Cook: 17 to 20 minutes   Serves: 4

1 1½- to 2-pound spaghetti
   squash
2 medium zucchini, cut into
   ½-inch slices
1 large red or green bell
   pepper, cut into ½-inch
   dice
1 celery stalk, sliced
½ teaspoon basil

½ teaspoon salt
¼ teaspoon pepper
4 tablespoons butter
2 large tomatoes, coarsely
   chopped
¼ cup grated Parmesan cheese
   Chopped parsley, for
   garnish

1. Pierce squash deeply in several places with a long-pronged fork. Elevate on a rack if you have one. Cook on HIGH 7 minutes. Turn squash over and cook 4 to 7 minutes, or until slightly soft to the touch. Set aside to cool.

2. In a 1-quart casserole, combine zucchini, bell pepper, celery, basil, salt and pepper. Toss to mix. Dot with butter. Cover with lid and cook on HIGH 3 minutes. Add tomatoes. Cover and cook 3 minutes.

3. With a large sharp knife, cut squash in half lengthwise. Scoop out seeds. With 2 forks, scrape up squash strands and transfer to a serving platter. Spoon vegetables over top. Sprinkle with cheese and parsley.

241 RATATOUILLE WITH MUSHROOMS

Prep: 15 minutes   Cook: 20 to 22 minutes   Serves: 4 to 6

1 medium eggplant (about 1½
   pounds)
¼ cup extra-virgin olive oil
2 garlic cloves, minced
1 onion, thinly sliced
½ pound zucchini, sliced
2 bell peppers, red or green,
   sliced

¼ pound mushrooms, sliced
1 large tomato, cut into
   wedges
1 6-ounce can tomato paste
½ teaspoon herbes de
   Provence or basil
1 teaspoon salt
½ teaspoon pepper

1. Pierce eggplant several times with long-pronged fork. Elevate on a rack if you have one. Cook on HIGH 5 minutes. Turn eggplant over and cook 3 to 5 minutes longer (about 7 minutes per pound), until it feels slightly soft to the touch. Set aside until cool enough to handle. Cut lengthwise in half and scoop out flesh; coarsely chop eggplant.

2. In a 3-quart casserole, place oil, garlic and onion. Cook on HIGH 5 minutes, stirring once. Stir in chopped eggplant, zucchini, peppers, mushrooms and ⅔ of the tomato wedges. Cover with waxed paper. Cook 5 minutes longer.

3. In a small bowl, combine tomato paste, herbes, salt and pepper. Stir to blend well. Mix into vegetables. Arrange remaining tomato wedges on top. Cook on HIGH 2 minutes, until hot.

242 GARLIC CUSTARD
Prep: 10 minutes   Cook: 13 to 14 minutes   Serves: 4

An excellent accompaniment to grilled lamb chops or roast chicken.

12 garlic cloves, crushed
    through a press
1¼ cups heavy cream
3 egg yolks

Dash of freshly grated
    nutmeg
¼ teaspoon salt
⅛ teaspoon white pepper

1. In a 2-quart casserole, combine garlic and cream. Cover with vented microwave-safe plastic wrap. Cook on HIGH 7 minutes.

2. In a small bowl, lightly beat egg yolks. Gradually whisk in ½ cup of the hot cream. Whisk warmed yolks into remaining garlic cream. Season with nutmeg, salt and pepper.

2. Pour equal amounts of garlic custard into each of 4 buttered 3- to 4-ounce ramekins or custard cups. Arrange on a plate or round baking dish in a ring. Cook, uncovered, on MEDIUM 6 to 7 minutes, or until just set. Turn plate if custards appear to be cooking unevenly.

243 BAKED ONIONS WITH PARMESAN CHEESE
Prep: 5 minutes   Cook: 9 to 10 minutes   Serves: 6

2 large onions, unpeeled
¼ cup extra-virgin olive oil
    Salt and pepper

⅓ cup grated Parmesan cheese
    Paprika

1. Cut each onion crosswise in thirds, leaving the skin in place. Arrange in a single layer in a circle in a 10-inch pie plate. Place ends skin-side down. Cover with waxed paper. Cook on HIGH 7 to 8 minutes, until slightly tender.

2. Drizzle olive oil over onion pieces. Season liberally with salt and pepper. Top with Parmesan cheese. Cook, uncovered, on HIGH 2 minutes. Sprinkle lightly with paprika and serve hot.

244 MAPLE BUTTER SQUASH
Prep: 5 minutes   Cook: 18 to 22 minutes   Serves: 6 to 8

The microwave is a real time-saver when it comes to hard-shelled squash.

2 1½-pound acorn squash
1 cup pure maple syrup
8 teaspoons butter

½ cup chopped pecans
    Cinnamon

1. Pierce each squash several times with a long-pronged meat fork. Cook on HIGH 10 minutes. Turn squash over. Continue to cook 7 to 10 minutes longer, until soft to the touch. Set aside until cool enough to handle; cut each squash into 4 wedges.

2. Remove metal cap from glass bottle of maple syrup. Cook on HIGH 1 to 2 minutes, until hot. Using a mitt or pot holder, remove bottle from microwave, replace cap and shake syrup briefly.

3. Arrange squash in a single layer in a large shallow serving dish. Place 1 teaspoon butter on each wedge. Spoon 2 tablespoons maple syrup and 1 tablespoon pecans over each. Sprinkle with cinnamon. Serve hot.

---

245   EGGPLANT PARMESAN
Prep: 20 minutes   Cook: 15 to 20 minutes   Serves: 3 to 4

1 medium eggplant (about 1¼ pounds)	6 tablespoons grated Parmesan cheese
1 egg	2 cups Thick Spaghetti Sauce (recipe follows)
1 tablespoon olive oil	
⅓ cup Italian-seasoned bread crumbs	6 ounces mozzarella cheese, shredded (about 1½ cups)
1 tablespoon cornmeal	

1. Cut eggplant crosswise into ½-inch slices. In a pie plate, beat together egg and oil. In a shallow bowl, blend bread crumbs, cornmeal and 3 tablespoons Parmesan cheese.

2. Dip each eggplant slice in egg, then dredge in bread crumb mixture to coat. Arrange slices, overlapping slightly if necessary, in a 12-inch round baking dish. Cover with paper towel. Cook on HIGH 10 to 14 minutes, or until eggplant is tender.

3. Remove from microwave and spoon sauce over eggplant. Sprinkle with mozzarella and remaining Parmesan. Cook, uncovered, on HIGH 5 minutes, until cheeses melt. Serve hot.

---

246   THICK SPAGHETTI SAUCE
Prep: 10 minutes   Cook: 17 to 20 minutes   Makes: about 4 cups

This sauce improves if made a day ahead and refrigerated overnight. It freezes well.

2 medium onions, chopped	¼ cup chopped parsley
3 garlic cloves, minced	1 teaspoon salt
3 tablespoons extra-virgin olive oil	½ teaspoon sugar
	½ teaspoon basil
1 14-ounce can Italian peeled tomatoes, coarsely chopped, liquid reserved	½ teaspoon oregano
	¼ teaspoon black pepper
	⅛ teaspoon crushed hot red pepper, or more to taste
1 6-ounce can tomato paste	
½ cup grated Parmesan cheese	

1. In a 2-quart glass measure or bowl, combine onions, garlic and oil. Cook on HIGH 5 minutes, stirring once.

2. Add tomatoes with liquid, tomato paste, Parmesan cheese, parsley, salt, sugar, basil, oregano, black pepper and hot pepper. Cover with waxed paper and cook 12 to 15 minutes, until sauce is slightly thickened.

247 BROCCOLI-CORN CASSEROLE WITH COTTAGE CHEESE
Prep: 10 minutes   Cook: 14 to 17 minutes   Serves: 6

2 10-ounce packages frozen
   chopped broccoli
1½ cups cottage cheese
½ cup sour cream
1 tablespoon flour
3 eggs, beaten

1 small onion, finely chopped
1 teaspoon salt
¼ teaspoon pepper
1 17-ounce can corn kernels
½ cup grated Parmesan cheese

1. Place 2 packages of frozen broccoli on a plate. Cook on HIGH 7 minutes. Let stand 5 minutes to complete thawing. Drain thoroughly.

2. In a large mixing bowl, combine cottage cheese, sour cream, flour, eggs, onion, salt and pepper. Blend well. Fold in broccoli and corn. Turn into a 2-quart casserole. Sprinkle Parmesan cheese over top. Cover with lid and cook on MEDIUM-HIGH 7 to 10 minutes, or until edges appear set. Let stand, covered, 5 minutes to allow center to set up.

248 SALT-BAKED ROSEMARY POTATOES
Prep: 5 minutes   Cook: 17 to 20 minutes   Serves: 4

4 tablespoons butter
2 pounds small red potatoes

¼ cup coarse (kosher) salt
2 tablespoons rosemary

1. Put butter in a 1-cup glass measure. Cook on HIGH 1 minute, or until melted.

2. Wash potatoes but do not peel. In a 10-inch shallow round baking dish, combine salt and rosemary. Toss to blend. Place potatoes on top and brush with ½ the melted butter. Cover with waxed paper. Cook on HIGH 8 minutes.

3. Turn pototoes over with tongs. Brush with remaining melted butter. Cover again and cook on HIGH 7 to 10 minutes, just until potatoes are fork tender. Do not overcook. Brush off excess salt and rosemary with pastry brush and serve hot.

249 ZESTY TOMATO SAUCE WITH BASIL
Prep: 10 minutes   Cook: 25 minutes   Makes: about 2 cups

1 14-ounce can Italian peeled
   tomatoes, liquid reserved
1 6-ounce can tomato paste
2 tablespoons minced fresh
   basil or 1 teaspoon dried
¼ cup minced onion

¼ cup minced green bell
   pepper
2 garlic cloves, minced
¼ teaspoon sugar
¼ teaspoon pepper
Pinch of cayenne pepper

1. Place tomatoes and liquid in a food processor or blender. Add tomato paste and puree until smooth.

2. In a 2-quart measure or bowl, combine tomato puree and all of the remaining ingredients. Cover with waxed paper and cook on HIGH 5 minutes. Reduce power to MEDIUM and cook 20 minutes, or until thickened.

250   CARROT TIMBALES
Prep: 10 minutes   Cook: 13 to 15 minutes   Serves: 6

1 **pound carrots, peeled**	½ **cup half-and-half or light**
1 **tablespoon butter**	**cream**
1 **teaspoon sugar**	**Parsley leaves, for garnish**
2 **eggs**	

1. Cut carrots into 1-inch pieces. Place in a casserole just large enough to hold them. Add butter and sugar. Cover with lid and cook on HIGH 6 to 7 minutes, stirring once to coat with butter, until fork tender. Let carrots cool slightly. Then puree in food processor or blender.

2. In a medium bowl, beat together eggs and half-and-half until blended. Add carrot puree and blend well. Fill six 6-ounce buttered ramekins or custard cups with an equal amount of carrot custard. Arrange ramekins in a circle on a plate.

3. Cook on MEDIUM 7 to 8 minutes, or until set. Turn dish if they appear to be cooking unevenly. Let cool slightly. Run knife around edges to loosen and unmold onto serving plate. Garnish with parsley leaves.

251   KOREAN-STYLE BEAN SPROUTS
Prep: 10 minutes   Cook: 4 to 5 minutes   Serves: 4 to 6

This is a light, refreshing, slightly spicy salad that goes well with grilled meats.

2 **teaspoons sesame seeds**	1 **tablespoon rice wine**
1 **tablespoon vegetable oil**	**vinegar or cider vinegar**
1 **pound fresh bean sprouts**	1½ **teaspoons Asian sesame oil**
2 **scallions, chopped**	½ **teaspoon crushed hot red**
2 **garlic cloves, minced**	**pepper**
1 **tablespoon soy sauce**	½ **teaspoon salt**
	¼ **teaspoon black pepper**

1. In a 1-cup glass measure, combine sesame seeds and 1 teaspoon oil. Cook on HIGH 1 to 2 minutes, stirring once, until lightly toasted.

2. In a 2-quart bowl, place bean sprouts and 3 tablespoons water. Cover and cook on HIGH 3 minutes. Drain sprouts well.

3. Using same bowl, combine scallions, garlic, soy sauce, vinegar, sesame oil, hot pepper, salt, black pepper and remaining 2 teaspoons vegetable oil. Mix well. Add bean sprouts and toss to coat. Serve chilled or at room temperature.

252   FOUR-BEAN BAKE
Prep: 10 minutes   Cook: 13 to 15 minutes   Serves: 6 to 8

1 large onion	1 16-ounce can pinto beans
2 green bell peppers, cut into ½-inch pieces	1 16-ounce can chili beans in sauce
2 garlic cloves, minced	1 16-ounce can stewed tomatoes
2 tablespoons vegetable oil	¾ teaspoon ground cumin
1 16-ounce can red kidney beans	1 teaspoon Italian seasoning
1 16-ounce can garbanzo beans (chick-peas)	Salt and pepper

1. In a 3-quart casserole, combine onion, bell peppers, garlic and oil. Cook on HIGH 4 minutes.

2. Drain kidney beans, garbanzo beans and pinto beans. Add to casserole. Add chili beans with sauce, stewed tomatoes with liquid, cumin and Italian seasoning. Cover and cook on HIGH 9 to 11 minutes, stirring once. Season with salt and pepper to taste.

253   ARTICHOKES ITALIAN-STYLE
Prep: 5 minutes   Cook: 10 to 15 minutes   Serves: 1

The microwave does a great quick job on artichokes, sealing in all their delectable flavor.

1 large artichoke	½ lemon, thinly sliced
1 garlic clove, halved	1 tablespoon olive oil

1. Cut off artichoke stem and about 1 inch of top. Trim sharp tips of leaves with scissors. Place artichoke upside-down in 4-cup glass measure. Add cut garlic and lemon slices. Pour in enough water to cover about ⅓ of the artichoke. Pour oil over artichoke.

2. Cover measure tightly with microwave-safe plastic wrap. Poke 2 or 3 steam vents in wrap with tip of sharp knife. Cook on HIGH 10 to 15 minutes, or until stem is fork tender. Turn artichoke in liquid to moisten all leaves. Let stand, covered, for about 5 minutes before serving.

NOTE: To cook more than 1 artichoke, increase garlic and lemon and add 3 to 5 minutes for each additional artichoke.

254   COUNTRY FAIR CORN ON THE COB
Prep: 10 minutes   Cook: 10 to 12 minutes   Serves: 4

This is my favorite method for cooking corn on the cob. Try it and you'll never have it any other way.

4 unhusked ears of corn	Butter and salt

1. Discard any brown or soiled outer leaves of the husk. Soak ears in bowl of cold water 10 minutes.

2. Lift corn out of water and let excess run off. Place still-moist corn in husk on plate. Cook on HIGH 10 to 12 minutes (about 3 minutes per ear). Peel back husks; discard silk. Serve hot, with butter and salt.

255 ORANGE-BAKED YAMS
Prep: 10 minutes   Cook: 9 to 12 minutes   Serves: 6 to 8

2 pounds fresh yams or sweet
    potatoes
½ cup orange juice
½ cup brown sugar

½ teaspoon cinnamon
4 tablespoons melted butter
½ cup coarsely chopped
    pecans

1. Wash yams but do not dry. Pierce skin in center. Wrap each yam separately in a paper towel. Arrange in a circle, on a rack if you have one. Cook on HIGH 4 to 6 minutes, until potatoes are slightly soft to the touch. Remove any that are done before the others. Let cool slightly.

2. Peel yams and cut into ½-inch-thick slices. Arrange slices in concentric circles in a 9- or 10-inch deep dish pie pan or quiche dish. Mix orange juice, brown sugar and cinnamon. Pour over yams.

3. Drizzle melted butter over yams and sprinkle with chopped pecans. Cover with waxed paper. Cook on HIGH 5 to 6 minutes, until top is slightly caramelized.

256 WILTED CHEF'S SALAD WITH CAESER DRESSING
Prep: 15 minutes   Cook: 2 minutes   Serves: 4

8 cups torn mixed salad
    greens: spinach, chicory,
    leaf lettuce
¼ pound thickly sliced roast
    turkey, cut into 1½ ×
    ¼-inch strips
¼ pound thickly sliced cooked
    ham, cut into 1½ ×
    ¼-inch strips

¼ cup thickly sliced Swiss
    cheese, cut into 1½ ×
    ¼-inch strips
1 small red onion, thinly
    sliced
1 8-ounce glass bottle Caesar
    salad dressing

1. In a large salad bowl, place salad greens, turkey, ham, Swiss cheese and onion. Toss to mix.

2. Shortly before serving, shake dressing well. Remove metal cap. Place bottle in microwave and cook on HIGH 1½ minutes. Using mitt or pot holder, remove bottle. Replace cap and shake again. Pour over salad, toss and serve.

257   ORANGE GINGERED CARROTS
Prep: 10 minutes   Cook: 8 to 9 minutes   Serves: 4

1 **pound carrots, peeled**	1½ **teaspoons minced fresh**
¼ **cup sugar**	**ginger**
3 **tablespoons water**	¼ **cup orange juice, preferably**
1 **teaspoon cornstarch**	**fresh**
⅛ **teaspoon salt**	2 **tablespoons butter**

1. Slice carrots crosswise on the diagonal about ¼ inch thick. Place in a small casserole with the sugar and water. Cover and cook on HIGH 6 to 7 minutes, stirring once, until just fork tender. Set aside, covered.

2. In a 4-cup glass measure, combine cornstarch, salt, ginger and orange juice. Stir until cornstarch is dissolved. Cook on HIGH 1 minute; stir. Cook 1 minute longer. Add butter to sauce and stir until melted. Drain carrots and place in a serving dish. Pour ginger sauce over carrots and toss to coat. Serve hot.

258   SNOW PEAS WITH FRESH GINGER
Prep: 5 minutes   Cook: 3½ minutes   Serves: 2

2 **teaspoons Asian sesame oil**	1 **teaspoon sesame seeds**
1 **teaspoon minced fresh**	¼ **pound snow peas**
ginger	

1. In a small casserole, combine oil, ginger and sesame seeds. Cover and cook on HIGH 1½ minutes.

2. Stir in snow peas. Cover and cook on HIGH 2 minutes.

BABY FOOD

It is so simple to prepare vegetables and fruits for your baby in the microwave that you might never buy store-bought again. You have the assurance of knowing exactly what is in your baby's food, and it is certainly the way to retain as many vitamins and nutrients as possible, since so little liquid is required and the cooking time is so short.

One important tip: when reheating the baby food, remember to just warm it, don't cook until boiling hot. Stirring and testing are important. Think in terms of seconds in the microwave, not minutes. Store baby fruits and vegetables in small covered jars in the refrigerator. Reheat in custard cups on MEDIUM, stirring once or twice, 30 to 60 seconds.

Puree and strain vegetables and fruit with liquid as needed, depending on the age of the baby. Younger babies need a smoother, more liquid texture. If in doubt, consult with your pediatrician.

259 BABY'S PEACHES
Prep: 5 minutes   Cook: 4 to 5 minutes   Makes: about 1 cup

3 ripe peaches   ¼ cup water

1. Peel peaches, cut in half and remove pit. Cut peaches into 1-inch chunks. Place in a 1-quart casserole. Add water. Cover and cook on HIGH 4 to 5 minutes, until peaches are soft.

2. Place peaches and liquid in a blender or food processor and puree until smooth. Strain if necessary. Store in a covered jar in the refrigerator for up to 3 days, or freeze.

260 BABY'S PEARS
Prep: 5 minutes   Cook: 5 minutes   Makes: about 1 cup

3 medium pears   ¼ cup unsweetened apple
                                            juice or water

1. Peel and quarter pears; cut out stem and cores. Cut pears into 1-inch chunks. Place in a 1-quart casserole. Add apple juice. Cover and cook on HIGH 5 minutes, until soft.

2. Place pears and liquid in a blender or food processor and puree until smooth. Strain if necessary. Store in a covered jar in the refrigerator for up to 3 days, or freeze.

261   BABY'S SWEET POTATOES
Prep: 5 minutes   Cook: 7 to 8 minutes   Makes: about 1 cup

2 large sweet potatoes (7 to 8   ¼ to ⅓ cup purified water
ounces each)

1. Scrub sweet potatoes. Pierce once with a fork. Wrap completely in paper towels and set on a microwave rack or on the floor of the oven with folded ends of towel underneath. Cook on HIGH 7 to 8 minutes, until soft to the touch. Let cool slightly.

2. Peel sweet potatoes and slice. Puree with ¼ cup purified water until smooth. If too thick, thin with more water. Strain if necessary. Store in covered jar in refrigerator for up to 3 days, or freeze.

262   BABY'S ACORN SQUASH
Prep: 5 minutes   Cook: 8 to 10 minutes   Makes: about 1 cup

1 acorn squash, about 1¼   Purified water
pounds

1. Cut squash in half; scoop out seeds and fibers. Place squash, cut-sides down, in pie plate. Cook on HIGH 8 to 10 minutes, or until soft to the touch. Let cool slightly.

2. Scoop out squash and place in a blender or food processor. Puree until smooth. Add purified water to thin if squash is too thick. Strain if necessary. Store in a covered jar in the refrigerator for up to 3 days, or freeze.

263   BABY'S CARROTS
Prep: 10 minutes   Cook: 6 to 7 minutes   Makes: about 2 cups

1 pound tender young carrots,   ¼ cup water
preferably with tops on

1. Cut off tops and peel carrots. Cut into thick slices. Place in a casserole just large enough to hold carrots. Add water. Cover with lid and cook on HIGH 6 to 7 minutes until carrots are tender. Set aside, covered, and let cool slightly.

2. Place carrots with liquid in a blender or food processor and puree until smooth. Strain if necessary. Store in covered jar in refrigerator for up to 3 days, or freeze.

264   BABY'S APPLESAUCE
Prep: 5 minutes   Cook: 4 to 5 minutes   Makes: about 1 cup

2 cooking apples   **¼ cup unsweetened apple
                                                     juice or water**

1. Peel and quarter apples; cut out cores. Cut apples into 1-inch cubes and place in a 1-quart casserole. Add apple juice. Cover and cook on HIGH 4 to 5 minutes, until apples are very soft.

2. Place apples and liquid in a blender or food processor and puree until smooth. Strain if necessary. Store in a covered jar in the refrigerator for up to 3 days, or freeze.

Chapter 11

Take a Baked Potato . . .

In recent years, the potato has come into its own, recognized not only for its soul-satisfying flavor and delightful versatility, but for its excellent nutritional benefits. At only about 100 calories per medium potato, it acts as a delicious filler in many diets. Purely from a health standpoint, it is rich in fiber, complex carbohydrates and potassium. And it is a good source of vitamin C, which is bonded to the starch in the potato in such a way that it is well preserved even after cooking. Since prolonged heat does tend to destroy most nutrients, the microwave's quick-cooking process retains as many vitamins and minerals as possible.

Of all the ways of cooking a potato, the hands-down favorite is—without a doubt—baking. Even the sound of the words—baked potato—makes my mouth water. No question, it's delicious, and it involves the least possible preparation. Just pop it in the oven and wait. Well, that's the only drawback. In a conventional oven you have to wait for about an hour. Remember all those nights you came home from work tired and hungry and sat there smelling that baked potato baking and wishing it were done. Or more often than not, thought of that baked potato, but turned to something else because you didn't have the time to wait.

Well, the marriage of the baked potato and the microwave oven is probably one of the happiest that's ever taken place, even if it is a marriage of convenience—yours! A potato baked in the microwave takes only minutes. And, oh, what you can do to that potato, beyond smothering it in melted butter or sour cream and chives.

Make a quick one-dish meal out of a microwave baked potato. Make it Pizza Potatoes with Italian sausage, fresh mushrooms, pepperoni, mozzarella cheese and plenty of sauce. Turn it into a light Chicken Potato Orientale, with broccoli and a savory sesame-soy sauce, or Salmon-Stuffed Potatoes. Or fill up on Chili-Stuffed Potatoes, for tasty comfort at its best.

Turn quick-baked potatoes into salad: German Potato Salad with Hot Bacon Sauce or Skinny Potato Salad with low-cal dressing. Snack on Potato Nachos.

Create irresistible side dishes like Tomato Potato with Basil-Cheese Topping, Potatoes with Mixed Garden Vegetables and Corny Potatoes. Vegetarian and most meatless eaters will find plenty to fill them up in this chapter.

The trick to baking potatoes in the microwave is choosing the right kind of potato and cooking it so that you lock in the moisture. I use russet baking potatoes because their dense texture and low moisture content makes them ideal for the microwave. They become mealy and soft when cooked, easy to mash, slice or dice.

To protect potatoes in the microwave, they should be wrapped in a paper towel designed for use in the microwave. This holds in internal moisture and helps to prevent the skin from becoming soggy from condensing moisture.

PERFECT POTATOES

For baking, choose russet baking potatoes, such as Idahos. Wash but do not dry potatoes. Pierce each one once through the skin in the center. Wrap the potato in a microwave-safe paper towel, which will help to hold in the moisture.

Bake the potato according to the time chart below. If cooking more than one potato, arrange them end to end in a circle, about 1 inch apart. Be sure to wrap each potato individually.

Feel potatoes to test for doneness. Naturally, smaller potatoes will be ready faster than larger ones, just as they are in a conventional oven. The potato is done when it reaches 200° on a microwave probe or instant-reading thermometer. It should pierce easily to the center. Let the potato stand, wrapped in the paper towel, for about 5 minutes to complete cooking after you remove it from the microwave.

Whether or not your potatoes need to be turned depends on your microwave and its cooking pattern. If you have a microwave rack, use it to elevate the potatoes; they will cook more evenly. Also, wrapping the towel so that several layers are tucked underneath allows the towel to absorb excess moisture and provides an even cooking pattern.

Cut open the potato and fluff with a fork. Top with butter, sour cream and chives, blue cheese or one of the wonderful toppings that follow.

POTATO COOKING CHART:
(Assuming each baking potato weighs 8 ounces)

1 potato—6 to 7 minutes
2 potatoes—9 to 12 minutes
3 potatoes—13 to 16 minutes
4 potatoes—18 to 22 minutes

265 PIZZA POTATOES

Prep: 10 minutes   Cook: 25 to 32 minutes   Serves: 4

Here are all the traditional flavors of the popular pizza on top of a baked potato instead of a bread crust. Kids will love this one.

4 **large baking potatoes**	4 **mushrooms, thinly sliced**
½ **pound Italian sausages,**	12 **pepperoni slices, cut into**
sweet or hot to your taste,	**slivers**
casings removed	1 **cup shredded mozzarella**
1½ **cups prepared pizza or**	**cheese**
spaghetti sauce	¼ **cup grated Parmesan cheese**

1. Bake potato as described on page 131. Let stand, wrapped, 5 minutes. Crumble sausage into a 4-cup glass measure. Cook on HIGH 2 to 3 minutes, until sausage is no longer pink, stirring once to break up any lumps. Drain off fat and set aside.

2. In a 2-cup glass measure, combine sauce and mushrooms. Cover with waxed paper. Cook on HIGH 4 minutes. Set aside, covered, to keep warm.

3. Open each potato, fluff with a fork and make a well to hold sauce and toppings. Spoon sauce with mushrooms into each potato. Top each with ¼ of the sausage and pepperoni. Sprinkle ¼ cup mozzarella and 1 tablespoon Parmesan cheese over each potato. Return to microwave and cook on HIGH 1 to 3 minutes, just until cheese melts. Serve hot.

266 CHICKEN POTATO ORIENTALE

Prep: 10 minutes   Cook: 19 to 24 minutes   Serves: 3

Here's a light one-dish supper that's perfect for a busy day. Accompany with a green salad and serve fresh fruit for dessert

3 **8-ounce baking potatoes**	¾ **teaspoon minced fresh**
1 **whole skinless, boneless**	**ginger**
chicken breast, cut into	1 **tablespoon cornstarch**
thin strips	½ **cup canned chicken broth**
1 **cup broccoli florets**	2 **tablespoons soy sauce**
2 **tablespoons vegetable oil**	1 **tablespoon dry sherry**
2 **garlic cloves, minced**	1 **teaspoon sugar**
	1 **teaspoon Asian sesame oil**

1. Bake potatoes as described on page 131. Let stand, wrapped, 5 minutes. In a 2-quart casserole, combine chicken, broccoli, vegetable oil, garlic and ginger. Cover with lid and cook on HIGH 3 to 4 minutes, stirring once, until chicken turns white.

2. In a small bowl, combine cornstarch, chicken broth, soy sauce, sherry and sugar. Stir to dissolve cornstarch and sugar. Add sauce to chicken and stir to mix. Cover and cook on HIGH 3 to 4 minutes, stirring twice, until thickened. Stir in sesame oil. Cut potatoes in half lengthwise and fluff with fork. Top with chicken, broccoli and sauce.

267 TOMATO POTATO WITH BASIL-CHEESE TOPPING

Prep: 10 minutes   Cook: 8 to 9 minutes   Serves: 1

1 8-ounce baking potato
1 teaspoon butter
1 teaspoon chopped fresh basil
Salt and pepper

¼ cup diced tomato
2 tablespoons shredded Cheddar cheese
Basil leaves, for garnish

1. Bake potato as described on page 131. Let stand, wrapped, 5 minutes. Place butter in a small bowl and cook on HIGH 30 to 45 seconds, until melted. Stir in chopped basil. Cut potato open and season with salt and pepper to taste. Drizzle basil butter on top.

2. Sprinkle diced tomato and cheese over potato. Cook on HIGH 1 minute, or until cheese melts. Garnish with fresh basil leaves.

268 GREEK STUFFED POTATOES

Prep: 15 minutes   Cook: 16 to 20 minutes   Serves: 3 or 6

3 8-ounce baking potatoes
½ pound fresh spinach
⅓ cup chopped scallions
¼ teaspoon nutmeg

3 tablespoons butter
¼ pound imported feta cheese, crumbled
¼ cup plain yogurt

1. Bake potatoes as described on page 131. Let stand, wrapped, 5 minutes. Rinse spinach well, remove stems and tear leaves into pieces. In a 1-quart casserole, combine spinach, scallions, nutmeg and butter.

2. Cover with lid and cook on HIGH 2 to 3 minutes, until spinach is limp but still bright green. Stir in cheese and yogurt.

3. Cut potatoes in half lengthwise. Fluff with a fork. Arrange potato halves on a serving platter. Spoon spinach-cheese mixture on top. Cook on HIGH 30 to 45 seconds, until just heated through.

269 POTATO SALAD FOR TWO

Prep: 5 minutes   Cook: 9 to 12 minutes   Serves: 2

2 8-ounce baking potatoes
½ cup mayonnaise
¼ cup chopped celery
2 tablespoons chopped pimiento
2 tablespoons finely chopped onion

1 tablespoon white wine vinegar
2 teaspoons Dijon mustard
½ teaspoon salt
¼ teaspoon pepper

1. Bake potatoes as described on page 131. Let stand, wrapped, 5 minutes. Set aside until cool enough to handle. Peel and cut into ½-inch dice.

2. In a medium bowl, combine all remaining ingredients. Whisk to blend. Add potatoes and toss to coat.

270 BAKED POTATOES TOPPED WITH BLUE CHEESE

Prep: 5 minutes   Cook: 18 to 22 minutes   Serves: 4

4 8-ounce baking potatoes
⅓ cup crumbled blue cheese

¾ cup sour cream
2 scallions, chopped

1. Bake potatoes as described on page 131. Let stand, wrapped, 5 minutes. Meanwhile, in a small bowl, combine blue cheese and sour cream. Mix to blend well.

2. Cut potato open and fluff with fork. Top with blue cheese and sour cream and garnish with chopped scallions.

271 POTATOES WITH BROWNED ONIONS

Prep: 10 minutes   Cook: 20 to 26 minutes   Serves: 4

3 8-ounce baking potatoes
2 medium onions, sliced
2 tablespoons butter
1 teaspoon salt

¼ teaspoon thyme
¼ teaspoon pepper
⅛ teaspoon paprika

1. Bake potatoes as described on page 131. Let stand, wrapped, 5 minutes. Unwrap and let stand until cool enough to handle. Peel, then slice.

2. Place onions and butter in a 2-quart glass bowl. Cover and cook on HIGH 5 to 7 minutes, stirring several times, until onions are tender and beginning to brown slightly.

3. Add sliced potatoes to onions. Season with salt, thyme, pepper and paprika. Toss gently to mix potatoes and onions. Cover and cook on HIGH 2 to 3 minutes, until heated through.

272 CRABBY CHEESE POTATOES

Prep: 10 minutes   Cook: 20 to 25 minutes   Serves: 4

4 8-ounce baking potatoes
6 ounces crabmeat, drained
4 tablespoons butter
1 teaspoon salt
½ teaspoon pepper

Dash of cayenne pepper
½ cup chopped scallions
1 cup shredded Cheddar
   cheese
Paprika

1. Bake potatoes as described on page 131. Let stand, wrapped, 5 minutes. Meanwhile, pick over crabmeat to remove any bits of cartilage. Flake crab.

2. Cut off top ¼ of each potato. Scoop potato into bowl, leaving ¼-inch shell. Mash potatoes with butter, salt, pepper and cayenne. Fold in scallions, ¾ cup cheese and ¾ of the crab.

3. Spoon potato mixture back into shells. Top with remaining crab. Sprinkle 1 tablespoon cheese over each potato and top with a dash of paprika for color. Place on a plate and cook on HIGH 2 to 3 minutes, until cheese melts and potatoes are hot.

273   GERMAN POTATO SALAD WITH HOT BACON SAUCE

Prep: 10 minutes   Cook: 9 to 12 minutes   Serves: 4

2 8-ounce baking potatoes
½ cup sliced celery
1 2-ounce jar chopped
   pimientos
2 scallions, thinly sliced

2 tablespoons chopped
   parsley
⅛ teaspoon pepper
   Hot Bacon Sauce (recipe
   follows)

1. Bake potato as described on page 131. Let stand, wrapped, 5 minutes. Unwrap and set aside to cool. Peel and slice.

2. In a large serving bowl, combine sliced potatoes, celery, pimientos, scallions and parsley. Season with pepper. Pour Hot Bacon Sauce over potatoes and toss lightly. Serve warm or at room temperature.

274   HOT BACON SAUCE

Prep: 10 minutes   Cook: 9 minutes   Makes: 1½ cups

This also makes a very special dressing for spinach and mushroom salad or for chicory. You can make it ahead and store it in a covered glass jar in the refrigerator. Before using, remove the lid, set the jar in the microwave and reheat on HIGH for 1 to 2 minutes.

6 slices of bacon, diced
1 medium onion, chopped
¼ cup cider vinegar
2 tablespoons water

2 tablespoons vegetable oil
2 teaspoons sugar
¼ teaspoon salt
⅛ teaspoon pepper

1. Put diced bacon in a 4-cup glass measure. Cover with paper towel and cook on HIGH 4 minutes, or until crisp. Remove bacon pieces with a slotted spoon.

2. Add onion to bacon drippings. Cook on HIGH 3 minutes, stirring once. Add vinegar, water, oil, sugar, salt and pepper. Cook on HIGH 2 minutes. Stir in bacon and use while hot.

275   SKINNY POTATO SALAD

Prep: 15 minutes   Cook: 13 to 16 minutes   Serves: 4 to 6

3 8-ounce baking potatoes
1 10-ounce package (frozen)
   cut green beans, thawed
½ cup sliced radishes
½ cup pitted black olives,
   halved

¼ cup chopped red onion
½ cup reduced-calorie creamy
   Italian dressing

1. Bake potatoes as described on page 131. Let stand, wrapped, 5 minutes. Set aside until cool enough to handle. Peel potatoes. Cut into ½-inch dice.

2. In a serving bowl, combine diced potatoes with green beans, radishes, olives and red onion. Toss to mix. Add dressing and toss to coat.

276   SALMON-STUFFED POTATOES
Prep: 10 minutes   Cook: 21 to 27 minutes   Serves: 4

4 8-ounce baking potatoes
4 tablespoons butter
2 tablespoons flour
1 cup milk
2 scallions, chopped
1 tablespoon minced fresh dill
   or 1 teaspoon dried

½ teaspoon lemon juice
½ teaspoon salt
¼ teaspoon pepper
1 7¾-ounce can salmon,
   drained and flaked

1. Bake potatoes as described on page 131. Let stand, wrapped, 5 minutes. Unwrap and let cool slightly. Meanwhile, in a 4-cup glass measure or bowl, cook butter on HIGH 1 to 2 minutes, until melted. Add flour and stir until smooth. Stir in milk. Cook on HIGH 2 to 3 minutes, stirring once, until thickened. Add scallions and dill and blend well. Season with lemon juice, salt and pepper. Stir in salmon.

2. Cut potatoes in half lengthwise. Fluff with fork. Spoon creamed salmon over potatoes.

277   POTATO NACHOS
Prep: 5 minutes   Cook: 8 to 9 minutes   Serves: 2

1 8-ounce baking potato
¼ cup taco sauce
2 to 3 teaspoons chopped
   pickled jalapeño peppers

2 tablespoons coarsely
   chopped pitted black
   olives
½ cup shredded Cheddar
   cheese

1. Bake potato as described on page 131. Let stand, wrapped, 5 minutes. In a 1-cup glass measure, combine taco sauce, jalapeño peppers and olives. Cook on HIGH 45 seconds, until hot.

2. Cut baked potato in half lengthwise. Fluff with a fork. Top each half with ¼ of the taco sauce mixture. Sprinkle ¼ cup cheese over each potato half. Cook on HIGH 30 to 60 seconds, until cheese melts.

278   CHILI-STUFFED POTATOES
Prep: 10 minutes   Cook: 18 to 22 minutes   Serves: 3

3 8-ounce baking potatoes
1 15-ounce can chili
¾ cup shredded Cheddar
   cheese

6 tablespoons sour cream
3 tablespoons chopped
   scallion or red onion

1. Bake potatoes as described on page 131. Let stand, wrapped, 5 minutes. Pour chili into a medium bowl. Cover with waxed paper. Cook on HIGH about 4 minutes, stirring once, until heated through.

2. Cut potatoes lengthwise in half. Arrange on a large plate or platter. Spoon chili over potatoes, dividing evenly. Sprinkle 2 tablespoons cheese over each potato half. Cook on HIGH 1 to 2 minutes, until cheese is melted. Top each half with 1 tablespoon sour cream and ½ tablespoon chopped scallion. Serve hot.

279 POTATOES WITH MIXED GARDEN VEGETABLES
Prep: 10 minutes   Cook: 26 to 33 minutes   Serves: 4

4 8-ounce baking potatoes
1 small onion, thinly sliced
1 garlic clove, minced
2 tablespoons butter
1 cup sliced fresh mushrooms
1 cup broccoli or cauliflower florets (about 1-inch)

1 cup sliced zucchini
1 red bell pepper, cut into thin strips
½ teaspoon salt
¼ teaspoon pepper
½ cup sour cream
2 tablespoons minced chives

1. Bake potatoes as described on page 131. Let stand, wrapped, 5 minutes. In a 1-quart casserole, combine onion, garlic and butter. Cook on HIGH 3 minutes. Stir in mushrooms, broccoli, zucchini and bell pepper. Cover with lid and cook on HIGH 5 to 8 minutes, until vegetables are tender. Season with salt and pepper.

3. Cut potatoes open and fluff with fork. Spoon mixed vegetables into each. Mix together sour cream and chives and spoon a dollop on top of each potato.

280 CORNY POTATOES
Prep: 10 minutes   Cook: 28 to 35 minutes   Serves: 4

4 8-ounce baking potatoes
2 slices of bacon, chopped
½ cup chopped onion
¼ cup chopped celery
2 tablespoons flour

1 cup milk
1 12-ounce can vacuum-packed corn kernels
½ teaspoon salt
¼ teaspoon pepper

1. Bake potatoes as described on page 131. Let stand, wrapped, 5 minutes. Place bacon in a 4-cup glass measure. Cover with paper towel and cook on HIGH 2 to 3 minutes, or until bacon is crisp. Remove bacon with slotted spoon and set aside. Pour off all but 2 tablespoons drippings.

2. Stir onion and celery into bacon drippings. Cook on HIGH 3 to 4 minutes, until tender. Stir in flour until smooth. Slowly blend in milk. Cook on MEDIUM 3 to 4 minutes, until thickened.

3. Stir in corn, salt and pepper. Cook on HIGH 2 minutes, or until heated through. Place potatoes on serving plates. Cut open and fluff, making a well in the center. Spoon corn mixture into well, dividing evenly. Sprinkle bacon on top and serve hot.

281   TACO TATERS
Prep: 10 minutes   Cook: 27 to 32 minutes   Serves: 4

  4 8-ounce baking potatoes
  1 pound lean ground beef
  1 medium onion, chopped
  1 4-ounce can chopped green
       chiles
1½ teaspoons chili powder
  ¾ teaspoon ground cumin

  ½ teaspoon salt
  1 8-ounce can tomato sauce
      Garnishes: shredded lettuce,
       chopped tomato,
       shredded Cheddar
       cheese, diced avocado or
       guacamole

1. Bake potatoes as described on page 131. Let stand, wrapped, 5 minutes. Place beef and onion in a 1-quart glass bowl. Cook on HIGH 3 minutes. Stir to break up any lumps. Cook 2 minutes longer. Pour off any fat.

2. Add chiles, chili powder, cumin and salt to beef, breaking up lumps with a fork. Add tomato sauce and mix well.

3. Cook filling on HIGH 5 minutes, until hot. Open up potatoes, fluff and make a well in the center of each. Spoon about ¼ of taco filling into each potato. Pass the garnishes separately and let everyone choose among them.

Chapter 12

Microwave in the Morning

If there's one time of day when effort saved is appreciated, it's first thing in the morning. Quick, fast and clean could be my motto for sun-up cooking.

Whole grains, like Old-Fashioned Oatmeal and Breakfast Buckwheat, are made for the microwave. They'll be done before you pour your first cup of coffee. Eggs can be a bit of a challenge in the microwave, but I've developed any number of highly successful dishes. The problem is that because eggs are so delicate and set so quickly at a certain point, tiny variations in individual microwave ovens will affect the cooking time. For that reason, I recommend you practice my basic Scrambled Eggs recipe in your microwave. Once you get the exact timing in your oven, all the others will be a snap.

For variety, try Scrambled Eggs and Potatoes, Scrambled Eggs with Onions and Smoked Salmon or a snappy Denver Omelet. Having a brunch? Make it easy with perfect Eggs Benedict, Huevos Rancheros or Quick and Easy Corned Beef Hash Muffins.

I've also included an assortment of easy microwave preserves. Made in small batches with less sugar, these rich fruit spreads are designed to be stored in the refrigerator; no water bath processing is required.

So remember, the microwave is not just for frozen products, and not just for reheating that cold cup of coffee. It's as useful in the morning as it is all day long.

---

282 SCRAMBLED EGGS
Prep: 5 minutes   Cook: 2 to 3 minutes   Serves: 1

You *can* cook eggs in the microwave. The secret is in the timing.

1 teaspoon butter
2 eggs

2 tablespoons milk
Salt and pepper

1. In a small bowl, cook butter on HIGH 30 seconds, or until melted.

2. In another small bowl, whisk together eggs, milk and salt and pepper to taste. Pour into melted butter. Cook on HIGH 1 minute. Stir, drawing the firmer egg from the edges toward the center, and pushing the less-cooked egg from the center toward the outside. Continue to cook 30 to 60 seconds longer, stirring once more, until eggs are slightly softer than you like them. They will continue to cook after removing from the microwave.

283   HERBED SCRAMBLED EGGS
Prep: 5 minutes   Cook: 2 to 3 minutes   Serves: 1

1 teaspoon butter	1½ teaspoons minced chives
2 eggs	1 teaspoon minced parsley
2 tablespoons milk	⅛ teaspoon dried tarragon
Salt and pepper	

1. In a small bowl, cook butter on HIGH 30 seconds, or until melted.

2. In a small bowl, whisk together eggs, milk and salt and pepper to taste. Toss together chives, parsley and tarragon.

3. Pour eggs into melted butter. Cook on HIGH 1 minute. Sprinkle on herbs and stir, pushing less-cooked eggs from center to edges. Continue to cook 30 to 60 seconds longer, stirring once more, until eggs are barely set.

284   HUEVOS RANCHEROS
Prep: 5 minutes   Cook: 3½ minutes   Serves: 1

1 6- to 7-inch corn tortilla	1 to 2 teaspoons minced fresh
2 tablespoons refried beans	green chile, to taste
2 eggs	Salt and pepper
2 tablespoons milk	2 tablespoons taco sauce or
3 tablespoons shredded	salsa
Monterey jack cheese	

1. Place tortilla between 2 sheets of paper towel and cook on HIGH 1 minute, to soften. Transfer to plate. Spread beans over tortilla and cook 30 seconds, to heat.

2. In a small bowl, whisk eggs, milk, cheese, chile and salt and pepper to taste. Cook on HIGH 1 minute. Stir, drawing firmer egg from edge toward center and pushing less-cooked egg from center toward edge. Cook 30 to 60 seconds longer, stirring once more, until eggs are barely set. Spread eggs over tortilla and drizzle sauce over top.

285   KIPPERS
Prep: 3 minutes   Cook: 7 to 8 minutes   Serves: 1 to 2

Kippers are smoked herring. The English love them with scrambled eggs and sliced potatoes for breakfast or brunch. I prefer the vacuum-sealed plastic pouches to the canned variety.

1 medium onion, thinly sliced	2 kippers
1 tablespoon vegetable oil	Lemon wedges

1. In a small shallow baking dish, place onion and oil. Cook on HIGH 3 minutes.

2 Place kippers, skin-side down, in dish and spoon onions on top. Cover with waxed paper. Cook on HIGH 4 to 5 minutes, until tender. Serve hot, with lemon wedges to squeeze over the kippers.

286 EGG IN A BASKET

Prep: 5 minutes   Cook: 1 to 2 minutes   Serves: 1

1 slice white or whole wheat
   bread, toasted
1 egg

Salt and pepper
1 slice favorite cheese

1. With a small glass or biscuit cutter, remove a 2½-inch circle from the center of the toast. Place cut-out bread on a serving plate. Break egg and slip into center of toast. With toothpick, pierce center of yolk about 3 times. Season egg lightly with salt and pepper.

2. Cover dish with waxed paper. Cook on MEDIUM 1 minute, or until white appears almost set. Place cheese on top and cook 30 to 45 seconds longer, until melted.

287 QUICK AND EASY CORNED BEEF HASH MUFFINS

Prep: 5 minutes   Cook: 3 to 6 minutes   Serves: 4

2 English muffins, split
4 teaspoons Dijon mustard
1 15-ounce can good-quality
   corned beef hash

½ cup shredded sharp
   Cheddar cheese
Minced fresh parsley

1. Toast muffins in toaster. Spread 1 teaspoon mustard over each muffin half. Remove both ends from can of hash. Press firmly on one end until hash is pushed from can in one piece. Slice into 4 equal patties.

2. Arrange corned beef hash patties in a circle on a round plate. Cover with paper towel. Cook on HIGH 2 to 4 minutes, until slightly crisp.

3. Place muffin halves on a serving plate. With wide metal spatula, carefully lift patties and place on muffins. Sprinkle 2 tablespoons cheese over each. Cook on HIGH 1 to 2 minutes, until cheese melts. Garnish with a sprinkling of minced parsley and serve hot.

288 COUNTRY BRUNCH CASSEROLE

Prep: 5 minutes   Cook: 7 to 8 minutes   Serves: 4

¼ pound bulk pork sausage
½ cup sliced mushrooms
6 eggs
½ cup sour cream

2 teaspoons chopped chives
¼ teaspoon salt
⅛ teaspoon pepper

1. In an 8-inch round or oval baking dish or quiche pan, cook sausage on HIGH 2 minutes, stirring once to break up any lumps. Add mushrooms. Cook 1 minute, or until sausage is no longer pink. Drain off fat.

2. In a medium bowl, beat eggs lightly. Whisk in sour cream until blended. Mix in chives, salt and pepper. Pour eggs over sausage and mushrooms. Cook on HIGH 4 to 5 minutes, stirring eggs from center toward edge several times, until eggs are just set but still moist. Serve at once.

289   THELMA'S MONDAY DIET EGGS
Prep: 5 minutes   Cook: 2 to 3 minutes   Serves: 1

The cottage cheese here keeps the eggs moist. If you prefer your eggs dry and firm, this is not the recipe for you.

2 eggs
¼ cup low-fat cottage cheese
3 tablespoons shredded low-fat Monterey jack cheese

1 scallion, chopped
Salt and pepper

1. In a 2-cup glass measure, combine eggs, cottage cheese, jack cheese, scallion and salt and pepper to taste. Whisk briefly until ingredients are well blended.

2. Cook on HIGH 2 to 3 minutes, stirring twice to keep mixture fluffy, until eggs are just cooked. They will look spongy and soft, like a soufflé.

290   THELMA'S LOW-CHOLESTEROL DIET EGGS

Prepare recipe as described above, but use egg whites only.

291   DENVER OMELET
Prep: 10 minutes   Cook: 7 to 9 minutes   Serves: 2

2 tablespoons butter
3 tablespoons diced ham
2 tablespoons diced green bell pepper
2 tablespoons minced onion

4 eggs
¼ cup milk
Salt and pepper
¼ cup shredded Cheddar cheese

1. In a 9-inch pie plate or microwave omelet pan, cook butter on HIGH 1 minute, until melted. Stir in ham, green pepper and onion. Cook on HIGH 2 minutes, stirring once.

2. In a small bowl, beat eggs with milk until blended. Season with salt and pepper to taste. Pour over ham and vegetables. Cook on HIGH 3 to 5 minutes, gently stirring eggs from center toward edge several times, until eggs are just set but still moist; do not overcook.

3. Sprinkle cheese over top and cook on HIGH 1 minute, just until cheese melts. Serve at once.

292   POACHED EGGS
Prep: 5 minutes   Cook: 30 to 45 seconds   Serves: 1

Whenever you poach eggs in a microwave, the yolk must be pierced, or it will explode. Use a small toothpick to perforate the yolk in several places; it will not run. Cook the egg in a tea cup or in a small custard cup. In either case, place it on a saucer to make it easy to remove. I also use a saucer as a cover.

If your first few efforts to produce a perfect poached egg are not to your liking, continue to cook until the egg is hard-cooked and use for salads.

1 egg	**Salt and pepper**

1. Carefully crack shell and slip egg into custard cup or tea cup without breaking yolk. Pierce yolk in several places with a toothpick.

2. Cover with a saucer and cook on MEDIUM 30 to 45 seconds, or until white appears almost set; do not overcook. Egg will continue to cook for several seconds after removing.

NOTE: Add 30 seconds for each additional egg you cook at the same time.

---

293 SCRAMBLED EGGS WITH ONIONS AND SMOKED SALMON
Prep: 5 minutes   Cook: 3 to 4 minutes   Serves: 1

Because smoked salmon is salty, I don't add any extra salt to this recipe.

2 tablespoons finely chopped onion	**Pinch of pepper**
2 teaspoons butter	**1 slice (about ½ ounce) smoked salmon, diced**
2 eggs	**1 tablespoon sour cream**
2 tablespoons milk	

1. In a small bowl, combine onion and butter. Cook on HIGH 1 to 2 minutes.

2. In another small bowl, whisk eggs, milk and pepper. Pour into eggs and onions and stir. Cook on HIGH 1 minute.

3. Add smoked salmon and stir, pushing less-cooked egg from center to edge. Cook 30 to 60 seconds longer, stirring once more, until eggs are barely set. Transfer to a plate and top with sour cream.

---

294 SCRAMBLED EGGS AND POTATOES
Prep: 5 minutes   Cook: 11 to 15 minutes   Serves: 3 to 4

1 large baking potato (about ½ pound)	**¼ cup milk**
	½ teaspoon salt
1 medium onion, chopped	**¼ teaspoon pepper**
2 tablespoons olive oil	**Dash of cayenne**
6 eggs	

1. Rinse potato but do not dry. Pierce once with fork. Wrap in paper towel and cook on HIGH 4 to 5 minutes, until tender. Let stand until cool enough to handle; peel and cut into ½-inch dice.

2. In a 9-inch pie plate or quiche dish, combine onion and oil. Cook on HIGH 3 to 4 minutes, until onion is softened. Stir in potatoes.

3. In a bowl, whisk together eggs, milk, salt, pepper and cayenne. Pour over potatoes. Cover dish with waxed paper. Cook on HIGH 2 minutes. Stir, drawing set eggs from edges toward center. Continue to cook 2 to 4 minutes longer, stirring once more, until eggs are just barely set. Let stand 1 minute before serving.

295　EGGS BENEDICT

Prep: 5 minutes　Cook: 3½ to 4½ minutes　Serves: 2 or 4

2　English muffins, toasted (in toaster) and split	4　eggs
4　thick slices Canadian bacon or boiled ham	Perfect Hollandaise Sauce (recipe follows)

1. Place muffin halves in a circle on a paper towel-lined plate. Top each muffin with a slice of Canadian bacon. Cook, uncovered, on MEDIUM 1½ to 2 minutes, until ham is hot. Transfer muffins to 4 serving plates and cover with foil to keep warm.

2. Carefully crack eggs and slip each into a small custard cup set on a saucer (for easy handling). Pierce yolks several times with a toothpick. Cover each with a saucer or microwave-safe plastic wrap. Arrange cups in a circle in microwave. Cook on MEDIUM 2 to 2½ minutes, until white appears just set.

3. Slip a poached egg on top of each piece of ham. Spoon Hollandaise sauce on top and serve.

296　PERFECT HOLLANDAISE SAUCE

Prep: 5 minutes　Cook: 1½ to 2 minutes　Makes: ⅔ cup

3　egg yolks	1　stick butter, at room temperature
2　tablespoons lemon juice	Salt and white pepper

1. In a 4-cup glass measure, whisk egg yolks lightly. Beat in lemon juice. Cut butter into 3 equal pieces. Add 1 piece of butter to egg yolk mixture. Cook, uncovered, on HIGH 30 seconds. Whisk vigorously to incorporate butter into yolks.

2. Add second piece of butter. Cook on HIGH 30 seconds. Whisk until butter is absorbed.

3. Add third piece of butter. Cook on HIGH 30 seconds. Whisk vigorously. Sauce should be smooth and thickened. Season with salt and white pepper to taste.

NOTE: To reheat, cook on MEDIUM 30 seconds; whisk well. If necessary, repeat.

297　BREAKFAST BUCKWHEAT

Prep: 3 minutes　Cook: 7 to 8 minutes　Serves: 2 to 3

1　cup whole-grain buckwheat kernels	Garnishes: butter, milk or cream, sugar, berries, peaches, bananas
1½　cups water	

1. In a 2-quart casserole, combine buckwheat and water. Cover with waxed paper and cook on HIGH 7 to 8 minutes, until water is absorbed.

2. Serve buckwheat in breakfast bowls, garnished with your choice of butter, milk, sugar and fresh fruit.

---

298   OLD-FASHIONED OATMEAL
Prep: 1 minute   Cook: 3 to 4 minutes   Serves: 1

⅓ cup regular (not instant) rolled oats
⅔ cup water

Pinch of salt
Butter, milk and brown sugar to taste

1. In a 2-cup or larger cereal bowl, combine oats, water and salt. Cook on HIGH 1½ to 2½ minutes, just until mixture comes to a rolling boil. (Watch to make sure it doesn't boil over.)

2. Stir and continue to cook 45 seconds, or just until it returns to a boil. Stir in butter and or milk and sweeten with brown sugar to taste.

---

299   MAPLE-FLAVORED SYRUP
Prep: 5 minutes   Cook: 5 to 6 minutes   Makes: about 2 cups

There's no reason not to make your own maple-flavored syrup. It takes minutes in the microwave and costs a mere fraction of the real thing.

1 cup water
1 pound brown sugar

½ teaspoon maple flavoring, or to taste

1. Place water in a 2-quart glass measure or bowl. Cook on HIGH 3 minutes, until boiling.

2. Stir in brown sugar. Cook on HIGH 2 to 3 minutes, stirring once, until sugar is dissolved. Stir in maple flavoring.

---

300   BLACKBERRY-APPLE JAM
Prep: 10 minutes   Cook: 22 minutes   Makes: 6 half-pints

1 pound blackberries
½ cup water
2 tablespoons lemon juice
5 cups sugar

1 pound tart green apples, such as Granny Smith
1 3-ounce pouch liquid pectin

1. In a 4-quart casserole, coarsely mash blackberries. Stir in water, lemon juice and sugar.

2. Peel and quarter apples. Cut out cores. Cut apples into 1-inch chunks. In a food processor or blender, coarsely chop apples; do not puree. Immediately add apples to blackberry mixture. Cook on HIGH 15 minutes, stirring several times, until sugar dissolves.

3. Add liquid pectin all at once and stir to blend well. Cook on HIGH 7 minutes, stirring twice. Remove from microwave and skim foam off top. Ladle jam into clean, hot canning jars. Cover with lids and let cool. Refrigerate or freeze.

301   CRANBERRY-PINEAPPLE JAM

Prep: 10 minutes   Cook: 20 minutes   Makes: 5 to 6 half-pints

This preserve appears thin when it is first made, but it thickens upon standing overnight.

1   **pound fresh cranberries (4 cups)**
1   **cup water**
1   **20-ounce can crushed unsweetened pineapple**

6   **cups sugar**
1   **3-ounce pouch liquid pectin**
¼   **cup lemon juice**
2   **tablespoons grated orange zest**

1. In a 4-quart casserole, combine cranberries and water. Cook on HIGH 8 minutes, stirring once.

2. Stir in pineapple and sugar. Cook on HIGH 12 minutes, stirring once or twice.

3. Stir in pectin, lemon juice and orange zest. Let cool 30 minutes. Ladle jam into clean, hot canning jars. Cover with lids and let cool completely. Refrigerate or freeze.

302   KIWIFRUIT JAM

Prep: 30 minutes   Cook: 16 minutes   Makes: about 5 half-pints

1¼   **pounds kiwifruit**
¼   **cup lemon juice**
½   **cup water**

1   **1¾- to 2-ounce package powdered pectin**
4   **cups sugar**

1. Peel fruit with a small knife or swivel-bladed vegetable peeler. Thickly slice fruit and place in a 4-quart bowl. Mash coarsely with a fork or potato masher.

2. Add lemon juice, water and pectin to kiwi. Blend well. Cook on HIGH 10 minutes, stirring every 3 minutes. Stir in sugar. Cook on HIGH 6 minutes, stirring every 2 minutes.

3. Remove jam from microwave and skim foam off top. Ladle into clean, hot canning jars. Cover with lids and let cool. Refrigerate or freeze.

303   WINTER FRUIT CONSERVE

Prep: 10 minutes   Cook: 7 to 9 minutes   Makes: 6 half-pints

A conserve usually means a preserve containing a mix of fruit and nuts. This one is made with dried fruit, so it needs no added sugar, and you can enjoy it year-round.

6   **ounces dried apricots**
6   **ounces pitted prunes**
6   **ounces golden raisins**
6   **ounces pitted dates**
½   **cup amaretto liqueur**

½   **cup water**
    Grated zest from 2 oranges
½   **cup fresh orange juice**
    Grated zest from 1 lemon
1   **tablespoon lemon juice**

1. Place all ingredients in a 2-quart bowl. Cover with a lid or a plate. Cook on HIGH 7 to 9 minutes, just until simmering.

2. Remove from microwave and ladle into 6 clean, hot half-pint jars. Cover with lids and let stand until cool. Refrigerate or freeze.

---

304 ORANGE-LEMON MARMALADE
Prep: 20 minutes   Cook: 30 minutes   Makes: 5 half-pints

3 **navel oranges**	¼ **teaspoon baking soda**
3 **lemons**	5 **cups sugar**
1½ **cups water**	1 **3-ounce pouch liquid pectin**

1. Wash oranges and lemons with soapy water. Rinse well. Dry thoroughly. Using a swivel-bladed vegetable peeler, remove colored zest from oranges and lemons. With a sharp knife, cut zest into thin shreds.

2. Holding fruit over a bowl to catch juices, use a stainless steel paring knife to cut off bitter white pith. Cut fruit into thin slices.

3. In a 5-quart casserole with lid or a glass bowl, combine fruit slices, any collected juices, water and baking soda. Stir to dissolve baking soda. Cover with lid or plate and cook on HIGH 25 minutes, stirring once or twice.

4. Stir in sugar. Cover and cook on HIGH 5 minutes, or until mixture boils hard for 2 minutes. Remove from microwave and stir in pectin. Skim off foam from top. Ladle marmalade into 5 clean, hot half-pint canning jars. Cover with lids and let cool. Refrigerate for at least 2 weeks before serving.

---

305 SPICED PEAR JAM
Prep: 30 minutes   Cook: 20 minutes   Makes: 6 half-pints

2½ **pounds ripe pears**	1 **1¾- to 2-ounce package**
3 **tablespoons lemon juice**	**powdered pectin**
1 **teaspoon ground cinnamon**	3 **cups sugar**
½ **teaspoon ground allspice**	6 **cinnamon sticks**

1. Peel and quarter pears. Cut out stems and cores. Place pears in a 4-quart bowl and mash coarsely with a fork or potato masher.

2. Stir in lemon juice, ground cinnamon, allspice and pectin. Blend well. Cook on HIGH 12 minutes, stirring every 3 minutes. Stir in sugar. Cook on HIGH 8 minutes, stirring every 3 minutes.

3. Place a cinnamon stick in each of 6 clean, hot half-pint canning jars. Ladle in pear jam; cover with lids and let cool. Refrigerate or freeze.

Chapter 13

Kids Are Cooks Too

Cooking can be fun—for kids as well as grown-ups. There's a kind of magic in that transformation of objective ingredients into a finished dish you can eat and enjoy that fascinates children and makes for great rainy-day projects. What's more, the ability to feed themselves or to prepare dinner for the whole family breeds important self-confidence along with useful skills. For moms and dads who both are working, it provides a tremendous relief to know that dinner can be served without them when necessary. With the microwave, kids can cook with no mess and most importantly, they can cook safely, with little fear of fire or burns.

All microwave ovens are designed for safety. They have double back-up mechanisms that make it impossible for the machine to operate when the door is open. Consequently, there is absolutely no danger from the microwaves. Children must be taught only a few simple rules.

1) With the exception of microwave-safe paper plates and towels, *never* put any paper or metal into the microwave. This includes twist ties and metallic butter wrappers. Remove all metal lids from jars.

2) If using plastic wrap, be sure it is microwave-safe. Plastic wraps that change composition in the oven are highly toxic.

3) Use only plates and cooking utensils designed for use in the microwave. It is a nice idea to set these aside in a separate place.

4) Always use a mitt or pot holders when removing jars or bowls containing hot ingredients, particularly liquids. The glass itself can get extremely hot.

Of course, young children should always be supervised in the kitchen.

With these few safety rules, kids of all ages can make their own Super Hero Melts or Sloppy Joe Chili. They can snack on Cheesy Bacon Sticks and Hot Chocolate. Many youngsters will enjoy the thrill of preparing for their own party with BBQ Roast Beef Dippers, Tex-Mex Cheese Dip, Pizza on a Stick and Kid's Cake, a whimsical candy popcorn creation. For the sweet tooth in every kid, there are "baked" Nutty Cocoa Cookies, Caramel Apples, Rocky Road Fudge and more.

306 CHOCOLATE-COATED COOKIES
Prep: 10 minutes   Cook: 2 to 3 minutes   Makes: 24

24 rectangular butter biscuit
   cookies
	24 miniature (¼ ounce)
	   chocolate bars
	   Colored sprinkles

1. Place 12 cookies in a circle on a 12-inch round baking dish. Place a bar of chocolate in the center of each cookie. Cook on HIGH 1 minute. (If chocolate is still partly hard, cook 30 seconds longer.)

2. With a short spatula or the back of a spoon, spread the chocolate across the top of each cookie. Decorate with sprinkles. Refrigerate until chocolate sets. Repeat with second batch.

307 CHOCOLATE-COVERED MARSHMALLOWS
Prep: 15 minutes   Cook: 1 to 2 minutes   Makes: 10

6 ounces semisweet chocolate chips	10 large marshmallows 10 walnut halves

1. In a 2-cup glass measure, melt chocolate on HIGH 1 minute. Stir until smooth. If chocolate is not completely melted, cook 30 seconds longer. Stir until completely melted and smooth.

2. With a fork, dip each marshmallow into chocolate to cover completely. Place on a plate covered with waxed paper. Swirl top and decorate each with a walnut half. Refrigerate until chocolate hardens, about 1 hour.

308 BBQ ROAST BEEF DIPPERS
Prep: 20 minutes   Cook: 2 to 3 minutes   Makes: 16 to 20

I like to serve these as appetizers, though they'd make a fine supper, accompanied by French fries or chips.

2 small carrots, peeled and cut
   into 4 × ¼-inch strips
	2 thick slices Swiss cheese, cut
	   into 4 × ¼-inch strips

1 celery rib, cut into 4 ×
   ¼-inch strips
	1 pound thinly sliced roast
	   beef

1 small red bell pepper, cut
   into 4 × ¼-inch strips
	1 18-ounce bottle barbecue
	   sauce

1. Place 2 carrot strips, 1 or 2 celery and pepper strips and 2 cheese strips near one end of each slice of roast beef. Roll up and secure with a wooden toothpick.

2. Remove metal lid from bottle of barbecue sauce. Cover with paper towel. Cook on HIGH 2½ to 3 minutes, stirring once, until hot. Using pot holders, carefully remove bottle from microwave. Stir and pour into a heatproof serving bowl. Arrange roast beef dippers around sauce. Dip into sauce and eat.

309   APPLE CRISP SUNDAE
Prep: 2 minutes   Cook: 2 to 2½ minutes   Serves: 6 to 8

1 15-ounce glass jar chunky applesauce	1 cup granola
1 8-ounce glass jar honey	1 quart vanilla ice cream Cinnamon

1. Remove metal lids from applesauce and honey. Cover with paper towels. Cook on HIGH 1 minute. Holding jars with pot holders or mitt, stir to mix. Cook, covered, 1 to 1½ minutes longer, until hot. Carefully remove jars, using mitts or pot holders. Stir again.

2. To make sundaes, layer hot applesauce, granola and then a scoop of ice cream into ice cream coupes or dessert dishes. Drizzle about 2 tablespoons honey over each sundae. Sprinkle with cinnamon and serve at once.

310   SLOPPY JOE CHILI
Prep: 5 minutes   Cook: 12 to 13 minutes   Serves: 4

Kids can make this themselves after a grown-up chops the onion and tomato. The whole family will love these, especially for a quick Saturday lunch or Sunday supper.

1 pound lean ground beef	1 tablespoon chili powder
1 small onion, chopped	½ teaspoon ground cumin
1 large tomato, chopped	4 hamburger buns, split and
1 16-ounce can chili beans in sauce	toasted, if desired

1. With clean hands, crumble beef into a 2-quart casserole. Add onion and stir to mix well. Cover with a paper towel. Cook on HIGH 3 minutes. Stir to break up any lumps of meat. Cook 2 minutes longer. Pour off any fat.

2. Add tomato, chili beans with sauce, chili powder and cumin. Stir to mix well. Cover with paper towel. Cook on HIGH 7 to 8 minutes, until hot.

3. For each serving, set 2 bun halves, cut-sides up, on a plate. Spoon chili over bun. Eat with a knife and fork.

311   KID'S CAKE
Prep: 15 minutes   Cook: 3 to 4 minutes   Serves: 10 to 12

Great for a birthday party, and kids can make it themselves. This is best eaten out of hand.

4 quarts popped corn (p. 9)	1 16-ounce package
1 cup dry-roasted peanuts	marshmallows
1 cup M & Ms	2 sticks (½ pound) butter or
1 cup assorted colored gum drops	margarine Gummy bears (optional)

1. Generously grease a 9- or 10-inch tube pan. In a 2-quart bowl, combine popcorn, peanuts, M & Ms and gum drops. Toss to blend.

2. In a 2-quart bowl, place marshmallows and butter. Cook on HIGH 3 to 4 minutes, stirring once or twice.

3. Pour marshmallow butter over popcorn mixture and stir to coat evenly. Pack into greased tube pan. Refrigerate until cooled and set. Remove from pan; place on doily-covered serving plate. Decorate with gummy bears, if desired. Cut into wedges to serve.

---

312   PIZZA ON A STICK
Prep: 10 minutes   Cook: 4 to 5 minutes   Makes: 12

6 ounces unsliced dry Italian salami (about 1½ inches in diameter)	12 6-inch wooden skewers
	1 15-ounce glass jar spaghetti sauce
½ small loaf sourdough or Italian bread	Grated Parmesan cheese

1. Using a serrated knife, cut salami into 6 slices about ½ inch thick. Cut each slice into 4 wedges. Cut bread into 2 dozen ¾-inch cubes. Onto each skewer, thread 1 piece of salami, 1 cube of bread, another piece of salami and a second cube of bread.

2. Remove metal lid from jar of spaghetti sauce. Cover with paper towel. Place jar in microwave and cook on HIGH 1½ minutes. Using a mitt or pot holder to hold jar, stir up sauce. Cover and continue to cook 1 to 1½ minutes longer, until sauce is hot. Use mitt or pot holders to carefully remove hot jar from microwave.

3. Arrange skewers on a heatproof plate like spokes on a wheel, leaving center open. Cook on HIGH 45 to 60 seconds, until just hot. Stir sauce and holding with mitt, place in center of plate. To eat, dip skewers in sauce and sprinkle on grated cheese.

---

313   CHICKEN BURGER
Prep: 5 minutes   Cook: 3 to 4 minutes   Serves: 1

Here's an easy, nutritious sandwich kids can make for themselves. Serve with carrot and celery sticks and potato chips.

½ chicken breast	1 slice tomato
1 tablespoon mild mustard	3 pickle slices
1 hamburger bun, split	1 lettuce leaf
1 tablespoon mayonnaise	

1. Place chicken, skin-side up, in a glass pie plate. Cover with waxed paper. Cook on HIGH 3 to 4 minutes, just until chicken is white throughout but still juicy. Let cool for 5 minutes. Pull off skin. With your fingers, pull chicken meat off bone and tear into strips.

2. Spread mustard over one side of hamburger bun. Spread mayonnaise over other side. Pile chicken strips on bottom half of bun. Top with tomato, pickle slices and lettuce leaf. Set top of bun on sandwich and enjoy.

314 HOT CHOCOLATE
Prep: 2 minutes   Cook: 1½ to 2½ minutes   Serves: 1

2 to 3 tablespoons chocolate
   syrup

⅔ cup milk
1 marshmallow

1. Place syrup to taste in mug. Stir in milk until blended. Cook on HIGH 1½ to 2 minutes, until hot.

2. Add marshmallow. Cook on HIGH 10 to 20 seconds, until melted. Serve hot.

315 CARAMEL APPLES
Prep: 5 minutes   Cook: 4 minutes   Makes: 5

1 14-ounce bag light caramels
2 tablespoons water
5 wooden ice cream sticks

5 medium apples, washed
   and dried, stems removed
½ cup chopped nuts

1. Remove wrappers from caramels. In a 2-quart bowl, place caramels and water. Cook on HIGH 3 to 4 minutes, just until caramels begin to melt. Stir until smooth.

2. Push wooden sticks into center of apples from bottom. Dip each apple into hot caramel, turning to coat completely.

3. Spread out nuts on waxed paper. Roll each apple in nuts until lightly coated. Place apples on buttered waxed paper to cool and set.

NOTE: If the caramel hardens before all the apples are dipped, reheat on HIGH for 30 to 45 seconds and continue.

316 CHEESY BACON STICKS
Prep: 10 minutes   Cook: 5 to 7 minutes   Makes: 6

3 slices wafer-thin bacon
6 crisp bread sticks

1 8-ounce glass jar cheese
   sauce

1. Cut bacon slices in half lengthwise. Wind each bacon strip around the top two-thirds of a bread stick, barber pole fashion. The bacon will adhere by itself.

2. Remove metal lid from jar of cheese sauce. Put jar in microwave and cook on MEDIUM 1½ minutes. Using a mitt or pot holder to hold the jar, stir the sauce. Continue to cook 1 to 2 minutes longer, or until hot. Carefully use the mitt or pot holder to remove the jar; it will be hot.

3. Place 2 folded sheets of paper towel on a paper plate. Set bacon sticks in a single row on towel. Cover with another paper towel. Cook on HIGH 2 to 3½ minutes, just until bacon is crisp. Set jar in center of serving dish. Arrange bacon sticks around jar, with the plain ends facing out. Dip each stick in hot cheese sauce and eat.

317   BAKED BEANS WITH MAPLE SYRUP
Prep: 5 minutes   Cook: 4 to 7 minutes   Serves: 1 to 2

Doctor up a can of beans for a great after-school snack or side dish.

3 slices bacon	1 teaspoon maple syrup
1 8-ounce can baked beans	

1. On a paper plate, place a double layer of paper towels. Set bacon slices in a single layer and cover with another paper towel. Cook on HIGH 2 to 4 minutes, until bacon is crisp.

2. Open can of beans; spoon beans into microwave-safe bowl. Add maple syrup to beans and crumble bacon on top. Stir to mix in. Cook on HIGH 2 to 2½ minutes, until hot. Stir before eating.

318   TEX-MEX CHEESE DIP
Prep: 2 minutes   Cook: 5 to 7 minutes   Makes: about 3 cups

1 12-ounce glass jar thick and chunky salsa, mild or hot, to your taste	1 16-ounce glass jar pasteurized process cheese spread Tortilla chips

1. Remove metal lids from glass jars of salsa and cheese spread. Place jar of salsa in microwave. Cover with paper towel. Cook on HIGH 2 minutes. Using mitt or pot holder to hold jar, stir to mix salsa. Continue to cook 1 to 2 minutes, or until salsa is hot. Using mitts or pot holders, remove from microwave and set aside.

2. Place jar of cheese spread in microwave. Cover with a paper towel. Cook on HIGH 1 minute. Using a mitt or pot holder to hold jar, stir cheese. Cook 1 to 2 minutes longer, or just until hot. Using mitts or pot holders, remove from microwave.

3. Again using mitt or pot holders, dump hot jars of salsa and cheese spread into a heatproof serving bowl. Stir well to mix. Serve at once, with a basket of tortilla chips on the side for dipping.

319   MELTED CHEESE SANDWICH
Prep: 5 minutes   Cook: 45 to 60 seconds   Serves: 1

2 slices of bread, white or whole wheat	2 slices American cheese
	1 large slice tomato

1. Toast bread in toaster.

2. Place toast slices side by side on a paper plate. Place a slice of cheese on each piece of toast. Cook, uncovered, on HIGH 45 seconds, or just until cheese is almost melted.

3. Sandwich tomato between two slices of toast with melted cheese and enjoy.

320 TUNA NOODLE CASSEROLE WITH POTATO CHIPS
Prep: 5 minutes   Cook: 15 minutes   Serves: 4

1 12-ounce package egg
   noodles
2 cups water
1 6½-ounce can tuna
1 10¾-ounce can condensed
   cream of mushroom soup

1 10-ounce package frozen
   peas
½ cup crushed potato chips

1. Put noodles and water in a 2-quart casserole that has a cover. Cover with lid and cook on HIGH 5 minutes. Stir gently. Cook 5 minutes longer.

2. Open can of tuna and drain off water or oil. With a fork, break up tuna into large flakes. Add tuna to noodles. Add can of soup and frozen peas. Cover and cook on HIGH 3 minutes. Stir and cook 2 minutes longer. Sprinkle potato chips over the top of the casserole and serve hot.

321 HOT DOG BEAN BURRITO
Prep: 5 minutes   Cook: 1 to 1½ minutes   Serves: 1

1 flour tortilla (8 or 10 inches)
½ cup refried beans
1 hot dog, thinly sliced into
   rounds

2 tablespoons shredded
   Cheddar cheese
Taco sauce (optional)

1. Place tortilla flat on counter. Pile refried beans in center. Scatter hot dog over beans and top with cheese. Drizzle with a little taco sauce if desired. Fold over right side of tortilla. Then fold left side over to cover filling. Roll up from the bottom.

2. Place burrito on a plate. Cover with a paper towel. Cook on HIGH 1 to 1½ minutes, or until hot. Let stand 1 minute before eating.

322 CHILI CON CARNE FOR KIDS
Prep: 5 minutes   Cook: 3 minutes   Serves: 1

Look for small vacuum-packed cans of chili in your market. They are a perfect size for a meal or a hearty snack

½ cup tortilla chips
1 7-ounce can chili con carne
   with beans
½ cup shredded Cheddar
   cheese

2 tablespoons chopped
   scallion (optional)

1. With your fingers, crumble tortilla chips into a 2-cup cereal bowl. Spoon chili con carne with beans over chips. Cook on HIGH 2 minutes. Stir chili.

2. Sprinkle cheese on top. Cook on HIGH 30 to 45 seconds, just until cheese melts. Sprinkle scallions on top if you like them. Eat while hot.

323   QUICK FETTUCCINE WITH SAUSAGES

Prep: 10 minutes   Cook: 7 to 9 minutes   Serves: 3 to 4

½   pound fettuccine
¾   pound sweet Italian
        sausages, sliced
1   small green bell pepper,
        chopped

½   cup chopped onion
1   15-ounce glass jar spaghetti
        sauce
    Grated Parmesan cheese

1. In a large pot of boiling salted water, cook fettuccine according to package directions. Drain and place in large bowl. (Parents may wish to do this for small children.)

2. Meanwhile, in a 4-cup casserole, place sausages, green pepper and onion. Cover and cook on HIGH 3 minutes. Stir and cook 2 to 3 minutes longer, until sausages are no longer pink. Pour off fat and juices.

3. Remove metal lid from jar of spaghetti sauce. Cover jar with paper towel and cook on MEDIUM 1 minute. Holding jar with pot holders, stir. Cook 1 to 1½ minutes longer, until sauce is hot. Using pot holders, carefully remove jar. Stir again.

4. Pour sausage mixture and hot spaghetti sauce over fettuccine. Toss to coat. Pass Parmesan cheese on the side.

---

324   NUTTY COCOA COOKIES

Prep: 20 minutes   Cook: 8 to 9 minutes   Makes: about 30

It's a fact that cookies taste best when baked in a hot, dry conventional oven. But for kids, the ease and safety of a microwave is unbeatable.

1½   sticks (6 ounces) butter or
        margarine, at room
        temperature
1¼   cups sugar
1   egg
1¾   cups flour

¼   cup unsweetened cocoa
        powder
1   teaspoon baking powder
½   teaspoon salt
1   teaspoon vanilla extract
½   cup chopped pecans

1. In a medium bowl, combine butter, ¾ cup sugar and egg. Beat with electric hand mixer until light and fluffy, about 2 minutes.

2. In another bowl, put flour, cocoa powder, baking powder and salt. Stir or whisk gently to blend ingredients. Add flour-cocoa mixture to butter mixture. Beat just until blended. Stir in vanilla and nuts.

3. Pinch off pieces of dough and roll into 1-inch balls. Put remaining ½ cup sugar on a plate and roll balls in sugar to coat. Place on a flat dish and cover with plastic wrap. Refrigerate until ready to bake. Bake all at once in batches, or just a few at a time for a snack.

4. To bake, place balls of dough about 1½ inches apart on a paper plate. Flatten tops slightly with back of a spoon. Bake on HIGH until cookies are puffed: about 1 minute for 2 cookies, 1 minute 15 seconds for 4 cookies, 2 minutes for 8 cookies, 3 minutes for 12 cookies. For crispier cookies, cook a few seconds longer. Let cool slightly before removing from plate. Transfer to rack to cool completely. Cookies will firm up as they stand.

325   SUPER HERO MELT
Prep: 5 minutes   Cook: 45 to 60 seconds   Serves: 2

1 **12-ounce loaf of crusty Italian or French bread**
4 **slices salami**
2 **slices ham**
2 **slices bologna**
2 **slices American cheese**

2 **slices Monterey jack cheese**
   Mayonnaise and mild mustard
1 **large tomato, sliced**
   Lettuce
   Sweet pickle slices

1. Cut bread in half crosswise; split each half horizontally. Layer the bottom of each bread half with salami, ham, bologna, American cheese and jack cheese.

2. Place paper towel on a paper plate. Place open sandwiches on towel. Cook on HIGH 45 to 60 seconds, or until cheeses begin to melt.

3. Spread mayonnaise and/or mustard on top halves of bread. Place tomato, lettuce and pickles on top of melted cheese. Top off sandwiches with bread and serve.

326   TOASTED PUMPKIN SEEDS
Prep: 20 minutes   Cook: 2 to 4 minutes   Makes: about 1 cup

1 **pumpkin**   **Coarse (kosher) salt**

1. Scoop out seeds from pumpkin with your hands and large spoon. With clean hands, pull off large pieces of pumpkin clinging to seeds.

2. Spread out seeds in a single layer on a plate. (If there are too many, do this in 2 batches.) Sprinkle with coarse salt to taste. Cook on HIGH 1 minute; stir. Cook 30 seconds; stir. Cook 1 to 2 minutes longer, or until seeds are dry and slightly crisp.

327   ROCKY ROAD FUDGE
Prep: 5 minutes   Cook: 2 minutes   Makes: about 1½ pounds

1 **pound confectioners' sugar**
1 **cup unsweetened cocoa powder**
⅓ **cup milk**
1 **stick butter or margarine**

1 **tablespoon vanilla extract**
1 **cup walnuts or pecans, coarsely chopped**
1½ **cups miniature marshmallows**

1. Butter an 8-inch square or round baking pan (this one doesn't have to be microwaveable).

2. In a 2-quart glass bowl, place confectioners' sugar, cocoa powder, milk and butter. Cook on HIGH 2 minutes.

3. Remove bowl from microwave, add vanilla and stir to blend well. Add nuts and marshmallows and stir to combine. Immediately pour into greased pan. Refrigerate until set before cutting into squares.

328 CHOCOLATE SYRUP

Prep: 2 minutes   Cook: 5 minutes   Makes: about 2 cups

4 ounces (4 squares)
   unsweetened chocolate,
   broken in half
1 cup water

1 cup sugar
½ teaspoon vanilla extract
⅛ teaspoon cinnamon
   (optional)

1. In a 4-cup glass measure, place chocolate and water. Cook on HIGH 4 minutes, stirring twice. Stir until chocolate is completely blended and smooth. If any hard bits remain, cook 30 to 60 seconds longer until completely melted.

2. Stir sugar into chocolate. Cook on HIGH 1 minute, stirring once. Stir in vanilla; add cinnamon if desired. Let cool, pour into a jar, cover and store in refrigerator for up to 3 months.

329 PLAY DOUGH

Prep: 5 minutes   Cook: 4 to 6 minutes   Makes: about 2 cups

Here's a fun project that's magic in the microwave.

1 pound baking soda
1 cup cornstarch

1¼ cups cold water
3 drops food coloring

1. In a 2-quart glass measure or bowl, combine all of the ingredients. Stir until blended and smooth. Cook on MEDIUM 4 to 6 minutes, whisking briskly once every minute, until mixture is the consistency of moist mashed potatoes.

2. Whisk well, turn out onto a plate and cover with a damp cloth. Let stand until cool enough to handle. Pat gently until smooth, and it's ready to play.

Chapter 14

Desserts

We use the microwave for so many things, but too often, we forget about dessert. In fact, the microwave is an extremely useful tool for poaching fruit in a flash, reducing sugar syrups quickly and safely, melting butter and melting chocolate.

When melting chocolate in the microwave, keep in mind that it will not melt until it is stirred. The key to when it is ready is visual: it will turn shiny. Cooking beyond that point can cause the chocolate to scorch. As soon as it is shiny, remove it from the microwave and stir. Then the chocolate will take on a familiar melted appearance.

It may surprise you to see so many pies in this book. While baking is not its forte—cakes and pastry do better in a hot, dry conventional oven—the microwave can produce a fine pie if the crust and filling are prepared separately before being combined. The pie shell will be very pale. If you prefer a browner, more caramelized crust, you always have the option of baking the crust in a conventional oven and then adding the filling.

Following is a collection of some of my favorite microwave desserts. There is an Old-Fashioned Blueberry Pie, Apple Pie à la Mode and Raspberry Custard Tart, just for starters. For banana lovers, there is a Banana Cream Pie and a cake baked in a ring. For lemon lovers, there is a Sunny Lemon Tart, Lemony Ice Cream and Chocolate Lemon Wafers. And speaking of chocolate—how about brownies, plain and glazed, Chocolate Velvet, bittersweet Chocolate Truffle Torte, Black and White Chocolate Terrine and lots more.

Homemade candy is quick, easy and fuss-free in the microwave. For eating or gift-giving, there are recipes like Almond-Pecan Buttermilk Fudge, Mocha Taffy, White Chocolate Almond Bark and Chocolate-Covered Strawberries. Make your own sauces—chocolate, caramel, marshmallow, raspberry—in minutes in the microwave. Store them in glass jars and reheat in the microwave just before serving.

330 LEMON CURD
Prep: 5 minutes   Cook: 6½ to 7½ minutes   Makes: about 1 cup

Use as a filling for tarts or layer cakes, as an easy lemon pie with meringue topping or as a spread for biscuits or toast.

1 stick butter	**1½ teaspoons grated lemon zest**
½ cup sugar	**3 eggs**
⅓ cup lemon juice	

1. In a 4-cup glass measure, place butter, sugar, lemon juice and lemon zest. Cook on HIGH 4 minutes; stir.

2. In a small bowl, beat eggs until blended. Gradually whisk about ⅓ cup hot lemon mixture into eggs to warm them. Whisk eggs into remaining lemon mixture. Cook on HIGH 1½ minutes. Whisk until smooth. Continue to cook 1 to 2 minutes, until thickened. Whisk until smooth. Cover and refrigerate for up to 3 days.

331 KAHLUA FUDGE TOPPING
Prep: 5 minutes   Cook: 4 minutes   Makes: 2½ cups

1 cup unsweetened cocoa powder	**1 cup heavy cream**
⅔ cup granulated sugar	**¼ cup Kahlua**
½ cup (packed) light brown sugar	**1 stick butter**
	1½ teaspoons vanilla extract

1. In a 2-quart glass measure or bowl, combine cocoa, granulated sugar and brown sugar. Stir in cream and Kahlua. Add butter. Cook on HIGH 2 minutes.

2. Stir sauce well. Cook on HIGH 2 minutes longer. Stir in vanilla. Serve warm or let cool. Store in covered jar in refrigerator. To reheat, remove lid and cook on MEDIUM 2 to 3 minutes before serving.

332 THICK AND CREAMY CARAMEL SAUCE
Prep: 5 minutes   Cook: 9 to 10 minutes   Makes: about 2 cups

1 cup heavy cream	**3 cups miniature marshmallows**
1¼ cups (packed) light brown sugar	**4 tablespoons butter**
¼ cup coffee liqueur, such as Kahlua or Tia Maria	**1½ teaspoons vanilla extract**

1. In a 2-quart glass measure or bowl, combine cream, brown sugar, coffee liqueur and marshmallows. Cook on HIGH 9 to 10 minutes, stirring once or twice, until a microwave-safe candy thermometer registers 224 degrees, or until a small amount dropped in cold water forms a soft ball.

2. Add butter and vanilla. Stir until blended. Let caramel sauce cool. Pour into covered jars and store in refrigerator. To reheat, place amount desired in microwaveable pitcher and cook on MEDIUM about 1 minute per cup.

333 SUNNY LEMON TART
Prep: 10 minutes   Cook: 9 to 11 minutes   Serves: 6 to 8

A refreshing dessert for lemon lovers. If you prefer a browner crust, pre-bake the pie shell in your conventional oven at 325 degrees for about 12 minutes; then begin the microwave recipe at Step 2.

1 **cup flour**	2 **teaspoons cornstarch**
½ **cup confectioners' sugar**	½ **teaspoon baking powder**
1 **stick butter, cut up**	2 **teaspoons minced lemon**
2 **whole eggs**	**zest**
2 **egg yolks**	⅓ **cup lemon juice**
1 **cup granulated sugar**	

1. In a medium bowl, combine flour, confectioners' sugar and butter. Pinch and rub with your fingers until crumbly like oatmeal. Pat dough into 9-inch pie plate. Cook on HIGH 5 to 6 minutes, until crisp.

2. In another medium bowl, whisk together whole eggs and egg yolks until blended. Gradually whisk in granulated sugar and beat until mixture forms a slowly dissolving ribbon. Whisk in cornstarch, baking powder, lemon zest and lemon juice until well blended.

3. Scrape lemon filling into pie shell. Cook, uncovered, on HIGH 4 to 5 minutes, just until center appears set. Turn dish if pie appears to be cooking unevenly. Let cool completely. Sprinkle with additional confectioners' sugar just before serving.

334 CHOCOLATE-COVERED STRAWBERRIES
Prep: 5 minutes   Cook: 2 to 3 minutes   Makes: 15

If you have any chocolate left over after dipping the strawberries, let it cool until hardened, wrap well and save for another time.

½ **pound semisweet or white chocolate**	15 **large strawberries, with stems if available**

1. Place chocolate in a 4-cup glass measure. Cook on MEDIUM 2 to 3 minutes, just until chocolate appears shiny. Stir until chocolate is melted and smooth.

2. One at a time, hold a strawberry by stem and dip into melted chocolate to coat about ⅔ of berry. Place in candy cups or on waxed paper and let stand until set. If chocolate does not harden after 10 minutes, refrigerate until set.

335 CREAMY VANILLA PECANS
Prep: 5 minutes   Cook: 7 minutes   Makes: about 1 pound

Serve these lovely sweets after dinner with coffee or for a sweet tea.

1½ **cups sugar**	3 **cups pecan halves**
½ **cup sour cream**	2 **teaspoons vanilla extract**

1. In a 2-quart glass measure or bowl, combine sugar and sour cream. Blend well. Cook on HIGH 7 minutes, stirring twice.

2. Add nuts and vanilla. Stir until mixture turns creamy. Quickly turn out onto a baking sheet and let cool. When candy is crisp, break into pieces. Store in airtight container.

---

336 OLD-FASHIONED BLUEBERRY PIE
Prep: 10 minutes   Cook: 5 to 7 minutes   Serves: 6 to 8

⅓ cup flour
1 tablespoon lemon juice
½ cup plus 3 tablespoons cold
  water
¾ cup sugar

5 cups fresh or dry-pack
  frozen blueberries
1 teaspoon cinnamon
Sweet Pie Crust (recipe
  follows)

1. In a 2-quart glass measure or bowl, combine flour, lemon juice and 3 tablespooons cold water. Stir to make a smooth paste. Set aside.

2. In a 4-cup glass measure, combine sugar, remaining ½ cup water and 1 cup blueberries. Cook on HIGH 5 to 7 minutes, until mixture comes to a rolling boil and boils for 1 minute. (Watch to be sure it does not boil over.) Pour boiling blueberries into flour paste and stir until thickened. Mix in cinnamon. Set aside until cool.

3. Add remaining 4 cups blueberries to thickened blueberry mixture and stir gently to blend well without breaking too many of the berries. Turn blueberry filling into prebaked pie shell. Refrigerate if desired. Serve chilled or at room temperature, with sweetened whipped cream or vanilla ice cream.

---

337 SWEET PIE CRUST
Prep: 10 minutes   Cook: 6 to 7 minutes   Makes: 1 9-inch shell

1¼ cups all-purpose flour
½ cup cake flour
⅔ cup butter-flavored
  vegetable shortening

2 tablespoons sugar
½ teaspoon salt
¼ to ⅓ cup ice-cold milk
1 egg, beaten

1. In a food processor, combine all-purpose flour, cake flour, shortening, sugar and salt. Turn the machine quickly on and off until the mixture resembles coarse meal. Gradually add the milk through the feed tube while pulsing just until dough begins to mass together. (Or cut shortening into dough with pastry blender or two knives.) Turn out dough and gather into a ball. Flatten into a 6-inch disk; wrap in plastic wrap and refrigerate for 30 minutes.

2. Roll out dough between 2 pieces of plastic wrap to a round about ⅛ inch thick. Remove top sheet of plastic wrap and transfer dough to 9-inch pie plate or quiche dish. Peel off remaining wrap and fit dough into dish without stretching. Trim excess dough to about ½ inch from edge. Fold excess under and crimp edge decoratively.

3. Brush egg over rim and sides of dough. With a fork, prick the pie shell all over. Cook on HIGH 6 to 7 minutes, until shell looks dry and feels crisp to the touch. Remove pie plate with pot holders; it will be hot. Set aside to cool.

338   BANANA RING CAKE
Prep: 10 minutes   Cook: 7 to 7½ minutes   Serves: 8

4   tablespoons butter, at room
    temperature
½   cup sugar
1   egg
3   very ripe medium bananas,
    mashed
1   teaspoon vanilla extract

¼   cup milk
1½   cups flour
½   teaspoon baking soda
½   teaspoon salt
½   teaspoon lemon juice
½   cup chopped walnuts

1. In a large mixing bowl, combine butter, sugar, egg, bananas, vanilla and milk. Whisk to blend well. Combine flour, baking soda and salt. Stir into banana mixture. Mix in lemon juice and nuts.

2. Turn batter into a 4-cup ring mold. Cook on HIGH 7 to 7½ minutes, or until cake begins to pull away slightly from sides of pan. Turn dish if cake appears to be cooking unevenly. Set cake pan on a flat, heat-resistant surface and let set and cool thoroughly before serving.

339   CHOCOLATE CHIP-PECAN BROWNIES
Prep: 10 minutes   Cook: 6½ to 7½ minutes   Makes: about 20

2   ounces (2 squares)
    unsweetened baking
    chocolate
1   stick butter
2   eggs
¾   cup sugar
½   cup flour

2   teaspoons vanilla extract
1   teaspoon baking powder
¼   teaspoon salt
1   cup coarsely chopped
    pecans
1   cup chocolate chips

1. In a 1-quart bowl, cook unsweetened chocolate and butter on HIGH 1½ minutes, or until butter is just melted. Stir to melt chocolate. Blend well.

2. In another bowl, beat eggs. Add melted chocolate and butter, sugar, flour, vanilla, baking powder and salt. Blend well. Stir in pecans and chocolate chips. Turn batter into 9-inch pie plate or quiche dish.

3. Cook on HIGH 5 to 6 minutes, until brownies begin to pull away from side of pan. Cake will be moist but will firm up as it cools. Let cool completely before cutting into squares.

340   CHOCOLATE GLAZED BROWNIES
Prep: 10 minutes   Cook: 8½ to 10 minutes   Makes: about 20

Chocolate-Chip Pecan
    Brownies (recipe above)
4   ounces semisweet chocolate

1   stick unsalted butter
2   tablespoons honey

1. Make brownies as described in recipe. Let cool slightly, but do not cut.

2. In a 4-cup glass measure, combine chocolate, butter and honey. Cook on MEDIUM 2 to 2½ minutes. Stir until chocolate is completely melted and

glaze is smooth. Spread glaze over brownie cake. Let cool completely; cut into squares.

---

341   BANANA CREAM PIE
Prep: 10 minutes   Cook: 10 minutes   Serves: 6 to 8

½ cup plus 2 tablespoons sugar
¼ cup cornstarch
2 tablespoons flour
¼ teaspoon salt
4 egg yolks
2 cups milk
1 cup half-and-half or light cream

1 tablespoon butter
1½ teaspoons vanilla extract
1 9-inch Prebaked Pie Shell (recipe follows)
3 medium bananas, sliced into rounds
1 cup heavy cream

1. In a small bowl, combine ½ cup sugar, cornstarch, flour and salt. Stir to mix. In a 2-quart bowl, lightly beat egg yolks. Whisk in milk and half-and-half. Add dry ingredients and mix well until cornstarch is completely dissolved. Cook on HIGH 10 minutes, stirring every 2 minutes.

2. Add butter and vanilla to custard and blend well. Pour 1 cup of custard into pie shell. Layer half the banana slices over custard. Cover with 1 cup more custard and layer on remaining bananas. Pour remaining custard on top. Cover and refrigerate 2 to 3 hours, until set.

3. Beat heavy cream with remaining 2 tablespoons sugar. Cover pie with whipped cream. Swirl top decoratively with back of spoon. Serve chilled.

---

342   9-INCH PREBAKED PIE SHELL
Prep: 20 minutes   Cook: 6 to 7 minutes   Makes: 1 9-inch shell

This crust can be made a day ahead and set aside at room temperature before filling.

1½ cups flour
½ teaspoon salt
⅓ cup vegetable shortening

3 tablespoons butter
3 to 4 tablespoons ice water
1 egg, beaten

1. In a food processor, combine flour, salt, shortening and butter. Turn machine quickly on and off until mixture resembles coarse meal. (Or cut in with 2 knives or pastry blender.) Add 3 tablespoons ice water and pulse just until dough begins to mass together. If too dry, add remaining 1 tablespoon water and pulse briefly. Turn out dough and gather into a ball. Flatten into a 6-inch disk and wrap in plastic wrap. Refrigerate for at least 20 minutes.

2. Roll out dough to a round about ⅛ inch thick. Fit dough into a 9-inch microwave pie plate or quiche dish without stretching. Trim off excess dough to about ½ inch of edge. Fold excess dough under and crimp edge decoratively.

3. Brush egg over rim and sides of pie shell. With a fork, prick pastry all over. Cook on HIGH 6 to 7 minutes, until shell looks dry and feels crisp to the touch. Use pot holders to remove pie plate; it will be hot. Set aside to cool.

343 MOCHA TAFFY

Prep: 10 minutes   Cook: 15 to 20 minutes   Makes: about 1 pound

This is a dark, rich candy that is a cinch to make in your microwave. Because I use corn syrup instead of sugar, there is no stirring.

2 cups dark corn syrup	¼ teaspoon salt
¼ cup brewed strong coffee	1 tablespoon butter
2 ounces (2 squares) unsweetened chocolate	1 teaspoon vanilla extract

1. Generously grease an 8-inch square baking dish. Set aside. In a 2-quart glass measure, combine corn syrup, coffee, chocolate and salt. Mix to blend well. Cook on HIGH 15 to 20 minutes, until microwave-safe candy thermometer registers 255 degrees, or until a small amount dropped into a glass of cold water forms a soft ball.

2. Add butter and vanilla. Stir just until blended. Pour into greased pan. Set pan on a rack and let stand until taffy is cool enough to handle. Grease hands well with oil or butter and pull taffy until satiny, elastic and lighter in color. Cut into pieces. Wrap in waxed paper or colored cellophane. Twist ends closed or tie with ribbon. Store in an airtight container.

NOTE: If taffy cools and becomes too hard to pull, return to microwave and cook on HIGH 1 minute, or until softened.

344 WHITE CHOCOLATE ALMOND BARK

Prep: 5 minutes   Cook: 8 to 10 minutes   Makes: about 1¼ pounds

1 cup whole shelled almonds	1 pound white chocolate, broken into pieces
1 teaspoon butter	

1. Line a large baking sheet with waxed paper. Place almonds and butter in a 9-inch pie plate. Cook on HIGH 3 minutes. Stir and continue to cook 2 to 3 minutes, until almonds are lightly toasted. Set aside to cool slightly.

2. Place white chocolate in a 4-cup glass measure. Cook on MEDIUM 3 to 4 minutes, just until ends appear softened and chocolate looks shiny. Do not overcook. Stir with metal spoon until completely melted and smooth. Stir toasted almonds into melted white chocolate. Turn out onto baking sheet and spread evenly. Let cool until set. Break into pieces.

345 RASPBERRY CUSTARD TART

Prep: 5 minutes   Cook: 8 minutes   Serves: 10 to 12

¾ cup plus 1 tablespoon sugar	1 11-inch Prebaked Tart Shell (see NOTE)
¼ cup flour	
1½ cups milk	3 cups fresh raspberries
4 egg yolks	½ cup currant jelly
1 teaspoon vanilla extract	

1. In a 2-quart glass measure or bowl, combine ¾ cup sugar, flour, milk and egg yolks. Whisk to blend well. Cook on HIGH 7 minutes, stirring every 2 minutes, until custard begins to thicken. Stir in vanilla. Pour custard into prepared pie shell. Cover with waxed paper and let cool. Refrigerate for 2 hours, until well chilled.

2. In a food processor or blender, puree ½ cup raspberries with 1 tablespoon sugar. Spread puree over custard. Arrange remaining raspberries on top.

3. Put jelly in a 1-cup glass measure. Cook on HIGH 45 seconds, or until jelly melts. Brush glaze over raspberries. Refrigerate for up to 3 hours before serving.

NOTE: This recipe calls for an 11-inch prebaked pie shell. Either make a conventional pastry shell in an 11-inch tart pan with removable bottom, or fit pastry for 9-inch microwave shell into 11-inch quiche pan and bake as directed.

---

346   SOUTHERN PECAN PIE
Prep: 10 minutes   Cook: 11 to 13 minutes   Serves: 6 to 8

4 tablespoons butter	**3 eggs, lightly beaten**
½ cup granulated sugar	**1½ teaspoons vanilla extract**
½ cup (packed) brown sugar	**2 cups pecan halves**
1 cup dark corn syrup	**1 9-inch Prebaked Pie Shell**
1 tablespoon molasses	**(p. 163)**

1. In a 2-quart glass measure or bowl, cook butter on HIGH 1 to 2 minutes, until melted. Stir in granulated sugar, brown sugar, corn syrup, molasses, eggs and vanilla. Whisk to blend well. Stir in pecans. Pour into pie shell.

2. Cook on MEDIUM 11 to 13 minutes, turning dish if pie appears to be cooking unevenly, until filling begins to set in center. Let cool before serving. Pie will set upon standing.

---

347   FRUIT KEBABS WITH AMARETTO AND HOT FUDGE SAUCE
Prep: 15 minutes   Cook: 3½ to 4½ minutes   Makes: 12 kebabs

1 large firm banana, cut into ½-inch slices	**24 firm medium strawberries**
24 pineapple chunks, fresh or canned unsweetened	**2 to 3 tablespoons amaretto liqueur**
	1 19-ounce glass jar hot fudge

1. Using a dozen 6-inch wooden skewers, thread a banana slice, a pineapple chunk and a strawberry on each. Repeat so that there are 2 of each on each skewer. Arrange skewers like spokes of a wheel on a large round platter; leave the center open. Drizzle amaretto over fruit.

2. Place fudge sauce in a glass bowl. Cook on MEDIUM 2 minutes. Stir and continue to cook 1½ to 2½ minutes longer, just until fudge sauce is hot. Using pot holders, carefully transfer bowl of fudge sauce from microwave to center of platter. Dip and eat.

348   CHOCOLATE TRUFFLE TORTE

Prep: 15 minutes   Cook: 6 minutes   Serves: 12 to 16

1 13-ounce package pecan
   shortbread cookies
2 tablespoons brown sugar
¾ cup chopped pecans
1½ sticks (6 ounces) butter, at
   room temperature
4 cups semisweet chocolate
   chips

2 ounces (2 squares)
   unsweetened chocolate,
   cut into pieces
¼ cup sugar
2½ cups heavy cream
1 tablespoon vanilla extract
2 egg yolks, beaten
   Whipped cream

1. In a food processor or blender, combine cookies, brown sugar and pecans. Grind into crumbs. Dump crumbs into a medium bowl. Place 6 tablespoons butter in a small glass bowl or custard cup and cook on HIGH 1 minute, or until melted. Drizzle melted butter over crumbs and stir to moisten evenly. Press into bottom of a 10-inch springform pan, easing crust about ⅓ way up sides. Refrigerate crust.

2. In a 4-quart bowl, combine semisweet and unsweetened chocolate, sugar, heavy cream and vanilla. Cook on HIGH 5 minutes, stirring once. Remove from microwave and stir until chocolate filling is smooth and thick. Beat in egg yolks and remaining 6 tablespoons butter until smooth and well blended.

3. Turn chocolate filling into pecan crust. Cover and refrigerate or freeze until very firm, at least 4 hours or overnight. Run knife around rim to loosen. Remove side of springform and cut torte into very thin slices. Serve with whipped cream on the side.

349   BLACK AND WHITE CHOCOLATE TERRINE

Prep: 20 minutes   Cook: 3 to 6 minutes   Serves: 10 to 12

This sumptuous dessert can be made ahead and frozen. It is most attractive served with raspberry sauce. Serve both or freeze one for another occasion.

5 ounces white chocolate,
   broken into pieces
15 ounces semisweet chocolate,
   broken into pieces
4 tablespoons unsalted butter

1 cup heavy cream
1 teaspoon vanilla extract
2 recipes Raspberry Sauce
   (recipe follows)

1. Butter two 5¾ × 3 ½ × 2-inch mini-loaf pans; metal or aluminum foil are fine. Line with plastic wrap, allowing some extra on the short sides.

2. In a 4-cup glass measure, place white chocolate. Melt on MEDIUM 1 to 2 minutes, just until chocolate turns shiny. Stir chocolate until melted. Divide white chocolate equally between prepared pans; spread to cover bottom evenly. Cover pans and place level in freezer.

3. In another 4-cup glass measure, place semisweet chocolate and butter. Cook on MEDIUM 2 to 4 minutes, just until chocolate turns shiny. Stir until melted and smooth.

4. In a mixing bowl, whip cream until soft peaks form. Beat in vanilla. Fold in melted chocolate about ⅓ at a time. Divide chocolate cream between chilled pans. Cover and freeze until firm, about 3 hours. Unmold and using a hot, wet serrated knife, cut terrine into ½ inch thick slices. Spoon raspberry sauce around each serving.

350   RASPBERRY SAUCE

Prep: 5 minutes   Cook: 5 minutes   Makes: about 1¼ cups

Serve over fruit, ice cream, pound cake and chocolate mousse cake.

1 **10-ounce package frozen raspberries**	2 **tablespoons raspberry liqueur, such as**
1 **teaspoon cornstarch**	**Chambord or 1 tablespoon each lemon juice and water**

1. Place raspberries in a 4-cup glass measure. Cook on HIGH 2 to 3 minutes to defrost. Break up berries slightly with spoon. Sieve to remove seeds if desired.

2. Dissolve cornstarch in liqueur or diluted lemon juice. Stir into berries. Cook on HIGH, stirring once, 1½ to 2 minutes, until sauce thickens and clears.

351   APPLE PIE A LA MODE

Prep: 15 minutes   Cook: 15 to 20 minutes   Serves: 6 to 8

To make the perfect fruit pie in the microwave, cook the crust and the filling separately. For even greater convenience, you can use a store-bought premade shell and bake it in the microwave.

6 **large, tart cooking apples, such as Granny Smith**	2 **tablespoons dark corn syrup**
1 **tablespoon lemon juice**	4 **tablespoons butter**
3 **tablespoons flour**	1 **9-inch Prebaked Pie Shell (p. 163)**
½ **cup sugar**	1 **quart vanilla ice cream**
1 **teaspoon ground cinnamon**	

1. Peel and quarter apples. Cut out cores. Cut apple quarters into ½-inch-thick wedges. As apples are cut, place in a 2-quart bowl and toss with lemon juice to prevent discoloration.

2. Sprinkle flour, sugar and cinnamon over apples. Toss to coat and mix evenly. Add corn syrup and stir to mix. Dot with butter. Cover with a paper towel. Cook on HIGH 15 to 20 minutes, stirring gently with wooden spoon every 5 minutes, until apple filling has thickened. Let cool slightly.

3. Spoon apple filling into pie shell and let cool completely. Slice into wedges and top each with a scoop of vanilla ice cream.

352 INSTANT OLD-FASHIONED CHOCOLATE PUDDING

Prep: 5 minutes   Cook: 7 to 10 minutes   Serves: 4

The best place to cook puddings is in your microwave. No scorched pans, and no constant stirring.

⅔ cup sugar
⅓ cup unsweetened cocoa
    powder
3 tablespoons cornstarch

¼ teaspoon salt
2¼ cups milk
2 tablespoons butter
1½ teaspoons vanilla extract

1. Combine sugar, cocoa, cornstarch and salt in a 2-quart glass measure or bowl. Slowly whisk in milk. Stir until cornstarch is completely dissolved.

2. Cook on HIGH 7 to 10 minutes, stirring every 2 minutes, until pudding begins to thicken. Stir in butter and vanilla. Pour into 4 individual serving dishes. Cover with plastic wrap to prevent a skin from forming on top. Refrigerate until chilled.

353 ESPRESSO POTS DE CREME

Prep: 10 minutes   Cook: 9 to 11 minutes   Serves: 4

½ cup milk
½ cup brewed strong espresso
¼ cup heavy cream
4 egg yolks

2 teaspoons vanilla extract
¼ cup sugar
4 candy coffee beans
    (optional)

1. In a 4-cup glass measure, combine milk and espresso. Cook on HIGH 2 minutes. In a medium bowl, combine cream, egg yolks, vanilla and sugar. Whisk until frothy. Slowly whisk in hot milk mixture.

2. Divide coffee custard among 4 buttered 6-ounce custard cups. Arrange in a circle on a flat plate. Cook on MEDIUM 7 to 9 minutes, until edges are set and centers are just beginning to firm up. Do not overcook. Let stand 5 minutes to allow the centers to set up. Run a small knife around the edges and invert to unmold, or serve out of custard cups. Garnish each with a candy coffee bean.

354 CHOCOLATE VELVET

Prep: 15 minutes   Cook: 2 to 3 minutes   Serves: 6 to 8

4 ounces semisweet chocolate,
    broken into pieces
2 ounces (2 squares)
    unsweetened chocolate
3 tablespoons coffee liqueur,
    such as Kahlua or Tia
    Maria

1 teaspoon vanilla extract
5 eggs, separated
⅓ cup sugar

1. In a 4-cup glass measure, combine semisweet chocolate, unsweetened chocolate and coffee liqueur. Cook on HIGH 2 minutes, or just until chocolate appears shiny; do not overcook. Stir chocolate until melted and smooth. Mix in vanilla. Set aside to cool slightly.

2. In a mixer bowl, beat egg yolks until fluffy. Gradually beat in melted chocolate. Set aside and let cool completely.

3. In another mixer bowl, beat egg whites until soft peaks form. Gradually beat in sugar and beat until egg whites are stiff and shiny. Stir ⅓ of egg white mixture into chocolate. Fold in remaining egg whites. Turn into a 1-quart soufflé dish or individual serving dishes. Cover and refrigerate until set, about 2 hours.

---

355   CHOCOLATE LEMON WAFERS
Prep: 20 minutes   Cook: 3 to 4 minutes   Makes: about 20

Serve as a candy, or as an elegant treat with coffee after a fine dinner. Use a good-quality coating chocolate, preferably imported, if you can find it.

2 **large elongated lemons**	¾ **pound dark sweet or**
1½ **tablespoons solid vegetable**	**semisweet chocolate,**
shortening	**broken into pieces**

1. Using a sharp stainless steel or serrated knife, slice lemons as evenly as possible into ⅛-inch-thick rounds. Cut each round in half. Arrange lemon slices in a single layer on paper towels.

2. In a 4-cup glass measure, combine shortening and chocolate. Cook on MEDIUM 3 to 4 minutes, just until chocolate looks shiny. Remove from microwave and stir until chocolate is melted and smooth.

3. Using a fork, dip each lemon slice into chocolate, coating completely. Set on a waxed paper-lined baking sheet. Place sheet in freezer for 5 minutes, or until chocolate is firm.

---

356   PEANUT SESAME BRITTLE
Prep: 10 minutes   Cook: 10 minutes   Makes: about 1 pound

1 **cup granulated sugar**	½ **cup unhulled sesame seeds**
½ **cup light corn syrup**	1 **tablespoon butter**
2 **tablespoons water**	1 **teaspoon vanilla extract**
1 **to 1½ cups dry-roasted**	1 **teaspoon baking soda**
peanuts	

1. Grease a large baking sheet. Set aside. In a 2-quart glass measure or bowl, combine sugar, corn syrup and water. Cook on HIGH 4 minutes. Stir in peanuts. Cook 5 minutes. Stir in sesame seeds, butter and vanilla. Cook 1 minute longer

2. Stir in baking soda; mixture will foam and boil up. Stir until light and foamy. Working quickly, pour candy onto greased baking sheet. Spread quickly to edges using back of a wooden spoon. As candy cools, stretch out to a thin sheet, using palms of hands. Let cool completely until crisp before breaking into pieces. Store in an airtight container in a cool place.

357   BITTERSWEET TRUFFLES WITH APRICOTS AND GRAND MARNIER

Prep: 15 minutes   Cook: 4 minutes   Makes: 24

6 **tablespoons chopped dried apricots**
¼ **cup Grand Marnier**
¾ **pound bittersweet chocolate**

4 **tablespoons unsalted butter**
¼ **cup heavy cream**
1 **tablespoon solid vegetable shortening**

1. Place apricots and Grand Marnier in a 1-cup measure. Stir to moisten fruit. Cook on HIGH 30 seconds. Stir and set aside. Break 7 ounces chocolate into pieces. Place in a 4-cup glass measure or bowl. Add butter. Cook on HIGH 1 minute, or just until chocolate appears shiny. Stir until chocolate is melted and smooth.

2. Stir cream into apricots. Add apricot mixture to melted chocolate and blend well. Cover and refrigerate 10 to 15 minutes, stirring frequently, until truffle mixture is thick enough to hold its shape. Drop by heaping teaspoons onto a waxed paper-lined baking sheet. Freeze for at least 30 minutes to set.

3. In a 1-cup glass measure, combine remaining 5 ounces chocolate and shortening. Cook on MEDIUM 2 to 3 minutes, just until chocolate appears shiny. Stir until melted. One at a time, set a frozen truffle on a fork and dip into melted chocolate to coat. Return to baking sheet and refrigerate at least 2 hours, or until set. If chocolate thickens too much to dip last truffles, return to microwave on MEDIUM for 15 to 30 seconds and stir.

358   MARSHMALLOWS

Prep: 10 minutes   Cook: 6 minutes   Makes: 3 dozen

Here's a great rainy-day project the kids will love.

1 **envelope unflavored gelatin**
⅓ **cup water**
⅔ **cup granulated sugar**
½ **cup light corn syrup**

1 **teaspoon vanilla extract**
2 **tablespoons cornstarch**
3 **tablespoons confectioners' sugar**

1. In a 2-quart glass measure or bowl, combine gelatin and water. Let stand until softened, about 10 minutes. Stir in granulated sugar. Cook on MEDIUM 3 minutes. Stir and cook 3 minutes longer. Watch to be sure syrup does not boil over.

2. Place corn syrup and vanilla in large bowl of an electric mixer. Add cooked gelatin and sugar mixture and beat at high speed for 12 to 14 minutes, until mixture is thick and holds its shape.

3. Combine cornstarch and confectioners' sugar. Sift briefly over an 8-inch square pan to dust bottom. Spread fluffy marshmallow mixture in pan. Dust top with another sifting of cornstarch mixture. Let stand several hours, until dry.

4. Sift remaining cornstarch mixture onto a baking sheet. Loosen edges of marshmallow with sharp knife dipped in cornstarch mixture. Turn out onto baking sheet. Cut into squares with knife or scissors dipped in cornstarch mixture. Dust each square with cornstarch mixture. Let dry about 1 hour before storing in airtight container.

---

359 MARSHMALLOW SAUCE
Prep: 5 minutes   Cook: 10 to 12 minutes   Makes: 3 cups

Serve over ice cream, fruit salad or brownies. Mix with chocolate syrup to make Chocolate Marshmallow Sauce.

1 **cup sugar**	**Dash of salt**
⅔ **cup light corn syrup**	¼ **teaspoon vanilla extract**
½ **cup hot water**	¼ **cup mayonnaise**
2 **egg whites**	

1. In a 2-quart glass measure or bowl, combine sugar, corn syrup and hot water. Stir until sugar dissolves. Cover with waxed paper. Cook on HIGH 10 to 12 minutes without stirring, until syrup registers 248 degrees on a microwave candy thermometer, or until it forms a thread or firm ball when a small amount is dropped in a glass of cold water.

2. In a mixer bowl, beat egg whites with salt until stiff but not dry, about 2 minutes. Gradually beat in hot syrup until thick and fluffy. Blend in vanilla. Fold in mayonnaise until well blended.

---

360 ALMOND-PECAN BUTTERMILK FUDGE
Prep: 5 minutes   Cook: 19 minutes   Makes: 36 pieces

1 **cup buttermilk**	1 **cup whole natural almonds,**
1 **teaspoon baking soda**	**coarsely chopped**
2 **cups sugar**	1 **cup pecan halves, coarsely**
2 **tablespoons light corn syrup**	**chopped**
6 **tablespoons butter**	1½ **teaspoons vanilla extract**

1. In a 4-quart casserole, combine buttermilk and baking soda. Stir until soda completely dissolves. Stir in sugar and corn syrup. Add butter. Cook on HIGH 5 minutes, or until boiling. Remove from microwave.

2. Stir fudge with metal spoon. Place a sheet of microwave-safe plastic wrap over ¾ of casserole. If using microwave thermometer, clip onto open edge of casserole. Continue to cook on HIGH 14 minutes, until thermometer registers 245 degrees or until a small amount dropped into a glass of cold water masses together. Let cool until thickened, about 45 minutes.

3. Beat in almonds, pecans and vanilla. Turn fudge into a generously greased 8-inch square pan. Let stand 30 minutes, or until firm. Cut fudge into 1¼-inch squares.

361 PERFECT HOT CHOCOLATE SAUCE
Prep: 10 minutes   Cook: 6 to 7 minutes   Makes: 2 cups

1 **cup sugar**
½ **cup half-and-half or light cream**
4 **ounces (4 squares) unsweetened chocolate**

1 **stick (¼ pound) butter, cut into tablespoons**
2 **egg yolks**
1 **teaspoon vanilla extract**

1. In a 4-cup glass measure, combine sugar and half-and-half. Cook on HIGH 3 to 4 minutes, or until sugar dissolves and mixture boils. Stir in chocolate and butter. Cook 1 minute.

2. Whisk egg yolks in a small bowl. Gradually whisk in ½ cup hot chocolate mixture. Whisk egg yolk mixture into remaining chocolate. Cook on MEDIUM 2 minutes. Whisk in vanilla. Serve sauce hot or cold. To reheat, cook on MEDIUM 30 seconds, or until just warmed through.

362 CUSTARD SAUCE
Prep: 5 minutes   Cook: 6 to 8 minutes   Makes: 2 cups

¼ **cup sugar**
¼ **cup cornstarch**
2 **cups milk, at room temperature**

3 **egg yolks**
1½ **teaspoons vanilla extract**

1. In a 4-cup glass measure or bowl, combine sugar and cornstarch. Add about ¼ cup milk and stir until cornstarch is dissolved and smooth. Whisk in remaining milk. Cover with waxed paper and cook on HIGH 5 to 7 minutes, stirring twice, until mixture comes to a boil and thickens. Whisk until smooth.

2. In a medium bowl, beat egg yolks lightly. Gradually whisk in ½ cup hot milk mixture to warm egg yolks. Whisk in remaining milk mixture. Return custard to glass measure and cook, uncovered, on HIGH 1 minute. Blend in vanilla.

363 LEMONY ICE CREAM
Prep: 20 minutes   Cook: 5 to 7 minutes   Makes: 1 quart

1 **cup heavy cream**
1 **cup milk**
⅔ **cup sugar**

Grated zest and juice from 2 large lemons

1. In a 2-quart glass measure or bowl, combine cream, milk and sugar. Stir to blend well. Cook on HIGH 5 to 7 minutes, stirring twice, until sugar is dissolved and mixture is hot but not boiling. (Watch carefully; if it boils, it will bubble up and may spill over.) Set aside to cool.

2. Stir in lemon zest and juice. Pour mixture into ice cream maker and freeze according to the manufacturer's instructions.

364 CARAMEL GRAPES WITH SOUR CREAM AND TOASTED PECANS

Prep: 5 minutes   Cook: 3 to 4 minutes   Serves: 6

½ cup chopped pecans
1 teaspoon butter
3 cups seedless green or red
    grapes

½ cup sour cream
Thick and Creamy Caramel
    Sauce (p. 159) or a 12-
    ounce jar caramel sauce

1. Put pecans and butter in a 1-cup measure. Cook on HIGH 1 minute; stir. Cook 1 to 1½ minutes longer, until lightly toasted.

2. In a medium bowl, combine grapes and sour cream. Stir gently to coat grapes with cream. Divide among 6 dessert dishes.

3. Spoon caramel sauce into a pitcher or serving bowl. Cook on MEDIUM 1 to 1½ minutes, until warmed through; stir. Spoon 2 to 3 tablespoons caramel sauce over each serving. Sprinkle toasted pecans on top.

365 HOT BRANDIED MOCHA

Prep: 5 minutes   Cook: 3 to 4 minutes   Serves: 4

2 cups milk
¼ cup semisweet chocolate
    chips
2 teaspoons instant coffee

½ cup brandy
2 teaspoons sugar
Whipped cream, for garnish

1. In a 4-cup glass measure, combine milk and chocolate. Cook on HIGH 3 to 4 minutes, until hot; do not boil. Add coffee and stir until dissolved.

2. Divide hot mocha among 4 mugs. Stir 2 tablespoons brandy and ½ teaspoon sugar into each drink. Top with whipped cream and serve at once.

Index

About the Author

Thelma Pressman, a pioneer in microwave cooking since 1968, is the author of four books, including *The Art of Microwave Cooking* and *The Great Microwave Dessert Book*.